THE LAWS OF THE RING

URIJAH FABER

WITH

TIM KEOWN

WILLIAM MORROW
An Imprint of HarperCollinsPublishers

THE LAWS OF THE RING

For information address HarperCollins Publishers, 10 East 53rd Street, New York, NY 10022.

HarperCollins books may be purchased for educational, business, or sales promotional use. For information please write: Special Markets Department, HarperCollins Publishers, 10 East 53rd Street, New York, NY 10022.

A hardcover edition of this book was published in 2012 by William Morrow, an imprint of HarperCollins Publishers.

FIRST WILLIAM MORROW PAPERBACK EDITION PUBLISHED 2013.

Designed by Janet M. Evans

Library of Congress Cataloging-in-Publication Data has been applied for.

ISBN 978-0-06-211241-5

13 14 15 16 17 OV/RRD 10 9 8 7 6 5 4 3 2 1

This book is dedicated to my family:
My amazing mom, Suzanne; my carefree pop, Theo; and my fearless stepdad, Tom. My brother, Ryan, and my sister, Michaella. Rhino and KK, you have inspired me with your fighting spirit. You have both pushed through adversity that I may never fully experience or truly understand. Mom, Pop, and Tom, thank you for all the guidance through the good and the difficult! We have all grown stronger together. Love you guys.

Special thanks to all the teachers and coaches throughout my life, and Jim and Renata Peterson for their help in mapping out this book.

CONTENTS

THE FIRST FIGHT

Meet Jay Valencia, my first professional opponent: wide, strong, mean-looking. The first thing I notice is the tattoo across his stomach: *PRIDE* in Old English font. He has clearly seen more than me, experienced more than me, struggled more than me. The bend in his nose tells me all I need to know on those counts.

And those eyes—damn, those eyes are something else. They're wide and wild under his shaved head. They are fixed on mine, but I get the feeling they're not really focused. He is looking but not looking, which could be intimidating if I'd allow it. Tattooed like the ex-con he isn't, muscled like a bodybuilder, he is jumping around like a maniac. He is looking at me the way I imagine a fox looks at a crippled hen.

I look at the people in the stands and wonder how every roughneck—and his mother—found his way to the Colusa Casino, dropped down in the middle of rice fields and orchards north of Sacramento, California. They're here to watch something that's illegal everywhere in California but on sovereign Indian land. Maybe the semi-illicit nature of the spectacle has them amped up, or maybe it's the booze or whatever else is coursing through their veins. This is the Wild West of cage fighting, back before rules and money took MMA mainstream. These people are screaming and pounding the chairs, dying to see blood spilled. Tough-looking guys and tougher-looking girls, they look ready to fight, too, with eyes every bit as crazily detached as Valencia's. Teeth, I notice, seem optional.

Here's what these people see: a smiling, clean-cut, blond kid—fresh out of college—facing a tough, hardened Mexican. They see scars and tattoos on one side, shiny white teeth and no tattoos on the other. Everything society has taught them leads them to one conclusion: The college kid is going down, hard, and it's not going to be pretty.

It's the same thing Valencia sees. He sees someone he can intimidate, then destroy. There's nothing in his or anyone else's frame of reference that would lead them to believe anything else is possible. The tough barrio guy wants it more. He needs it more. He's overcome obstacles in his life, making him hungrier and more desperate.

What are the stakes? If the clean-cut college graduate loses, he might give up fighting and get a job with an investment bank, or make a career out of coaching college wrestling. If the other guy loses, who knows? He doesn't want to think about it, which is one more reason to believe he's going to mop the floor with the college kid.

Valencia is supposed to hold the power in this human dynamic. He has seen more and done more and has more to lose. Society tells me, in a whispery, judgmental tone, that I should be doing something better with my life. It tells me I should be embracing the advantages I've been afforded. I should be putting my college degree to good use with a solid, well-paying job with benefits and a clear path to advancement. I should be looking to buy a new car and maybe a house. I should be putting money away for my retirement and to fund the college educations of the kids I don't yet have.

Wherever I should be, I shouldn't be here, standing inches away from Jay Valencia's murderous eyes. This is something guys like me wouldn't do on a dare, and definitely wouldn't do for the small payout I've been promised.

Society has trained people to *get* Jay Valencia. They understand what he's doing here, and why he's doing it, and what's at stake. But what about me? What to make of this guy? Jay Valencia might *look* crazy, but these fans—including my buddies from college—are thinking *I'm* the truly crazy one. I'm the one they don't understand, because everything they've read or heard

or seen about sports, especially fighting sports, tells them I'm here on a lark, and Jay Valencia's here for keeps.

True or not, these are the unspoken messages emanating from the cage in the moments before the fight. As I walk toward the cage, I'm not scared or intimidated. However, one thought ricochets through my brain.

Why the hell did I get myself into this?

As soon as I step into the cage, that thought changes into something far different.

This dude is going down.

I believe there are laws at work in human interaction. These are laws that dictate success or failure, laws that portend a life of happiness or a life of regret. Put simply, they are Laws of Power. They are equally relevant to a salesman and a professional fighter. They work in the office or out. By maximizing your Laws of Power, you will lead a happier, more fulfilling life.

You'd be surprised how much you can learn when you make it your profession to stand in an enclosed cage with another man, with the intention of defeating him by simulating his murder—by strangulation, knockout, submission—the best you can. It's the history of the world compressed into a series of five-minute rounds: strength, wits, gamesmanship, creativity, adaptability—it's all on display.

And if you're observant and introspective, you can learn quite a bit. For instance, the way people carry themselves tells a lot about them. A fighter who comes into the cage talking garbage is telling me right away he's insecure, not sure of either his talent or his preparation. There's no need to talk; we're all dressed up to fight, so what good are words? What are you going to do, call me out? We have the means of settling it right in front of us. We're about to fight, so shut your mouth or expose yourself and your insecurities.

There are messages everywhere, some hidden, some not.

I must admit, a cage fight inside the Colusa Casino ballroom, at an event called "The Gladiator Challenge," is a strange place to begin a book intended to teach you how to find your passion and incorporate it into your life. If you were expecting a clear blue sky and a sandy beach, I apologize in advance.

But that night—the night of November 13, 2003—was the night my passion began to lead me. It was the night my life opened to the possibilities of following a dream even when it seemed outlandish and impossible. The events of that night set in motion a series of events I couldn't possibly have imagined.

The seeds for the Laws of Power were planted that night. Every one of them was in play at some point before, during, and after my fight with Jay Valencia. That night a rock was thrown into the water, and the ripples emanating from it tell the story you are about to read.

The lessons I learned are still with me, still leading. The laws that grew out of them are as pertinent today as they were then. If you live your life according to these laws, you will be happier and more productive. You will have more power over your life, and you will be more positive and successful.

They helped me, and they can help you.

There are things Valencia can't tell simply from looking at me, important things that might have changed his attitude some. He doesn't know the surge of adrenaline that shot through my entire body the first time I saw an MMA fight. He doesn't know that my commitment to the sport means I will attack him with single-minded devotion and a cold-blooded intensity that belie my looks. He doesn't know the words that are running through my mind as he is bouncing around and staring me down. As we stand waiting for the bell, any doubt or reserve is purged from my system. As I look into Valencia's wild, crazed eyes, there is just one thought remaining inside the mind of the pretty-boy blond college kid:

You're dead, dude.

Several of my buddies from college are in the stands. Dave Shapiro and Dustin Soderman, former UC Davis baseball players and my roommates at the time, sit out there wondering what the hell they've gotten themselves into. I can imagine them sitting in their metal folding chairs, paragons of young-adult responsibility and corporate potential, looking around at their fellow fight fans thinking they might not get out of the Colusa Casino alive.

My dad is there, happy as always, looking at this as just another example of life's good fortune.

I don't have any formal training in mixed martial arts. I go with a southpaw stance, which feels right (but lasts only three fights). As soon as the bell rings, I shoot out of the corner as if fired from a gun. Immediately I attack. I start punching, thudding my opponent on the head a few times. He fights back, but without much passion, and right there I've got the feeling Jay Valencia understands that he's gotten more than he expected.

I believe there's a certain energy that emanates from the human body. That energy is exaggerated in stressful moments like a fight. Right then, as I pop a few more good shots at Valencia's face, I feel a change in his energy. He goes from blustery confidence to uncertainty. This isn't going to be as easy as he thought, and his body tells me he wonders if he has the ability to change course and adopt a different approach. His energy is all doubt.

Valencia's formal training, like mine, is as a wrestler, and he double-legs me and takes me to the ground. It is his last good moment. I reverse it quickly, get back onto my feet, and knee him twice before we clinch against the cage. I am in complete control of this fight, and I know it. As we are leaning against the cage, I look out in the crowd and find my dad. I give him a quick nod and a smile, then I toss Valencia to the ground with a step-over throw and knee him three times in the head.

I jump on top of Valencia and choke him till he taps out at one minute, twenty-two seconds of the first round. I release him and punch the cage. I scream once and begin marching around the cage whooping and pointing to my buddies in the crowd. "Those are my dawgs!" I yell. I am pretty out-of-control happy at this point.

The crowd is going absolutely crazy. I can't describe the feeling. I've never been happier. This is beyond intoxicating. All the toothless and semi-toothed standing together, throwing air punches and yelling at the top of their lungs, happy to see someone get the shit kicked out of him, regardless of who it is. I wish I could find Dave and Dustin, just to see how wide their eyes were.

That settled it: I was hooked. This was all I wanted to do. The feeling I got in that funky place in front of all those funky people was worth every minute spent busing tables and teaching wrestling and wondering if I had enough money to pay rent. It took three minutes and forty-eight seconds for me to commit fully to this unconventional career path.

I couldn't have articulated it at the time, but that first fight encapsulated each of the Laws of Power that would take shape in my mind as my career progressed. As those fans howled their bloodthirsty approval and my buddies looked up at me like they couldn't believe what I just did, a future started to take shape.

I could get used to that feeling. I could make this work. It wasn't a profession yet—and there was no guarantee it ever would be—but at that moment I was following my heart and my passion. The feeling I had in that cage was something I was ready to follow wherever it might lead.

That was the easy part. Now I needed to weave it throughout the rest of my life. I needed to take this unconventional obsession and make it work for me. Along the way, I established rules—some intentional, some accidental—that served as a road map, guiding me toward my ultimate destination.

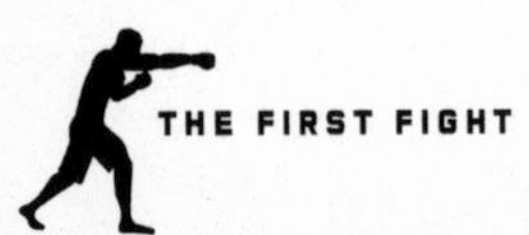

INTRODUCTION: WHAT'S YOUR PASSION?

It's a surprisingly difficult question to answer. I should know—I've asked it many, many times while speaking to groups and giving motivational speeches. I have come to expect a lot of blank faces, upraised arms, and embarrassed chuckles.

There's one reason a lot of otherwise successful people can't identify their passion: They haven't been conditioned to discover it. Sounds odd, but it's true. Most people go through their lives according to the guidelines set by society. You get an education and you get a job. You work hard at that job in order to make enough money and attain enough status to live comfortably. The particulars of the job are often mundane and unfulfilling. The forty hours a week spent working at that job are tolerated in order to reach an end point—a weekend at the lake, or a two-week vacation with the family—where you relax by doing something that takes your mind off your occupation.

Passion usually has no place in the equation. At best, it is compartmentalized, separated from "Work" and placed to the side, under "Pleasure."

First, a definition: Passion is what you would do if *you* got to choose. It's what you think about doing in the privacy of your own mind, without fear of dismissal or mockery. It might be something that makes you rich and happy, or something that simply makes you happy without financial reward.

But think about this: What if your choice—what you do when you are free of obligation—could be incorporated into your everyday life? What if your job and your passion merged? How much better would life be if you could make your forty-hour workweek as enjoyable as your weekends?

Right about now you might be asking yourself a question of your own: Why should I take life advice from a guy who beats people up—and occasionally gets beaten up—for a living? It's a valid question, and one I will answer plainly and directly: You should take advice from me because I have found a way to incorporate my passions into my life and work. I identified my passion early and did everything in my power to make sure I found ways to include my passion in every aspect of my life.

Part of my passion is to study people and their lifestyles. I was delivered by midwives in a Christian commune near Santa Barbara, where I spent the first five years of my life. My family moved to Sacramento, where my parents got divorced and I spent some time as a child model and small-time actor. From there, I moved to a nearby rural community called Lincoln, where I was a high-school football and wrestling star. The combination of a quirky background and my degree in human development from UC Davis, where I hold the record for most wins in the wrestling program's history, have made me intensely curious about lifestyles—and why people live the way they do.

My job makes it imperative for me to study both myself and my opponents. When you make your livelihood standing in a small, enclosed cage, fighting with another man whose stated goal is to separate your limbs from your body or your mind from its senses, introspection is a job requirement. It makes no sense for me to pretend I'm something I'm not; the reckoning will come in the cage, and it won't be pretty. Because of that, I have to be brutally honest when it comes to assessing my strengths and weaknesses. I have to do the same for my opponents.

You would be surprised what you can learn about yourself and other people when you engage in something as primal and basic as professional mixed martial arts. You probably know me as a fighter, but I'd like you to read this book with an open mind. My hope is that you picked up this book because you instinctively see why a fighter is qualified to offer insight into human nature, but that you pass it along to your friends and family because

you find something compelling and inspiring within its pages. This book is a result of me, ruminating on my experiences through thirty-some-odd years, asking myself a series of questions. Why has life gone this way for me? Why have so many good—and some bad—things happened? How did I become who I am today? How can I help others experience the good and avoid the bad? The lessons have not always been learned sequentially. Some have come about retrospectively. Their chronology unfolds as I unfolded.

When I first started jotting down ideas for a book, I always thought it would be called *Passion Runs the World.* It's my experience that the people who get the most out of life and have the most success are those who have found a way to incorporate their passion into every aspect of their existence. As I got deeper into the process, I came to the realization that community is the necessary by-product of passion. In my life, as you will see, community is primary. When it was proposed that we title the book *Laws of the Cage* in order to more accurately reflect my sport, I disagreed. The ring, with its symbolic inclusiveness, seemed the perfect embodiment of the community my passion has created. There are certain qualities that all successful, positive people share. *Passion* is the umbrella under which they all reside, and *community* is the collection of people who share the space, and the passion, under that umbrella. The umbrella is the perfect metaphor; it protects you, your passion, and your community from outside elements of negativity, distrust, and jealousy. As you read, think about yourself standing under the umbrella, inviting in more and more members of your community in order to protect your collective passion from the "elements."

Which gets us back to the original dilemma: What is your passion? I've asked this question and received the answer "I don't know" more often than I can count.

And that's okay. I have a response to that. I say, "Fine, here's what we're going to do, then. We're going to assign you a passion."

Sounds crazy, right? You ought to see the looks I get after I say that. Who do I think I am? How can I dictate someone's passion? How can I take someone I don't know and give him something to be passionate about?

Easy: The passion I assign is the same every time.

The passion is *you.*

I tell them this: For the time being, you are your own passion. You are going to invest in yourself. You are going to make it a point to work harder at whatever it is you're doing. You're going to celebrate your victories, no matter how small. If you do something well, you're going to compliment yourself for it. You're going to set goals. You're going to verbalize—and share—your plans. You're going to hold yourself accountable to those goals and plans. You're going to separate yourself from negative people who suck energy from you. You're going to surround yourself with people who are positive and have your best interests in mind. You're going to be healthier.

In short, you're going to start *consciously* doing things that will create a greater feeling of self-worth. You will be conscious of the choices you are making instead of simply autopiloting your way through your days, months, and years. Through this exercise, you will find something you like. By making yourself your passion, you will find a passion outside of yourself to follow on your way to a better life.

After all, we all start alone under our umbrella. From there, we seek out others who share our passion to join us and help us make it grow. However, there are many times when we need to stand on our own and make big decisions that can dictate the course of our passion. I relate it to a big fight: I enter the cage with the people from my corner—trainers and coaches—but when the bell rings I'm left alone to make decisions based on the teachings of the community. I am alone, but the community is with me in spirit and guidance. And then, when the battle is over, the cage opens up and I am reunited with my community to either rejoice or console in the aftermath of the fight.

It takes introspection to identify passion. It doesn't happen in a vacuum. There are no shortcuts. You have to think about yourself, your beliefs and desires. You may come to some uncomfortable truths about yourself, and that's okay. We live in a quick-hit, short-attention-span world, and introspection can often be in short supply. We want things, we want them now, and we are willing to compromise our lives in order to get them.

We don't have enough quiet moments to really look inside ourselves and conduct an honest assessment of our strengths and weaknesses. We roll through life in fast motion, feeling guilty if we aren't keeping as busy as pos-

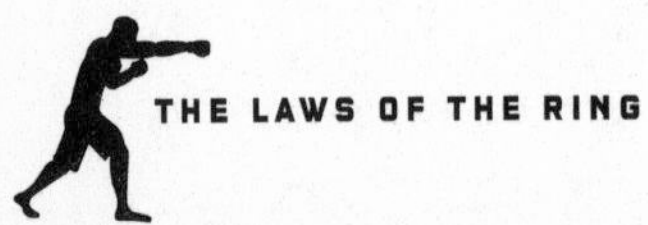

sible, and amid the hustle and bustle it's easy to lose sight of purpose and passion. This book, with its Laws of Power, is intended to be a caution sign on the lifestyle highway.

Slow down. Assess yourself. Define your passion. Make a plan. Execute it.

By first making yourself your passion, you are going to look inward and come to realistic conclusions about your strengths and weaknesses. You're going to learn how to stand under your umbrella and reach out to others who might need the protection and direction provided by a similar passion. More practically, you're going to develop a strategy to incorporate your passion into your life, depending on your available time, financial needs, and emotional burden.

You're going to take the first steps toward controlling your life rather than having it control you. In this book you will read examples of people who have gone through these same stages and come away with a changed outlook on life.

You'll read my story, about how I went against convention to pursue a career in fighting after deciding it was something for which I had both passion and talent. You'll read about the people who have combined talents in order to work together with me on business ventures outside the cage. You'll read about the courage shown by my older brother, Ryan, whose fourteen-year battle with mental illness has been a source of worry and inspiration. You'll read about top contender Joseph Benavidez, who showed up at my gym with nothing but a passion for fighting and a trunk full of the most basic worldly possessions.

The process isn't easy, though. I won't lie about that. It takes a unique person to ignore the pressures and expectations of society in order to chase a dream. It takes a strong person to stand alone under the umbrella and remain steadfast in the pursuit. Unknowns get in the way and cloud our thinking. Fear intrudes and we get stuck in stagnancy. We wait for something to happen instead of making it happen. We fear failure, so we don't take the kind of risks that could produce success.

You will learn that it takes more effort to wait than to act. Procrastination is tiring and soul-sapping. Waiting for the perfect opportunity is stifling and confining. You can wait for an opportunity, or you can *create* an opportunity.

Conventional society discourages risk taking. Oh, we pretend to embrace it, but this officially sanctioned risk taking occurs in a controlled environment. Risk, by this definition, is putting a hundred bucks on a fifty-to-one long shot, or buying a thousand dollars in penny stocks. Or it's reality-show risk taking, which is kind of like risk taking without the risk.

The kind of risk I'm suggesting in this book has nothing to do with bungee-jumping, or eating a cricket, or jumping in a frozen lake. I'm talking about life-changing risk, the kind that makes you take a deep breath, question everything you ever thought about your life, and still—even after acknowledging that standing pat would be easier and safer—putting your head down and charging forward into the unknown.

It's the kind of risk that turns your life from a poorly focused, passion-free existence into something happier, more positive, and far more fulfilling. By following the Laws of Power described in this book, you will feel more comfortable and confident about taking the kind of risk that will change your life. You will have the tools and the clear-eyed knowledge to take the smart risk that will pay big dividends.

My passion is risky. It's clearly not for everyone, and the style I employ while practicing it is high energy and exciting. Because of this, I've often been confused with someone who would be willing to take the contrived risk. I've heard, "Urijah, let's go bungee-jumping," or "Urijah, doesn't sky-diving sound like fun?"

No, it doesn't. I tell people, "Dude, my life is too good for me to take that kind of risk. I might screw up and miss out on the life I'm leading."

So here's my goal: If you live your life by the Laws of Power outlined in these pages, your life will be so good you won't want or need to take contrived risks. Metaphorically speaking, you will jump out of an airplane, but it will be a permanent, life-changing experience and not a cheap thrill. You, like me, will choose to embrace the real rather than chase the artificial.

PROLOGUE: KNOW WHAT YOU'RE FIGHTING FOR

It wasn't easy. My path to the cage at the Colusa Casino—and everything that followed—would not have happened if I hadn't been consumed with a sense of purpose.

The first task to complete on your way to a better, more passion-based life is this: Know what you're fighting for.

You're fighting for a lifestyle that allows you to incorporate your passion throughout your personal and professional lives. You're fighting to control your life instead of having it control you. In short, you're fighting for a life without compromise. It doesn't just happen organically. You can't wish it into being. You must push forward at all costs.

My pursuit began when my friend Tyrone Glover sold me a ticket to watch him compete in a new kind of professional fighting: MMA. He was fighting in Colusa—one of the few places in California staging fights—and from the moment the fight began, I knew I would do everything in my power to get inside that cage.

I got a queasy feeling the second Tyrone's fight started. It wasn't nerves, it was excitement. I wanted to jump into the cage right then and there. I didn't care that the sport was considered all but dead, pushed to the margins by Arizona senator John McCain's attempt to make it illegal in 2000. After watching tapes of the first UFC events, run under the motto "There Are No Rules," McCain called the sport "human cockfighting." He was right; the sport was badly in need of reform. It was primal. It was vicious. And it was incredibly exciting. I had watched early UFC fights when I was in high school, but seeing one in person was completely different. I couldn't imagine anything that would test a man's mettle to this degree. I was convinced I would be good at it; it seemed to be invented with me in mind. I immediately became consumed with the idea of pursuing it.

The butterflies in my stomach turned into bumblebees as I sat on a metal folding chair and watched Tyrone fight. This was my future, and I was ready for it to begin.

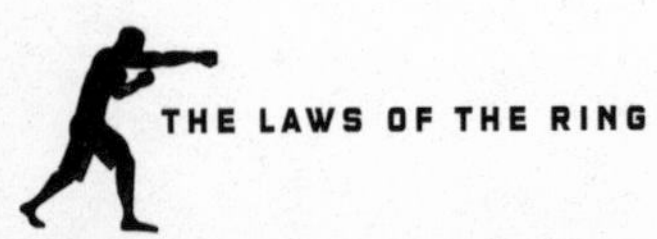

THE 1ST LAW OF POWER

POSITIVE THINKING BREEDS SUCCESS

Here's an easy question: Who would you rather hang out with, someone who is always *genuinely* happy and positive, or someone who is always grumpy and negative?

As part of your progress toward living your dream, you need to assess your attitude. Is negativity infecting your life and serving as a dream stopper? Is your mentality *limiting* your potential?

Remember this: Negativity takes no imagination. It's far easier to criticize someone's decisions after they make them than to propose better ones beforehand.

At some point between my first and second professional fights, when the prospect of making a career in a sport that then consisted of competing in semilegal fights on Indian reservations was still a wild long shot, I sat around with a group of friends and talked about my big plans. I have a tendency to do this—I just can't help it. I'm a motivated guy, and I want everyone around me to feel the same way.

During this particular conversation, my buddy Will Creger interrupted me and asked, "Why are you so confident about *everything*? Where does that come from?"

His tone wasn't angry or challenging. My attitude just blew him away, and he was both curious and amused. He was a successful guy who came from a successful family. His mother was a schoolteacher and his father was a top executive with a construction company. It's safe to assume he'd been around positive, happy people throughout his life, and yet he couldn't get his mind around the way I approached mine.

It's just the way I am. I make a point to stay positive and I'm always looking forward to the next thing to feed my excitement. When something bad happens in my life, I'm pretty good about shrugging it off and going forward. In reality you have to anyway, right?

I don't think I'd ever given my disposition a conscious thought until then. When I did give it some thought, though, I realized my upbringing was largely responsible for my mentality. My parents had me and my older brother, Ryan, while living in a commune situation modeled after the Early Church and started by Gene Edwards. My name, which means "God is my light," is a lasting symbol of those days. From the little I remember, the place had a heavy hippie vibe. You know, anything goes, love everybody, do what you do, and don't judge. It seems paradoxical today, in an age where fundamentalist Christianity is conservative and uptight, that such a place could also be based on religion. It *was*, though—charismatic Christianity carried the day.

Even after we left the commune, the strain of positivity that was cultivated in the commune proved pretty durable among the Fabers. It stuck around in separate households after my parents divorced. It has, in fact, stayed with me all these years later.

My dad, Theo, is the happiest, easiest-going person I have ever met. He had some difficult times following his breakup with my mom, with alcohol and despair darkening his disposition, but most of the time I think he's fundamentally *incapable* of feeling stress. His mind-set hasn't always produced the best results when it comes to his career and his finances, but he's sure a lot of fun to be around.

My mom Suzanne's positivity was more of the aggressive sort. She came from a broken family and was consequently adamant that her children grow up cultured, educated, and financially secure. She was highly disciplined and ambitious, and she expected her children to be the same. The walls of her home were always papered with inspirational sayings. She even made us write out goals and tape them to the wall in our rooms to serve as constant reminders of what we should be striving toward.

I vividly remember the saying that was on our refrigerator for years. It read:

Dream impossible dreams. When those dreams come true, make the next ones more impossible.

My mom was always running down a list of the things her kids could do. We could cook, we could play sports, we could build things. You name it, we could do it. She pushed confidence, positivity, and self-sufficiency on us like they were magic vitamins.

During my short stint as a child model and actor, I did commercial television shoots, for a radio station and a local hospital, among others. (It was all pretty small-time.) On one of the shoots, when I was in fifth or sixth grade, I remember talking with one of the producers, who asked if I liked to dance. "I can't really dance, but my brother is really good," I said frankly. Without a moment's hesitation, my mom butted into the conversation and corrected me. "Honey, you can dance. Any kid of mine can dance." I had to take her word for it at the time, but now that I think about it, I definitely have been known to get down on the dance floor on occasion. Without my mom's foresight and encouragement I might have had to stay sidelined on the dance floor, and my fight entrances might have had a little less bounce and energy when Tupac's "California Love" starts bumping.

We're not going to settle the nature vs. nurture argument in this book, but I can say with certainty that the cumulative effect of growing up in an environment where those kinds of messages were always front and center has something to do with who I am today. The combination of an aggressively positive mother and a naturally positive father resulted in an upbringing where nobody ever told me I couldn't do something. Mom taught me that anything was possible, and Pop taught me to shrug off misfortune and soldier on with a smile on my face. There were no barriers, no fears, no second thoughts.

Just because you haven't done something doesn't mean you can't, so *resist the urge to criticize*. This is harder than it seems. There's a difference between being a critical thinker and being a critic. A critical thinker comes up with constructive criticism after looking at a problem from all angles; a critic simply tosses out his or her caustic opinion with nothing substantive to back it up, and tends to lend mostly negative thoughts on any given topic. In pursuing your passion, accentuate the positive in yourself and other people, and never allow someone else's critiques to stop you from tackling your dreams. Don't confuse this with living in a fantasy world—remember, an umbrella can be used to protect you from the sun as well as the rain. So, to answer Will, there's a chance the confident attitude I took into the fight with Jay Valencia had its roots on my mom's refrigerator.

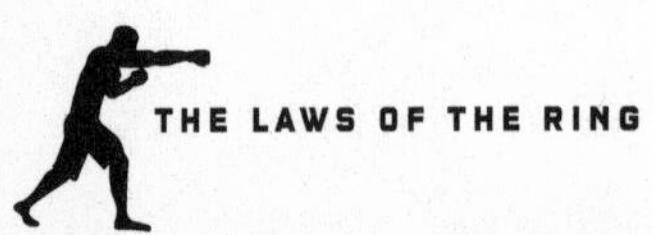

THE 2ND LAW OF POWER

ENJOY WHAT YOU HAVE

My brother and I spent a lot of time in the summers with our pop, who was always bouncing from one construction job to another. One year, Pop decided to buy a beat-up motor home for us to live in while he did his work rather than rent a house.

Ryan and I were probably ten and eight years old, respectively, and in the summer Pop would park the motor home next to a creek or a pond somewhere close to his job of the moment and head to work while we were left to our own devices until he returned.

You can debate the parenting aspects of this all you want—it's probably not in any of Dr. Spock's books—but some of the best times of my life happened that summer. Ryan and I would spend the day fishing, swimming, and exploring. This was before cell phones, of course, and before parents feared every moment for their children's safety. We were on our own, all day, without television or computers, and we had no problem filling up our days. We couldn't have asked for a better summer.

When I think back to that summer, I'm amazed at how many life skills Ryan and I developed as a result of that freedom. We carried our parents' values, but we grew confident in ourselves and our ability to handle our own problems without having constant parental intervention. We learned to be creative—without creativity, we would have grown bored quickly. We learned people skills; I won't say Ryan and I never had disagreements that summer, but we learned to work out most of our problems and reach a consensus on what we were going to do and how we were going to do it.

And there was nobody telling us that even our most harebrained schemes were too dangerous or impossible. Most of the time we got along great, but we had our typical sibling squabbles. We didn't have many creature comforts—no television, for example—but I did have a Game Boy that helped pass the time. One day we were sitting in the trailer on a hot afternoon, parked near a reservoir. We'd been outside all morning before coming in to grab some lunch and get out of the sun. I had been sitting on the couch playing with my Game Boy before getting up to get a drink of water. As soon as I got up, Ryan sat down, grabbed the Game Boy, and started playing with it.

"Give it back," I said.

"Make me," he said.

This classic highbrow childhood exchange went on for a few minutes before I decided to take a stand. I very deliberately put on my shoes right in front of him. My brother could tell I was up to something, so he started saying, "You better not." The whole time he kept his head in the Game Boy and refused to look at me.

After I put on the shoes, I walked slowly to the front door and propped it open.

"You better not." Still looking at the Game Boy.

The couch sat about five feet from the front door, facing the other direction. I could see the back of Ryan's head shaking back and forth as I plotted.

"You better not."

I stood behind him, between the door and the couch, and crouched into a sprinter's stance with my right hand upraised and ready to strike. Still, he kept his eyes on the Game Boy.

"You better not."

But I did. I punched him hard on the arm and started running out the door almost before my fist made contact. As I sprinted away I could feel Ryan in hot pursuit.

Ryan, two and a half years older, was stronger and faster than me, and even with the head start I could feel him gaining on me as soon as I leaped

out of the trailer door. He caught me within fifty yards and tackled me to the dirt. He popped me a few times but, all in all, went pretty easy on me.

Like animals in the wild, we each established our place in the pecking order. He was trying to teach me a lesson—as the older brother, he was in control and I better not be dumb enough to try to challenge his authority. As the younger brother just starting to assert himself and develop a mind of my own, I was letting him know that I understood his supremacy in the relationship, but that didn't mean I was going to let him pick on me.

Ryan and I found ways to amuse ourselves, which was a good thing. For better or worse, we were on our own until Pop finished his work and drove back to the trailer. The lesson from that summer was simple: We learned to enjoy what we had. We could have fixated on the things we didn't have, but instead we made the most of what we had. I guess you could say we didn't really know what we didn't have.

Popular culture inundates us with images of things we're told we should have. In order to have a good life, you need a certain kind of car, a certain size home, a whole roomful of high-tech electronics and gadgets. On top of that, you have to be able to eat at the right restaurants, drink at the right clubs, and hang out with people who are as upwardly mobile and as cool as you aspire to be. Whenever I find myself looking at the things I don't have, the old saying *ignorance is bliss* comes to mind. Looking back on that year in our little motor home and the fun times with my brother at parks and ponds just reminds me that satisfaction is relative. It's great to dream big, but always be content with what you have.

It's easy to jump outside the umbrella, to put passion aside and chase an image of the person the media say you should be. Whenever I feel I'm spinning on this endless hamster wheel of consumption, I remember one of my favorite sayings: *There are only two things that you have to do in life: You have to die, and you have to live until you die. The rest is up to you.*

So what gives you happiness? What do you love to do? Look at your life now, and find the things that already make you happy. Expand on them. At the same time look for other ways to feel excited and alive.

When you are making decisions in life, remember that it's okay to take the road less traveled. Society's norms may not be what's best for you.

THE 3RD LAW OF POWER

CREATE HEALTHIER HABITS

You can have all the knowledge in the world, but until you create good habits, that knowledge doesn't mean much of anything.

Your goal in life is to put yourself in position to "live the dream." I know those words are usually used ironically or sarcastically, coming from someone who's unplugging a toilet or struggling with a calculus equation.

Yeah, I'm living the dream.

But there's another way to think about those words—the way I choose to think about them. Living the dream is simply a form of living out your passion, of making that passion—gradually, through persistence and effort—a central part of your life.

Everyone's definition of this is different. Passion is an intensely personal thing, which is why you should make every effort to resist accepting opinions from people who do not understand your passion or have your best interests at heart.

I define living the dream this way: having a life where you spend all of your time doing things you love, with people you enjoy being around.

To get there, you have to fight through adversity. And by fight, I mean *fight.* You have to acquire strength through adversity. It isn't enough to simply overcome difficult times; you have to learn from them. You have to let the fight against adversity get inside you and empower you to achieve greater things.

I've explained some about my unique childhood. My older brother, Ryan, my younger sister, Michaella—the daughter of my mother and stepfather, Tom—and I were raised with love and affection.

But I also want you to know that it wasn't all sweetness and light. I was around six when the family began to break up. The radical Christian environment was getting old; the extreme celebration of life and religion got harder to celebrate in light of my pop's inconsistent career. He never developed a plan to create a comfortable life for himself and his family, and my mom was getting frustrated raising two hungry boys with very little money on hand.

My mom had grown up in a broken family that had money problems, and she was hoping for better. My pop was just content making a living and wasn't driven when it came to his business or money. Stress grew, fights happened, and the breakup was inevitable. While they were still together but after we left the commune, my mom decided to pursue a career in modeling and acting, and my dad began drinking heavily. Before long, the marriage split and we were left with an ugly breakup. My mom got work at a modeling agency. Pop kept working construction and partying hard. But the breakup affected him deeply.

One day my dad showed up at the apartment complex in Sacramento where my mom had relocated after the separation. Her apartment—our apartment—was across the courtyard from my uncle Danny's apartment, and the man who arrived at the apartment complex bore almost no resemblance to the joyful, carefree person I knew. He was both drunk and furious, a bad combination. My mom had already started dating, and she was in the apartment with her new boyfriend. My brother and I were sitting in Uncle Danny's apartment, watching an ugly scene play out.

As I said, I was five or six and couldn't make sense of what was going on. Ryan sat next to me, bawling. Danny's girlfriend Debbi attempted to console him. I didn't need consoling. I was too scared to cry. My stomach felt like it was in my throat. I couldn't stop watching.

Pop staggered up the outside stairs leading to my mom's apartment, yelling and threatening. He was going as fast as his altered state would allow.

We could hear my mom's frantic pleading from inside. "What are you doing, Theo? I'm calling the police!"

Pop, normally the most mild-mannered and happy person you could ever hope to meet, was distraught over the breakup. He'd been drinking heavily. Apparently the anger and the booze combined to produce the combustible mix we were watching.

As Pop reached the top of the stairs, he stumbled toward her door and started kicking and hitting it. I watched, transfixed. *My pop was trying to break down the door.* I didn't understand any of it. *Bam! Bam! Bam!* I was terrified, paralyzed by fear. I flinched with every strike and my eyes blinked hard as the door swelled from the hinges. I could hear both my parents yelling, but their voices had merged to the point where I couldn't make out the words.

Then, suddenly, the door cracked open. My mom's boyfriend appeared at the entryway. He and Pop met like rams at the threshold. Within seconds they had both hit the floor.

I could hear my mom crying and screaming. "Danny! Danny!" Out of nowhere, Uncle Danny flew up the stairs two at a time. He started ripping the two apart. His ego as torn as his clothes, Pop punched the window, slicing his hand, before stumbling down the stairs and out of my sight.

My pop had a drinking problem that was spurred by the upheaval in his personal life stemming from the divorce. I'll admit something: I tell this story partly for the shock value. It's a story that gets lost among all the good experiences growing up, but I feel like it's important that people look at the bad times and assess how they had an effect on their lives. How you deal with adversity is a choice, and every person, in every walk of life, has to face difficult times. You are defined most by how you push through. Never let negative experiences be excuses.

So despite their hard times, and the hard feelings, my parents worked through their differences and came out stronger people. They worked together to raise my brother and me, adopting principles of consistency and

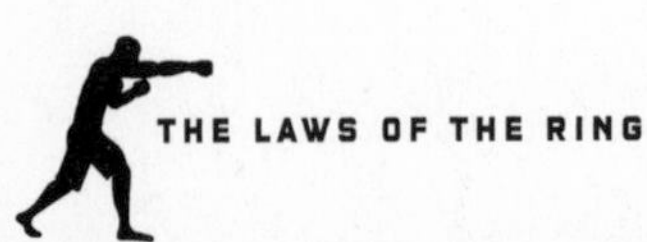

persistence along the way. It took work, and they both started from different places and advanced at different speeds, but they got there.

Your world might be turned upside down like Pop's was. You might be beside yourself with anger at a spouse or a boss or a colleague. The path to a dream life might begin by channeling that energy in a positive direction.

I'm not going to let the incident at the apartment complex be your lasting image of my pop. If that moment of weakness was indicative of who my pop really is, I wouldn't have included it. The truth is, showing him at his rawest and most vulnerable makes what I'm about to describe all the more powerful.

Early in 2011, Pop came to me and asked for a favor. He wanted me to come to his Alcoholics Anonymous meeting the next day and present him the chip commemorating his nineteenth year of sobriety.

I was touched, and honored. Of course I'd do it. I was proud of my pop for many reasons, and getting his life back on track after a difficult divorce was a big one. The way he maintained a positive attitude and attacked sobriety with persistence was an inspiration.

My pop traveled a long and difficult path from that day at the apartment complex to the day he asked me to present him the chip. If you had seen him enraged, drunk, and helpless back outside the apartment complex, you never would have known what a productive and happy person he was. He went through some hard times and had some bad habits, but the broken man of the postdivorce years is someone everyone has always loved to be around.

A victory over alcohol isn't incredible in the crazy world we live in, but it reminds us that there are always personal battles to be won. There is no such thing as a lost cause, or a dead end. Through persistence, attitude, and creativity, there's always an escape route.

Remember, the only two things you absolutely have to do in life are: (1) die; and (2) live every day until you do. If you've committed to making a change in your life, the past is irrelevant. It is the only thing you cannot change, so cleanse the regret and the guilt from your system.

My pop had a drinking problem, made worse by the upheaval in his personal life stemming from the divorce. My brother and I were always his true passion, and changing his habits was something he decided to do for us—and in doing so, he helped himself.

I don't know if it's customary for the presenter of a sobriety chip to give a speech, but I wasn't going to let the occasion pass without a few words about my pop. When they gave me the chip and called my pop to the front of the room, I said, "Congratulations to my pop—it's been nineteen years of sobriety. And to be honest with all of you, I don't remember much of the bad stuff about my dad's drinking, but I remember a ton of the great stuff with him *not* drinking."

I had planned to say a little bit more about my pop, but I never got there. I was too choked up to go on, and so the speech ended when Pop walked up to me and gave me a big hug and a kiss.

The fight I recounted from my uncle's apartment complex was the worst fight I remember, but there were a few others. Eventually, our lives calmed down and our days settled into a regular pattern. Ryan and I began doing our own modeling and acting—runway modeling at local fashion shows, some commercial work, and even live plays. Although my parents couldn't stand each other, they remained loving and supportive to my brother and me.

When I think back to my childhood, I tend to remember the positive things that built me into the competent and successful adult that I am today. The bad habits that sparked the divorce are mostly relegated to someplace in my subconscious, but have no doubt been an important part of who I am today.

The habits that were changed in my parents' lives served as a living lesson for me. You can always make changes to better your life. Start your new healthy habits today.

THE 4TH LAW OF POWER

LIFE IS ABOUT THE JOURNEY, NOT THE DESTINATION

Football was my first passion, and my style of play was fearless bordering on reckless. And I'm sure many people who watched me will tell you I crossed that border regularly. Despite my size, my goal on every play was to make a big hit. I wanted everyone on the other team to experience a Urijah Faber hit at one point or another.

There was a 250-pound running back who played for a rival high school my senior year. He was strong, too, and a load to bring down. On one play, I lined up at left cornerback and they ran him on a sweep to the other side of the field. He broke free down the sideline and I was the only guy left who had a chance to stop a touchdown. From the other side of the field, I had the angle on him and I was on a full sprint. Now, as I was running I wasn't thinking about the physics of this collision. I wasn't attempting to calculate what would happen when a 135-pound dude running full speed hits a 250-pound dude running full speed. I wasn't thinking I was at a disadvantage, or at risk for injury. In my head, I was never a little guy trying to play with big guys. My confidence had me thinking I was going to *destroy* this guy.

Just as I reached the big guy, he turned his shoulders toward me to take me on. I lowered my shoulder and hit him with all I had . . . he moved about a foot. That was enough—it got him out of bounds and saved a touchdown, but I couldn't believe he didn't go down or hardly even move. I accomplished my goal, I guess, but I remember thinking, *If I hadn't gone full speed and all out, he would have run right through me.* As it was, it was like a housefly trying to take down a bull. Whenever I see Coach Fowler from Lincoln High School, he brings it up. "Whenever I think of you, I think of that time you hit that 250-pounder from Marysville," he says. "You were just so fearless!"

For me, it was just something I did. There was no other way to play. But Coach Fowler doesn't remember that play because I saved a touchdown; he remembers it because of the kind of wild confidence and fearlessness it exemplified. That one crazy hit was an embodiment of what I was all about. Without giving it a conscious thought, I did more than get a 250-pound beast of a running back out of bounds. I gave someone a concise summary of my *personal credit* (a term I'll discuss more later, but, in short, a summation of one's *true* dedication and credibility).

Too often, people say, "If I can only achieve [insert accomplishment here], I will be happy." This is counterproductive and serves only to lower expectations. Try to resist imposing artificial limits on your dreams.

A bank might reward the officer who racks up the most new accounts in a month. He might get a bonus or a sweet parking spot for his work. But there might be another officer two cubicles down who starts half the number of accounts but takes extra time with each customer to make sure he sets them up with the right account for their needs. He might discover something about them and put his knowledge to work in making a difference in their lives. Rather than stockpiling awards, that bank officer is expressing his passion in a way that helps not just himself, his customers, and his employer, but his entire community.

Put simply, you don't want to be prisoner to a timetable. If you happen to come up short, the artificial deadline creates unnecessary doubt in your abilities. If you beat a deadline, the temptation will be to make the next one

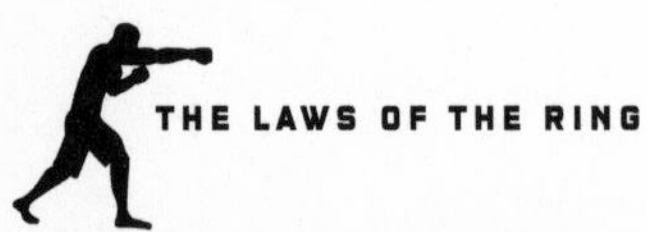

more stressful. Work persistently and creatively toward your goals. You'll know when you're making progress and moving forward. As time wears on, you'll be able to gauge the pace of the pursuit and adjust accordingly. It is vital to have goals and create a schedule, but it's unnecessarily confining to live by a calendar. It's important to set goals you can completely control, such as waking up at 6:00 A.M. every day and taking your vitamins. It's equally important to set big goals (dreams) that you can't completely control, such as winnning a presidential election.

My professional achievements are a matter of public record, and as someone who has defended world championships—small ones like *King of the Cage,* big ones like WEC—over an extended period of time, I'm often questioned about pressure and expectations. *What's next? Who's next?* In that context, it can be difficult to explain the way I live my life. Having a belt or a title is not what defines me. Being a public figure and getting recognized as I walk through an airport or eat in a restaurant has changed how *other people* define me, but not how I define myself. I define myself by my actions, work ethic, and my morals. I live for my supportive family and friends who have helped sculpt my persona and identity.

So, don't only set goals like "Salesperson of the Year" or "Employee of the Month." Short-term achievements are great, but can cloud the issue and get in the way of the bigger purpose. They also establish external forces—bosses, clients, etc.—as judges of your achievements. When artificial achievements become the journey *and* the destination, you run the risk of losing control of your passion. In other words, if I had been unable to get the 250-pounder out of bounds—which would have been a failure by statistical standards—I like to think Coach Fowler would still remember the incident as an example of what I was all about.

THE 5TH LAW OF POWER

KNOW YOURSELF

The decision to pursue wrestling in college was easy. In fact, you might say it was made *for* me. I was a good high-school football player. By my senior season I was an all-league cornerback and the third back in our Wing-T offense, but in the back of my head I always knew that no matter how much I loved football, it was never going to love me back in quite the same way. For a five-foot-five-and-a-half-inch 135-pounder, a future as a Division I football player was not impossible, yet not very likely either. But wrestling . . . wrestling was different. In this sport, I didn't need to hear someone else's thoughts on what was important, and a hundred pounds on a lesser athlete wasn't going to negate my hard work and grit.

Everyone has talents, but you can't be creative without a degree of self-knowledge that sometimes comes with a dose of brutal honesty about your talents. We all know people who have delusions about themselves. I'm not talking about "clinical" delusions, just, well, socially acceptable ones. The guy who thinks all the women love him, the woman who thinks she can be Miss America (despite all empirical evidence to the contrary), the old man who thinks he can go into a bar and beat up anybody forty years younger.

I had to understand the reality of my talents and how they matched up with my passion. The team nature of football was better suited to my personality, but wrestling was better suited to my mentality and physical talents, and so I threw myself into the sport with all-out zeal. I loved the individual nature of the sport, the one-on-one aspect of the competition.

I read whatever books I could lay my hands on and watched every instructional video I could find until the tape was worn out. I was determined to work harder than anybody else every day at practice. I not only watched college and Olympic wrestlers but I studied their habits and demeanor. I felt there were secrets locked inside those people, and if I learned their best attributes I would have an advantage over those competitors who didn't.

And I adopted Dan Gable, the great University of Iowa and Olympic wrestler, as one of my heroes. (Little did I know I would later be fortunate enough to break bread with Gable and have some one-on-one conversations with him.) I saw the fierce but quiet confidence he exuded when he stepped onto the mat, and I knew that his demeanor had an effect on the wrestlers who were faced with the task of competing against him.

Like Gable, I loved to compete, and I would contend that I *needed* to compete. Competition was like a drug for me. I loved looking into the eyes of my opponent and thinking about all the preparation that had gone into the moment. I loved the immediacy of the contest, and how it could turn one way or another in an instant.

There is a difference between creativity and self-delusion. Football, for the reasons described above, wasn't the best path for me to follow. Creativity comes after you have established your sense of purpose and are prepared to attack it with a positive attitude. You have to be realistic about your abilities. Shoot higher without being delusional. I don't plan on winning a jump ball against Shaquille O'Neal, but could I maybe play in the NBA? Who knows—Spud Webb did and he was barely an inch taller than me. Could Spud Webb have taken his talent and hard work into the Octagon as professional fighter? I'm almost positive he would believe that he could.

Shoot for the stars when you attack your passions, but give yourself every advantage to get there. Find your strengths and conquer your weaknesses.

THE 6TH LAW OF POWER

WORK HARDER AND SMARTER (STUMBLING VS. PLANNING)

There was very little wrestling history at Lincoln High School, so I wanted to create it. I arrived early and stayed late. The fitness aspect of sports never scared me—I *loved* to work out—but moderation wasn't one of my trademarks at this point.

So during my sophomore year, I had what I thought was a great idea. I was going to run to school in the morning. This would allow me to get in an extra workout, help me stay ahead of the competition. Wrestling had become a serious pursuit for me by this time, and as I've said, I approached it the way I did everything else in my life: with intent to win. I saw this running idea as a way of separating myself from the average wrestler—of doing just a little bit more than was expected of me.

We lived out in the country, a good distance from school; but "it's pretty far" was about as scientific as I got with my planning. I knew it took my mom fifteen or twenty minutes to drive to school but that was about as far as my research went.

When the appointed day arrived for me to embark on my journey, I made arrangements to have my backpack dropped off at school. I told my parents I would not be taking the bus.

So far, so good.

Since I didn't know the number of miles I would be running, I didn't have a good idea of how long it would take me to get to my destination. I had built this day up in my mind as epic—the day I would do something nobody else would even attempt—and the enormity of the feat led me to set my alarm for four-thirty. I wanted to make sure I left myself enough time, sure, but it was more than that: Something like this called for true sacrifice, not only in the running but in the amount of pain I would inflict on myself by getting up at this ungodly hour.

I got out of bed as soon as the alarm rang and headed outside to test the weather. The predawn winter air was brisk, so I dressed accordingly. Long johns, sweatpants, thermal long-sleeved undershirt, and sweatshirt, and capped it off—literally—with a beanie.

At four forty-five, I was out the door and running down the dirt driveway, ready for my big adventure. I was probably less than half a mile into the run when I realized I was seriously overdressed. Rivulets of sweat trickled down my back and beads began forming on my forehead.

Off came the sweatshirt, which I tied around my waist.

A few strides later I yanked the beanie off my head and crammed it into the pocket of my sweatpants.

I was in excellent shape for a sophomore in high school, and before long I found myself in a good running groove. Despite being weighed down by the extra clothes, I was on a good pace.

Too good, as it turned out.

My "long run" turned out to be nine miles, and my lack of planning caused me to arrive at school more than two hours before my first class, half undressed, clothes tied around my waist, stuffed into my pockets, and crumpled up in my hands.

It was not even six o'clock in the morning, and I was at school. I probably could have run back home, taken a shower, and still caught the bus.

This was an exaggerated case of poor planning. I didn't use any tools to calculate how long the run was, or the amount of time it would take for me to complete it. When I tested the morning weather and found it chilly, I didn't account for the heat my body would generate while running for more than an hour.

The run taught me a lesson: Passion without a plan is incomplete. It's great to be motivated and want to do more, but you want to be smart in your pursuit.

As I got older and wiser, I came to see this story as a parable of preparation. There are plenty of people out there with goals, people who desperately want to achieve something great. They have the passion to put those goals into motion. They aren't afraid to work for it. But too many people fall into the trap I call "Stumbling vs. Planning." My run to school was the perfect example of stumbling. I thought I had it planned, but my passion had blinded me to the importance of planning. I was stumbling, forced to make sense of it as I went along. To put your passion to work, you have to plan it out. There are going to be twists along the way, as we've seen in chapters 2 and 3 about persistence and creativity. But if you approach your passion with a realistic plan, you'll put yourself in a far better position to succeed—and succeed quickly. The less time you spend fixing problems after the fact, like wondering what you're going to do with the two hours before school, the more time you'll have to work on your passion.

If you don't plan, you'll end up in the same position as a fifteen-year-old Urijah Faber. You won't know where or how to start, and you won't understand the nuances of the old saying *Where there's a will there's a way.*

Possessing the will is important, but being smart in your pursuit will allow you to accomplish and achieve more.

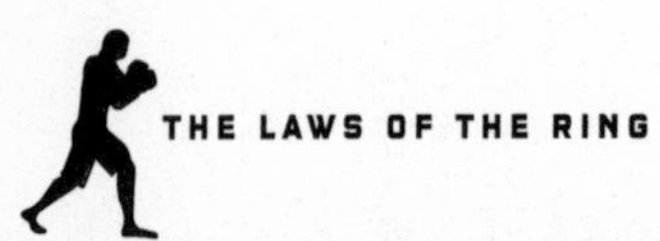

THE 7TH LAW OF POWER

PUSH THROUGH LIFE'S HICCUPS (DEALING WITH CHANGE)

I want to tell you the story of my brother, Ryan. It's not an easy story for me to tell. Ryan is two years older than me, and he's always been my hero. Our relationship was forged through a shared experience: the days and nights with our dad in the motor home, going back and forth between our mom and dad's places, being each other's rock during a bad divorce. My days watching in admiration as Ryan played high school football and wrestled. I remember when he started freshman football and I was in sixth grade, I would wake up each morning, fill a jug with ice-cold water, and ride my bike to the summer conditioning practice. I'd show up to watch the end of his practices, just in time to see him finish with the lead group on all the runs. He didn't have the best physique or style as a freshman in high school, but he was the hardest-working guy out there, and he led by example.

When I was a freshman in high school, he was a senior and the captain of the football and wrestling teams. He was a peer counselor in athletics. He was on the student council. He took all the available AP and honors courses, was fluent in Spanish after just three years of taking courses, he was off the charts in math. He had to take math classes at the junior college as early as his junior year because they didn't have a teacher at school who was at his level. Ryan never smoked, never drank, and as the MC brought spirit into all the pep rallies at school. I know there's no such thing as the perfect kid, but he came as close as humanly possible to fitting the definition.

He was so good, in fact, that I never wanted to let him know whenever I did anything bad. I wasn't a bad kid, but you have to understand Ryan. He was wall-to-wall good, and he had very little tolerance for missteps. I drank some in junior high and tried weed as an eighth grader, and I knew if Ryan caught wind of it there would be hell to pay. Besides, I didn't want to disappoint him.

Ryan was accepted into Cal Polytechnic in San Luis Obispo after he graduated from high school, but he decided to take the air force ROTC scholarship he was awarded and attend Citrus Community College near Los Angeles. It was all planned out: Ryan would attend Citrus, near my grandparents on my mother's side, for two years, and then transfer to Azusa Pacific University. After graduation, he would go on to become an air-force pilot.

Ryan was incredibly organized for a young man, and left nothing to chance. He had a job working in a Nordstrom's café in Sacramento (he would commute thirty minutes from Lincoln), and before he left for Southern California, he contacted the Nordstrom's closest to the campus and managed to transfer his job to that store. Then, at eighteen, scholarship and job in tow, Ryan moved to Los Angeles. He rented a room from a family in the area, went to school, and worked.

During his first year, he would come home for holidays. Though we noticed that he was getting more into our family's early roots of Christianity, it didn't set off any alarms in our family; Ryan was eight when we left the Christian commune, so he had a stronger religious education than I did. (I was five.) He got all As and continued to be the responsible, upstanding guy we all knew. But when he came back for the summer after his first year in college, I noticed *serious* changes. His beliefs were becoming more fanatical. It's not just seemingly innocuous stuff like the fact that he wouldn't check out girls like he used to—which to *me* was alarming—now he was getting up at four-thirty every morning to read his Bible.

Ryan doesn't do anything halfway, and we knew that he had become a member of the International Church of Christ (Boston Movement). It wasn't until later that we found out this Church of Christ is one of the fastest-growing and most destructive cults in America. *Time* magazine did a story on them, as did television information programs such as *A Current Affair,* a popular news show at that time. This group recruits almost exclusively on college campuses, and it uses young, good-looking people to do the recruiting. They target people like Ryan who are idealistic and away from home for the first time.

There is a big emphasis on fun activities, but the real push is to increase your monetary and time commitment to the church. In addition to the financial requests, each member was assigned to a group of peers with a "discipler," a person in charge, to keep him in line on his commitment to the International Church of Christ's interpretation of the Bible. He was expected to report to this person regarding every aspect and decision in his life. They twisted scriptures to encourage eating less, sleeping less, and giving more money to the church, even if you didn't have it—they didn't care if you were a young college student trying to make ends meet. Guilt was a major tool in the church's arsenal to control its members, so they went to great lengths to get members to tell anything and everything about their current self and their past and exaggerated "the sinfulness" of what they were coerced into sharing. Kip McKean, the leader of the group, saw to it that his disciplers were collecting everyone's money while (we are told) he and his family were living a lavish lifestyle in Malibu, apparently thanks to the devotion of his followers.

I had only just completed my sophomore year in high school when Ryan was first involved, and as time went on I began to see him getting more and more wrapped up in this church. I remember, during my junior year, questioning Ryan's thought process when he was home for Christmas. He had been praying for me to find a relationship with the Lord, which I guess I could understand, but he also told me he had been including our grandparents in his prayers. Our grandparents were immigrants from Holland and were about as devoted Christians as can be. They were part of the resistance during World War II and hid Jewish families in their home, which nearly cost them their lives, but helped save the lives of those families. My grandfather, Gerard Faber, was a music professor at Asbury Christian College in Kentucky, as well as the organist at his church. My grandmother, Gerry Faber, had her own seat reserved in the front row at church, and I've yet to receive a holiday, birthday card, or a phone call from them without a biblical quote or religious inspiration at the end.

Needless to say, the alarms went off when Ryan was extremely worried that my grandparents were going to hell because they weren't following the Bible the right way, like his church. I remember laughing hard at Ryan and saying, "Dude, are you being serious?" It was apparent that he was, even after I used my best logic and sarcasm to paint a picture of how crazy he was being. The conversation ended with Ryan frustrated, a little stumped, but holding on to his faith as he believed it was the only truth.

A few months later he took my entire family to one of his church's group baptisms in Sacramento, which was being held in a banquet room at the Hilton. Ryan didn't know anyone at the church (his group was in LA, the LAICC) but you couldn't tell. He walked in and, as a member of the church, was greeted like a family member. A man got up on the stage and began preaching about his relationship with a girl. He started out by saying their relationship was originally only about sex, and it got a little graphic. It was really odd and uncomfortable. Even my grandparents—who had been excited about Ryan's born-again Christianity—were so disturbed that they walked out. When I pointed this out to Ryan, he told me, "They were convicted."

Roughly six months after the meeting—on New Year's Eve 1997 to be exact—with Ryan one class shy of getting his AA degree and moving on to Azusa Pacific, my parents got a phone call from his boss at Nordstrom. His boss said, "I know this is not any of my business, but if he was my child, I would want to know. Ryan hasn't been showing up for work on time, and when he does, he acts strange. He's losing weight—we can't get him to eat when he is here—he will rarely talk, and doesn't smile. He walks around with his head down, and isn't able to perform his job duties as before. Even his regular customers are noticing and commenting. You know Ryan, he is always so fun and bubbly, joking around and making people laugh—he is no longer himself."

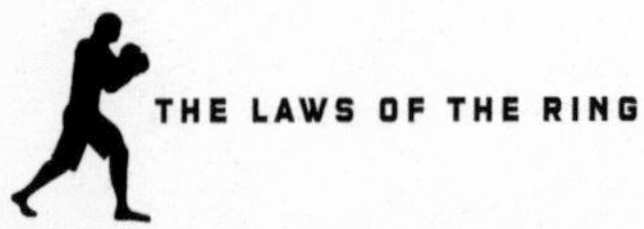

Both of my parents were remarried at this point, my mother to Tom and my father to a nice woman named Marrian. Both had their hands full. Pops was still recovering from a mild stroke he had suffered the previous summer, and my mom and Tom had Michaella, who was almost four.

But of course my mom snapped to attention and called the family Ryan had been renting from. Yes, they said, it seems like something's wrong. Ryan had moved in with some of his church friends earlier in the year, but had recently called the family and asked to move back with them.

Concern turned to panic. My mom, stepdad Tom, Pop, and stepmom Marrian left Michaella with me and drove seven long and anxious hours to Los Angeles to find Ryan. My mom had his ex-girlfriend's number and pieced together where he would be. They found him at a New Year's Eve party for the LAICC. It was on the college campus at Cal Poly SLO. When they finally found the ICC New Year's Eve party, Ryan was nowhere to be found. They looked relentlessly, asking various people if they knew or had seen him. Finally, my mom spotted him. Ryan was sitting by himself in a fetal-type position on a section of one of the lawns on campus. His arms were wrapped around his legs with his head almost in his lap.

"Ryan, is that you?" my mom asked. He looked up.

"Mom?" Ryan said faintly. My mom was horrified. It was him. Ryan was skin and bones, almost unrecognizable. He was so gaunt and starved-looking that you could see the outline of his teeth through his skin. It was as if he had been locked up as a prisoner of war. There was another church member standing nearby, just watching him as if not to let him out of their sight.

My mom and pop said, "Come on Ryan, we're taking you away from here."

He said, "I have to tell my discipler first and make sure it's okay." My parents were fuming by then, and my mom said, "What? You have to ask someone if you can leave with your parents? Who is your discipler?" My mom couldn't wait to be face-to-face with this person.

"Steve Burger."

"Okay then, let's go talk to Steve," my mom said. She said that when she met him, she could not believe this was a religious leader. He wore a white button-down dress shirt, almost completely unbuttoned to be sure everyone could see his chest, a gold chain, and a diamond earring in one ear. Mom said he looked more like a pimp. My mom had some very choice words with him, and my parents then took Ryan for a walk until they could convince him that they would just take a short ride.

Of course, they were kidnapping him, without much protest other than his mumbling attitude about needing to tell his discipler he was leaving. You could see the relief on his face as they drove off—he was very hesitant and scared but also relieved. They drove directly to the house where he was staying with his fellow church members, went to his room, packed up his belongings, and drove back to Lincoln. My mom called me at the house in Lincoln and gave me a warning: "Honey, I'm just letting you know your brother doesn't look good, we're driving home right now. We have all of his stuff."

I walked out front when they pulled into the driveway of my mom's house. Ryan walked up and a chill went through me. He looked like a shell of a person, devoid of emotion, completely emptied out of any trace of the Ryan we knew. Ryan is nearly six feet tall and weighed a lean and in-shape 165 pounds in high school; now he was maybe 120–125 pounds. Less than me. As I walked up to him I forced a smile and said, "What's up Ryan?" but he didn't even lift his arms to hug me back as I reached up to give him a hug. He was mute.

He lay down on the couch and slept for three days straight. And when he did wake up, he didn't stay awake long. It was obvious that he had been severely sleep deprived. He wouldn't eat at all and my mom feared that he would die. She finally got him to eat only by feeding him herself. He wouldn't talk but wrote, "They told me I am debaucherous." A word my mother had never heard of. "I am afraid of what they will do to my family if I talk." All of our lives were changed from that day on.

Almost immediately, my mom's life went from having two successful boys and a beautiful new daughter and enjoying our successful Lincoln business, the Morning Glory, to being obsessed with finding out what was wrong with Ryan. The quest consumed her. She took him to doctors. Psychologists, spiritual healers, and psychiatrists. More appointments than you

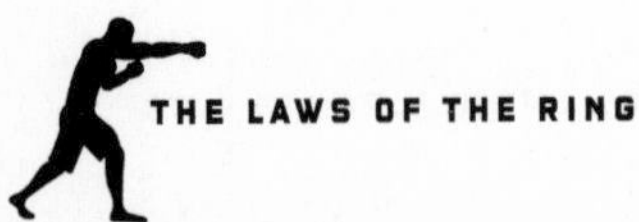

can imagine. She even sought out experts of every kind, including cult experts and deprogrammers. She took Ryan to the nation's leading cult abuse expert, now deceased, Margaret Singer. She flew another cult expert from the East coast for about five days and then she flew with Ryan to Boston to work with Steve Hassan, another leading cult abuse expert and deprogrammer. She was determined and obsessed with finding answers. I am sure she spent tens of thousands of dollars trying to help Ryan find his way back to himself.

It was my senior year when he came home, smack in the middle of wrestling season. I had been previously consumed by college prep, but now the only thing going through my mind was hoping Ryan could get better. When it came time to sit down and do my college applications, I had no idea what I was going to do or where I was going to go. My girlfriend Michelle sat down with me and helped me fill out applications, but we were all preoccupied with Ryan.

Ryan was one month away from his twenty-first birthday when he came home that night. The diagnosis was all over the place when he was first home. It seemed that with the help of these fanatical people he had pushed his strict lifestyle with food and sleep deprivation too far, which had caused some sort of mental, spiritual and emotional breakdown. Ryan went through all types of schizophrenic-like behaviors, acting out from intense fear that the cult would come and get him and his family. I would take him out to drive around and he would swear people were following us, constantly looking back in fear.

There were times when I would look into Ryan's eyes and his pupils would take up his whole eyeball, fluctuating big and small, big and small over and over again. He would be overcome with a glazed look. Completely dissociated as if out of his body, he didn't seem to even know we were there. Often strange behavior followed. To my mom, the behavior was the explanation and expression of the abuse and trauma that caused his breakdown. He would get real quiet, barely speaking for days and weeks on end. He would appear catatonic, even standing on one foot for hours at a time, oblivious to anything around him. He often behaved as if he were drugged and having withdrawals, especially at certain times of the day, though neither Ryan nor any of us had ever had drugs in our bodies. Other times he would sleep for days on end or stop eating or refuse to go to the bathroom. Ryan would take showers with his clothes on.

He would spit out random words one after another, exhibiting sometimes shocking and scary behavior. My mom is convinced that something horrific happened to him, and that it was all hints of the trauma and the abuse he experienced. It was like his mind was rebuilding itself after a total breakdown, his way of processing what he had been through and trying to make sense of it and cope in the best way he could.

One day passed, then months, then years. Progress still seems to be two steps forward and one step back, but there is always progress. Ryan has a place in our family, has had relationships and friendships and has worked for stints, but he is constantly battling the riddle of unpredictability. He is haunted—by what, we are to this day not really sure, and we don't know if we will ever know what happened. It is still a mystery.

There have been some really great times for Ryan, some scary ones, and a bunch of funny stories despite the misfortune of the situation. After fourteen years of dealing with the new adjustments brought about by Ryan's illness, any sadness or anger or disbelief has lain dormant and life just goes on. If you ever meet my brother, be prepared to laugh. Sometimes the comedy is by design, and other times it's accidental. He had a great sense of humor even before his breakdown, perhaps inherited from our great-grandfather Ford Leary (Jackie Gleason's understudy, and the trombonist and singer for the Larry Clinton Orchestra back in the day). He still has his brains and his wit, but you just never really know how it's going to come out. Over the years, occasionally Ryan's problems have caused situations where the police have been involved. The lack of understanding and appropriate training with regard to people like Ryan, who have had severe trauma, has caused misunderstandings. Thankfully, Ryan's behavior in these situations has always been innocent and explainable.

Suffice it to say, Ryan's illness completely changed our family dynamic, and this is true fourteen years later. Michaella, who is nineteen as I write this, never got a chance to meet the guy that I grew up with, but they are close, and she knows his great heart and what a sweet person he is. Michaella has been an important part of Ryan's life and healing. She has immense compassion for those in need and suffering. In a way she was born into this situation, because she was too young to remember how he was before this tragedy happened in Ryan's life.

He is someone I have looked up to my entire life as a mentor, as an athlete, a scholar, and a leader. Now I look up to him for different reasons. For being a fighter against a battle tougher than the ones I will ever face; fighting against the unpredictability of life and keeping a great attitude; never giving up and making the best of a situation he didn't get to choose. He has been a teacher to our family in many ways.

Millions of families deal with similar mental or emotional-health issues. Like us, they cope with the lack of services and true understanding. Mental illness is not a broken leg or a sprained ankle, where a cast or a limp makes it obvious there is something wrong. There's nothing Ryan did to bring this on, and there seems to be nothing he can do to completely rid himself of these problems and dilemmas he is faced with on a daily basis. My mom gets upset when I call it mental illness. She says it is unresolved emotional and spiritual dilemma, and that finding resolve has been the most challenging thing she has ever been faced with. It is particularly difficult because Ryan has never told us the full details of his trauma. Nor does he seem to be able to.

I'm proud of Ryan. He has worked harder and shown more courage than anyone I know. He is a vital member of our community, right next to me under the umbrella, but taking care of him has been a shared responsibility. I remember driving around the campus shortly after I was accepted at UC Davis, and feeling guilty for thinking I couldn't wait to get out of the house and come to live in this new, exciting place. The truth is, my mom has shouldered the vast majority of the burden, but we all try to do our best to give her a break.

Ryan is one of my biggest fans, but the emotions and energy surrounding a fight can be a little much for him to handle at times. He hasn't attended all my fights, but we have had some good fight stories together over the years.

My fifth fight took place at the Soboba Casino near Palm Springs, where I fought against Rami Boukai in the fall of 2004. This was still at the beginning of my career, when money and accommodations weren't what they should have been. Ryan was staying with me at the time and drove the nine hours from Sacramento with me and my friend Virgil Moorehead to watch the fight.

I won by decision, but was disappointed because I couldn't finish the fight. Rami was a good jujitsu fighter, and he got my back for two minutes of the last round and was holding me as I was punching at him behind me. I eventually reversed position and ended on top of him and won the fight.

It was my first fight in *King of the Cage,* and I walked away a winner, but afterward, Virgil—my harshest critic—who had been drinking, kept riding me.

"You couldn't finish him, you blew it. You shoulda KO'd his ass!"

"You don't have any power, and that was on pay-per-view."

Virgil was getting on my nerves more than usual. I was used to his heckling—it's kind of our unique way of communicating—but jeez, was he irritating. Virgil is a great friend, and usually his brand of honesty is something I appreciate, but he wasn't helping matters on this night. Ryan was with us, and although I knew this wasn't an ideal thing to do, he was coming with us to the bars to celebrate.

Anyway, we walked down the strip in Palm Springs—me, Ryan, Virgil, our friend Reed Shelger, and two of Reed's friends, who were bouncers from a bar in San Diego's Pacific Beach. Virgil, as it turned out, forgot his ID, and he couldn't get into a club. Our San Diego bouncer friends took over, talking to the Palm Springs bouncers as if there was some bouncers' code that supersedes California law.

"We'll vouch for him," they said. "He's with us."

The guys at the door were having none of it. No ID, no entry. Simple as that. Virgil and our bouncer friends weren't accepting this answer. They thought an exception could be made. I was tired, ready to get out of there and go somewhere else. They weren't. This had become an ego thing, and it escalated into a fight. My hands were swollen. I had a check for fifteen hundred bucks in my pocket. The last thing I wanted to do was have to get into

a brawl outside a club with a bunch of bouncers, drunk Virgil, Reed, and my brother.

So I stayed out of it. The fight was between the two sets of bouncers, and as far as I was concerned, it could stay that way. Ryan was out of it, Reed was mostly just talking from the margin, and Virgil—to this point—was just watching.

Unfortunately, that didn't last long. Virgil jumped into the fight, trying to help the bouncers who were trying to get him into the club. Virgil was going after one bouncer while the other, standing next to me but behind Virgil, reached down and grabbed a rope stanchion that was separating the lines to enter the club, primed to hit Virgil over the head.

So much for me staying out of the fight.

I hit him with a straight right to the jaw that he never saw coming. His feet stayed exactly where they were, the stanchion dropped harmlessly to the side, and his body slid to the sidewalk, out cold.

Virgil turned around and looked at me, his eyes wide.

"I told you I have power," I said.

Just as I was showing Virg how I saved him and proved him wrong, we saw a female Palm Springs cop jogging up the street wearing Daisy Duke shorts. "Hey you, come here," she said, pointing at me. I made a quick dumb decision to flee the scene rather than face the consequences, so I took off from the group, ducked into an alley, and sat there in the dark. My hands hurt like hell. I didn't know where anybody was, but figured they were all together. I was thinking that I would sit in the alley for a bit and then go find the group. Virgil was good with Ryan, so I didn't think much damage could be done in the next half hour before I rejoined them.

After about twenty minutes, I peeked out of the alley and saw a bike cop sitting about ten feet away scanning the area. It was clear the cop had seen someone run into the alley. Then I looked about fifty feet down and a cop car was sitting there also. They were surrounding the block and weren't going anywhere, so eventually I came out to face the music.

"What are you doing, why did you run?" the bike cop asked.

"My friends got in a fight, and I ran because everybody ran."

"Why are your hands messed up?"

"I'm an MMA fighter, and I fought tonight in the casino."

He either didn't believe me or didn't understand what I was talking about, so I pulled the check out of my wallet and showed him.

I was handcuffed and arrested for obstructing an officer from duty (running from the scene of the fight). I was in the back of a paddy wagon and was able to get my cell phone out of my pocket, so I put it on speaker and I called Virgil. Having my hands behind my back didn't help. I could hear someone had answered the phone and so I was yelling, "Virg, I got arrested! Make sure you take care of Ryan!" I was panicked and pissed, and knew Virgil had been drinking. I was worried about Ryan, but felt like my friends could all handle the situation until I was released. I spent the night in a cell (the drunk tank) for the first and only time in my life, and at five in the morning they called my name and let me go. I rushed back to the hotel, but I had no idea what room we were in. I simply couldn't remember. I asked the front desk and they refused to tell me. Finally, I had to give the guy thirty bucks just to tell me the room number, and the first thing I saw when I got there was a hole in the wall roughly five feet two inches above the floor—Virgil's height.

There were my friends sprawled out around the room. Nobody made it to the comfort of the two beds in the room. Virgil was there sleeping. Ryan was not in the room. I woke Virgil.

"Where's Ryan?"

"We thought he was with you."

"Me? I was in jail! I told you that!"

I was flipping out inside, but Virgil looked utterly clueless and quickly realized this was pointless. I took Virgil's keys and drove his pickup downtown. Panicked that I'd lost my brother forever, I drove from one street to the other until I suddenly saw Ryan. There he was, disheveled, sprinting across the street in my path then plopping down on a park bench, and looking at me like *where in the hell have you been*. I'd never been so happy to see him.

I rolled down the window and yelled over at him. He gave me the annoyed what-the-heck? gesture with his hands, and hopped on one foot to the street, a sign that he was stressed. I pulled the car up next to him.

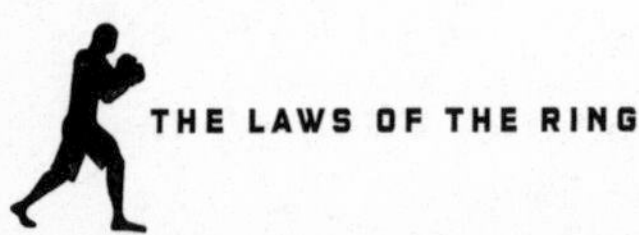

"Where the hell have you been?" I asked him.

"Where the hell have *you* been?" he replied.

Good point. "Get in the car," I told him as I reached over and opened the door. Ignoring my gesture, he did a three-step hurdle into the bed of the pickup, landing on his back. "What the heck are you doing? Get in!" I barked. He was pissed and just yelled back "Go!"—so I drove back to the hotel and we exchanged stories in the parking lot. He had just walked into the bar during all the commotion, ignoring the confrontation, and been on his own for the night. My friends had no idea I had been picked up by the cops and had all found each other after the senseless battle at the bar. Ryan spent the night roaming the main drag of Palm Springs. I couldn't help but laugh at how bitter he was about the situation, but I was more relieved than anything that I didn't have to face my mom without my big bro by my side.

Ryan and I had many adventures as kids, and we've had many more as adults. He and I still have a great relationship, it's just our roles have been reversed. It's almost as if I have become the big brother.

We have great hope for Ryan. After years of trying different solutions, we have all found that a healthy diet, a regimen of exercise, and family support suit him best. So far, it has worked well. Ryan lives a good life. He's loved unconditionally. Our whole family works together to create structure in Ryan's life. He works out two or three times a day. He goes to a local hyperbaric chamber, which he loves. Ryan is a hard worker and is always around to help the family with odd jobs. This last Thanksgiving Ryan ran the "Run to Feed the Hungry" 10K charity race, and is training for a half marathon in a few months. His bouts of hard times are inevitable, but he always gets through them and keeps on living. We may never know all the details of the trauma Ryan has lived through or the details of the cult experiences, but we know for sure that Ryan still has a great heart, lots of spirit and a good soul.

It takes strength for Ryan to stay positive and handle the ups and downs that life has dealt him. He knows his life has changed forever and that he is, in many ways, a different person from the eighteen-year-old scholar-athlete-mentor who was his little brother's hero. But the person he is now is equally inspiring and worthy of admiration.

Ryan has given me a whole new perspective on people in need. He and I used to ride the public bus as kids, and I was always the crack-up who would make jokes about the people who got on the bus. Silly kids' stuff like the big smelly guy, or the lady who would sit and argue with herself. Now I think about how many of those people might have had stories like Ryan's. Maybe a severe trauma that has never really been resolved and is eternally engraved in their mind, making them who they are now. Maybe they have no emotional support for whatever their mental torture is. Could be any number of heartbreaking scenarios. You never know when, in the blink of an eye, your whole world can be flopped over and rolled away, leaving you powerless to control it. Changed forever.

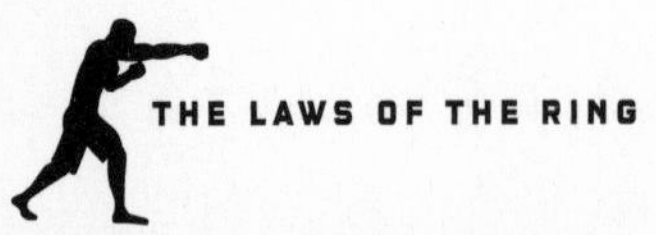

THE 8TH LAW OF POWER

LEARN FROM YOUR MISTAKES

It's great to grow up with freethinking and free-spirited parents. You get to experience life on your own terms and make your own mistakes (and, hopefully, learn from them). But when I got to UC Davis, I quickly discovered how poorly my upbringing and high school experience translated to the world of dormitories, roommates, and resident advisers.

I arrived at UC Davis fresh out of Lincoln, California, a town of about seven thousand people, mostly farmers and hardworking Mexicans. This, of course, was way after my Christian commune days. By this time my parents had split and my mom had married my stepdad, Tom. My friends and I had the run of the town. We'd go country-cruising around a local lake, and we'd hang out on my mom and stepdad's ten-acre lot and be as loud as we wanted. People in town knew us as good kids who sometimes got rambunctious. That's, of course, a nice way of saying we got away with a lot of stuff teenagers do, including driving around at all hours and partying at the local lake.

I was one of two boys from my class to attend a four-year college directly out of high school, and the number of college-bound girls didn't exceed us by much. But one of these was my high school sweetheart, who also chose Davis and was placed in the same dorm complex as me. To boot, it was less than an hour's drive from Lincoln to Davis, so it would be easy for my buddies from high school to come and visit—and party—in my new digs with me, my girl, and my new friends. The outspoken, friendly guy I am today is not an aberration of what I was at eighteen—so for better or worse (I like to think for better), everybody in the dorm knew me within a few hours of my arriving in college, and I quickly became friends with some excellent people like Dustin Soderman and my wrestling teammate Spanky Michaelis.

Because of wrestling practices and simply a desire to ingratiate myself in my new environment, I waited until about the third weekend of my college career before I invited Will Creger, Jim Cannon, and Brian Strand, three of my buddies who were still back home, to come experience college life with me. This was going to be my shining moment, when the best of my Lincoln and Davis worlds would collide.

Flash-forward . . . with beer in tow, Dustin, Spanky, and my other college friends were having a great time with my high school buddies. To me, this was the best. I was bringing my social circles together, and everybody was getting along as I'd hoped they would. But just as I convinced myself this new college atmosphere was easy to navigate, things got slightly out of hand. My buddies from high school started popping their heads into dorm rooms uninvited, flagrantly disregarding privacy and personal space. The alcohol was on full display in my room, and when word got around that the resident adviser was coming for heads, some people panicked and others just hung out. Spanky broke his leg jumping out of a second-floor window in an attempt to avoid being caught. My buddies from home, thinking they were re-creating our senior trip to Puerto Vallarta, followed suit and jumped off the second-floor balcony into the pool in the dormitory courtyard. And there were beer cases everywhere. With my friends cleared out, I quickly cleaned up some (which is to say, barely at all) and went to bed.

It was a wild night.

I'm not sure what time the night ended, but it was well into the morning. I wasn't in a position to take inventory of all the damage we had wrought, but the next day there was an official letter in my mailbox. I was being writ-

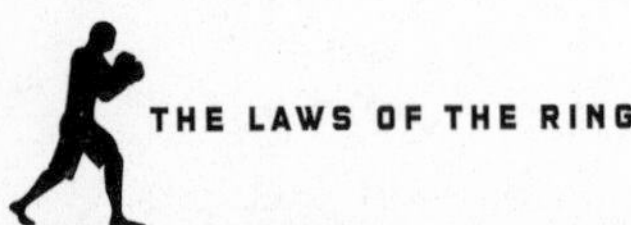

ten up for violations of noise, curfew, and alcohol, and I would need to appear before the resident adviser. I knew there were rules to living in the dorm, but I'd been too busy with wrestling and classes to consider them very closely. And let's be honest, I was still on Lincoln time, where everybody knew us and we could get away with being a little crazy without worrying about anyone getting too upset. Besides, we were just having a little fun and hindsight is always 20/20.

No big deal, I thought. *I've never been in trouble before, and this is just a minor deal.* I was so unconcerned that I neglected to write down the time and date of the meeting with the resident adviser.

Four or five days later, I got up around six in the morning to go for a long run. When I got back, I hopped into the dormitory spa in the courtyard. The rules stated that there was to be no spa use at that hour, but I concluded that since there was no one around and that if I was quiet, it would be no big deal. You can already see that by this point I was, unknowingly, compounding my mistakes.

On cue, the RD (resident director) came out of his room, which was directly across from the spa, and stopped in his tracks when he saw me.

"What are you doing?"

"Uh . . . relaxing after a run?" I said.

"Do you realize we're supposed to be having a meeting right now?"

"Oh, dude—I completely forgot. I'm sorry. I'll be right there."

Instead of heading to my room to change, I went directly to the RD's room to have the meeting. I had a towel around my waist and was wearing no shirt.

The RD looked at me with disgust. I didn't mean any harm, but I had broken nearly every rule in the book. I had shown no indication that I understood the severity of the situation. And now I showed up for the meeting bare-chested, seconds after breaking *another* rule by being in the spa at the wrong time. I was young, but not an idiot, and I pretty quickly realized that my state of *un*dress was going to fan the flames.

The RD started running down the list of offenses of the previous weekend. There was alcohol in the room. People were jumping off balconies. Curfew was broken. Noise rules were violated. A door was broken.

"Sorry," I said. "Those were my buddies. I guess they thought they were in Mexico." I wasn't mocking the guy; just trying to lighten the mood.

"*You're* responsible for your buddies," he said, clearly not amused.

He was getting more pissed off every minute. I was disrespecting him by dismissing what he had to say and sitting there in nothing but a wet towel.

"I'm going to recommend you meet with Judicial Affairs," he said. "You are in some trouble."

I immediately understood the implications of this. A meeting with Judicial Affairs was serious—not a student RA or even the head honcho of the dorms, the RD—and they had the authority to kick me out of school. I thought the guy had overreacted; surely he could have just disciplined me without passing me on to the big-time authorities, couldn't he?

"Dude, it was all in fun," I said, expressing more urgency.

"Just watch your mail for the notice of your next date to appear," he said.

Well, I immediately developed a phobia about that mailbox and the phone in our room. I thought every envelope was a dismissal notice and every phone call was informing me that I was through.

I still remember the name of the man at Judicial Affairs who would be determining my fate—Donald Moore. When I met with him, he immediately gave me a pretty thorough dressing-down.

"You have to understand that you are now living in an environment with neighbors and rules," he said sternly. "You have to respect those neighbors and be aware of the rules."

Of course, by now I had come to the conclusion that I couldn't wiggle out of this with my boys-will-be-boys defense. That might have cut it back home in Lincoln, but Donald Moore was here to tell me those days were over.

I promised to do better, and I apologized for screwing up, and Moore put me on some sort of probationary watch list that meant I better not make any more mistakes.

Two weeks later I got back from a wrestling tournament late on a Saturday and went with some of the guys over to another dorm to see some friends. It turned out to be a full-on party, and within three minutes—no joke—I saw two RAs heading our way ready to break it up. I hadn't had a

beer. I barely had time to say hello to anyone. But I panicked. *I can't be in here. I can't be in here. I can't be in here.*

I went into the back bedroom and crawled out the first-floor window. I thought I was home free, until I found a slip in my mailbox the next morning. I had either been seen leaving the party or someone had turned me in. Back to Donald Moore I went.

This time, as you can imagine, it was more serious. I got moved out of my original dorm, away from my girlfriend, away from my friends Dustin and Spanky. I was informed that I had run out of last chances. One more screwup and I was gone.

But despite all this, I was still hanging around the old dorm quite a bit. One night, I was with my girlfriend in the lounge when Dustin came home from the frat he had just pledged. He was drunk, his head was shaved (from being hazed), and he was jumping around like a wild man.

The RD's room was right across from us, and Dustin started flipping off the door in a move I took as a form of protest against my removal from the dorm. He was bouncing around, laughing and being stupid, and at some point he decided it would be a good idea to piss on the floor's copy machine. So he did.

I didn't condone the act, but if you knew Dustin, you, too, would find it kinda funny. But the laughter subsided the next morning when Dustin heard a knock on his door. It was the RD.

"Did you piss on the copy machine?"

Dustin denied it up one side and down the other, but the RD *knew* he was the one who pissed on the copy machine because he watched him do it through the peephole in his door.

So Dustin got kicked out of the original dorm and found himself a new room in the dorm across from mine.

By this point you might be thinking that I was incorrigible, but I was tired of fucking up and behaved myself for the rest of the year. I studied, wrestled, kept my nose clean. I didn't so much as leave a strand of hair in the communal bathroom sink.

During spring-quarter finals week, the last week before summer vacation, Dustin and I finished our last exam and were walking through the hallway one night with another of our friends. We weren't loitering—we had a destination (another friend's room), and we weren't being obnoxious, I don't think, but the rules were stricter for finals week—no loud talking, no after-hours mingling in the dorms. We sat on the floor outside of two of our girl friends' room in the hallway and were talking quietly about plans for the summer when, to our surprise, an RA popped his head out and said, "I'm going to write you guys up." Apparently, our voices carried.

Neither of us lived in this dorm and *this* RA was one of the few who didn't know either one of us, so Dustin decided to lie about his name. Stupidly, I did the same.

I don't know what led me to believe I could get away with this. Although the RA didn't know me, you couldn't go ten feet without finding someone who did. I was an outgoing wrestler with an unusual name and a desire to know everybody I came across. And of course, in the RA community, there was a target on my back. I got a phone call from Donald Moore.

"We know you were the one in the hallway," he said. "You and I need to have a meeting to discuss lying and the university's code of conduct. I also want to know who was with you; we can talk about that when you get here."

Dustin begged me not to give him up. "Dude, my parents—you don't understand," he said. "It will kill them if I get kicked out of school. My life will be miserable. You can't give me up. You can't."

Obviously, it would have been better if he'd considered all the collateral damage before he made poor choices, but I couldn't unwind the clock. I felt for him—he was my friend—and so I went along with him when he came up with a plan to talk to one of our friends who had no previous behavior warnings.

"Dude, I need a big favor," Dustin started with this guy, Darren.

Darren was a cool dude who hadn't had any write-ups or trouble throughout the year; he was a good friend also and realized that talking in the hallway was not going to get him into much trouble. A first write-up, especially for something so small, was basically just a warning and our time in the dorms was days away from being over.

Within minutes, Darren went from "no way" to "okay." Dustin is a good salesman.

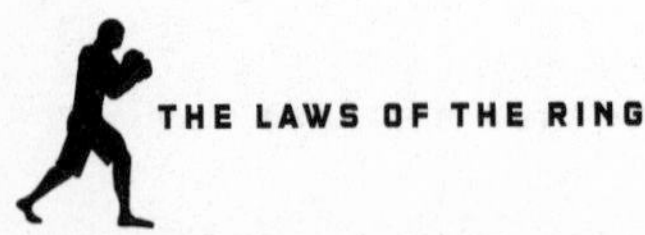

So, back to Donald. We were getting to be old friends now.

He got right to the point. "I'll let you off with a warning if you give up your friend."

I told him I was with Darren. He looked at me skeptically.

"Are you sure, Urijah?"

"Yes, I'm sure."

"You're *sure* you weren't with Dustin Soderman?"

Uh-oh.

I persisted for a few more sentences and then it was apparent I had to give in. "Why am I being punished for lying to you instead of giving up my friend?" I screamed out. "Do you understand the position I'm in here?" I launched into a passionate speech about friendship and loyalty and the unfairness of being singled out.

I was pretty pleased with my self-righteous explanation. Donald Moore wasn't. He couldn't stand my let-it-all-slide mentality. He was adamant that I be kicked out of school; according to the picture he painted, I had no other choice, and he proceeded to give me options for other schools I could attend once I was dismissed. I couldn't accept his punishment, however, and wasn't ready to lay down for his opinion on my future.

I researched the university's bylaws and discovered that a student has to agree to be dismissed. I had the ability to fight the decision and force the authorities to make their case. I decided to fight. Despite my occasionally juvenile behavior, I loved UC Davis, and I wasn't willing to give it up easily.

I spent the summer writing letters to anybody who would listen and requesting meetings with administrators. I acknowledged my mistakes and asked for their forgiveness. I selectively focused on the most recent event, which I wholeheartedly felt was unjust. I was protecting a friend. Someone *had* to see the nobility in that. But as I rewound the events through my mind, I could see that the Judicial Affairs board clearly felt I was making fools of them one time too many.

Over the course of four or five meetings, the board attempted to get me to agree to their terms. Each time I refused. I brought a folder to each meeting and took notes. I appealed to their sense of fairness and tried to show that my persistence and willingness to take this matter to the highest level was reason enough to keep me in school. That my efforts should demonstrate my ongoing loyalty to the university and my desire to do better.

Finally, *they* relented. They allowed me to remain in school under the most restrictive double- and triple-secret probation they could find. I walked on eggshells for the remaining four years of my college career, knowing one misstep would lead to expulsion. I changed my behavior and came away understanding the importance of honesty and owning my actions. In the process, I became a valued member of the UC Davis community and even worked for the university after I graduated. Getting disciplined during this time in my life was so valuable. The trial and error of living in a new environment with new people and new rules helped me realize how important success was in my life. After fighting for the right and opportunity to study at the university and to bust my butt in the UC Davis wrestling room every day, I knew that life is a privilege and to make the most of it. I often think back to that summer of meetings and letters and consider how much different my life would be if I had simply accepted the board's decision and left school.

The university put me to the test and asked, "How bad do you want it?" The first step was accepting the reality of my situation. If I had remained in denial and continued to make excuses for my behavior, I would surely have been kicked out. To this point I was just another kid who thought his own rules translated to the rules of the world. It wasn't until the university made a serious motion to expel me that I grasped how my actions—no matter how small—in aggregate, were reflecting my character. I know the university authorities saw me as a promising athlete, but the university, and Donald Moore in particular, didn't want any part of someone who disregarded the established rules of the community. And I liked this community. I liked it a lot. And by confessing to past violations and repeatedly vowing to do better, I convinced the people in charge that I understood the privilege not just of remaining in school, but of remaining in *this* school. I came away a stronger and more principled person, sure, but most important, adversity—which was about finding some self-awareness—reminded me what Davis meant to me.

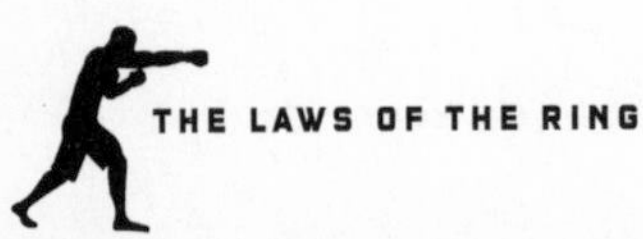

From a social standpoint, like many (dare I say most) kids, I started college without a clue. As I found, it can sometimes be preferable—in the long run—to be the guy who starts at a disadvantage. My missteps enabled me to understand adversity, and to develop the persistence to stand up for myself and be my own advocate.

Learning from your mistakes is not always a conscious act, but from here on out make a conscious effort to take lessons from your victories and your mishaps.

THE 9TH LAW OF POWER

UNDERSTAND YOUR TALENTS: THE COMPETENCY MODEL

I learned a valuable lesson about wins and losses during my years as a college wrestler. My sophomore year I won slightly more than half my matches (15–14) and many of those losses were by a point or two. More than a few were overtime or double overtime. I was so close. It was frustrating, and I watched video and racked my brain for ways to make up the difference. There had to be a formula that I could learn that would make up those very few points and give me the record I felt I deserved.

My junior year (second year of eligibility) was the first year I qualified for the national Division I tournament. All those close losses from the year before had turned into close wins. What made the difference? Was it watching the videos and vowing to overcome my frustration? I really don't think so. I'd gotten better, it was true, but the margin of victory was so slim that it was hard for me to pinpoint exactly what caused the change.

One of the losses I had that year was to a wrestler from Boise State named Jesse Brock. I lost to him by one point, and I was incensed afterward because I felt I'd been ripped off by the referee.

Brock was good, and I set a goal to beat him, and I felt cheated and powerless when I came up short.

Two weeks later, Brock and I met again in the Aggie Open at UC Davis. I approached the match with fierce resolve and it paid off. I beat Jesse Brock—by one point in overtime.

I was ecstatic. It was a huge win in my career, and it was made sweeter by the fact that I'd avenged a recent loss. But when the euphoria died down, I asked myself a question: *Why does this feel so much better?* Should this slimmest of victory margins—one single, solitary point—cause such a vast difference in how I felt about myself? How can a one-point victory and a one-point loss land with such a drastic difference on my psyche?

This little bout of self-examination changed my outlook on wins and losses. It hit me that I needed to be proud of what I'd done in both matches, not just in the match I'd won. If I let myself remain devastated by the loss and ecstatic over the win, I wouldn't be doing justice to the experience. I would be letting someone else's judgment—something as random and external as a scoring decision—determine how I perceived myself.

I had made some small adjustments since the match in which Brock beat me. I recognized his ability to defend the single leg shot on his right leg, and switched up the attack. His defense was his strongest attribute, so I was more calculated with the attacks and used better setups.

This led me to a realization: Making those little adjustments didn't require me to dwell on the negative emotions that come with experiencing a close loss. You don't have to enjoy losing, but enjoy the experience and do your best. I came to the conclusion that I loved to win, but I could be proud of myself even if a scoreboard was telling me I was losing.

One of my goals in writing this book is to explain the Laws of Power as guidelines to help you foster good habits in your push for a better lifestyle. Each of them taken individually will have some impact on your ability to develop better habits in dealing with life's challenges; taken together, they should have a major impact.

Consistency breeds good habits, but in fighting—and in life—bad habits can destroy promise. You can have a strong sense of purpose and a good plan, but unaddressed bad habits will keep you from your goal.

When someone asks me when I knew I had a particular fight won, I usually don't give the answer they want to hear. It's not something that happens during the fight; there's no "aha!" moment where everything comes together and I know beyond a shadow of a doubt that I have defeated Jens Pulver. Fights are often a blur of movement and countermovement, and I operate inside the cage with actions and reactions that are subconsciously acquired through constant practice.

Instead, the defining moment to me is often something you might find irrelevant to the actual event and it usually has something to do with self-awareness and being the master of my domain.

A good way to illustrate one's aptitude is with the competency model. There are four states of competency: conscious competence, unconscious competence, unconscious incompetence, and conscious incompetence. Understanding where you fall in these categories can help put you on the path to creating good habits.

Conscious Competence

I remember a great story that I heard one year at a wrestling camp during the summer of my junior year in high school. One of the coaches at the camp, Coach John, was talking about how proud he was of his twelve-year-old daughter, Cassie, who was selling Girl Scout cookies door-to-door one year. His daughter was young and, from his perspective, fairly shy. He hadn't really been keeping an eye on the task, other than to make sure she was going to be safe throughout the process. Coach John, of course, did his part as an encouraging father, but he didn't expect what was coming. By the end of the fund-raiser he was pleasantly surprised to hear that his daughter had not only been the leading salesgirl in her troop, but had set an all-time record for cookie sales in the region.

When he sat down to talk with his daughter, he was shocked to hear that she knew exactly why she had done so well. It turns out that she had allotted a one-hour period every day to selling the Girl Scout cookies. During the allotted time she started walking from door to door and then came up with a better idea—she would start jogging from house to house. By

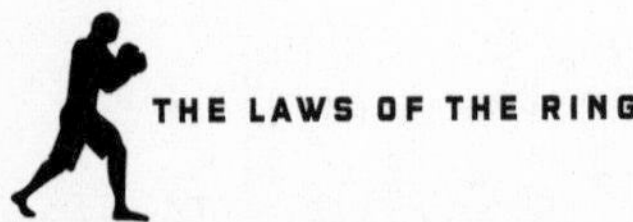

jogging instead of walking, Cassie reached about three times as many households as she would have by walking the cookies around the neighborhood. On top of reaching more homes, she started asking for referrals at the houses. She would ask politely if there was anyone else that the customer could call who might like some cookies. If the answer was yes, she would wait patiently, always saying please and thank you regardless of their answer. Her success was calculated; she was completely aware of the steps she'd taken to achieve her goal. This is the condition everyone should strive to create.

Conscious competence is the act of possessing the knowledge that you excel at something, and also the knowledge of why you excel at it. Being consciously competent allows you to do something correctly and also teach it to other people. Conscious competence flows outward to others. It also means you can identify when you begin to do something poorly, and you have the skills and the consciousness to be able to correct it. If Cassie wanted to share her strategy with the rest of the Girl Scouts, there is no doubt that she could easily have passed her system on to her peers. Knowledge of your success is priceless.

Unconscious Competence

Put simply, this is being good at something but having no idea why. Some of the most successful people go about their lives achieving great things through unconscious competence. In the fighting community, this seemed to be exemplified by one of my favorite fighters and good buddies Quinton (Rampage) Jackson. Rampage was one of the lucky fighters in our sport to be a coach on the UFC's hit reality series *The Ultimate Fighter.* Not to pick on Rampage, but he didn't seem to be able to pick fighters with potential when it came to coaching his first season of *The Ultimate Fighter.* Again, I could be wrong, but I imagine that if you had asked Rampage why he was such a great fighter, he might have had trouble pointing out exactly what it was (although you would probably get a hilarious story or reasoning). Often people fall into the trap of believing that a person's talent equates with their ability to identify or teach that talent. Sometimes, that talent just sits there and doesn't emanate beyond the individual. This is not exclusive to Rampage; there are tons of people in every field—athletics, chemistry, journalism, you name it—who are very good at what they do but can't explain it. Their talent doesn't extend beyond their reach. Rampage got a second chance to coach on *The Ultimate Fighter.* By his second season of coaching, Rampage had picked up some introspection and seemed to add some consciousness to his coaching regimen. It's always best when you can pinpoint a problem. Still and all, being great and not knowing why is a much better scenario than the condition described below.

Unconscious Incompetence

Here's the good thing about unconscious incompetence: It's fixable. The trick is being made aware of the areas in which you are being incompetent without understanding the reasons. Habits born of unconscious incompetence might include something you picked up from your parents—something as minor as poor grammar or as major as malnutrition.

I met Poppies Martinez at a fight in 2005 at the Tachi Palace Casino. Poppies grew up poor as a member of the Tachi Yokut tribe in a town near Fresno called Lemoore, where schools were not equipped with the resources to accommodate his severe learning disabilities. The casino, however, had drastically changed the economic conditions for every member of the tribe. It didn't provide a better school system or a community ethos that valued education, but the profits from the casino allowed a college fund to be set up for every young person in the tribe.

With his learning disabilities and the educational system's inability to deal with them, Poppies was not a viable candidate for college. He had a lack of role models and a lack of desire to succeed academically as well. Under different circumstances, with an educational system far better than the one that existed on the reservation and a family that valued education, things might have been different in the classroom for Poppies. As it stood, though, the die had been cast by the time he reached his late teens. There was no need for a college fund for Poppies. This meant he was free to put his college-fund money toward other forms of training and self-improvement. He decided to put his toward establishing a career as a fighter.

Poppies was an established fighter on the casino circuit when he introduced himself to me that day at the fight. He was the poster boy for the pre-UFC WEC, as the reigning Native American champion, and in the two fights of his I'd seen, I was impressed with his fire and fighting style. I also knew he had stamina and conditioning issues. Poppies started calling me periodically to express his desire to come to Sacramento and train at the gym I own and operate, Ultimate Fitness. He was ready to take the next step in his career, he said, and he knew that training with better people and in better facilities would help him reach his goals.

However, every time he got close to making the move, something would happen. Most often it was an issue that arose with his then wife, with whom he was having problems. But as the weeks went by, with the promises continuing and no follow-through, it became clear that Poppies was afraid to leave the reservation. He was literally afraid that he would be unable to adjust to living away from his comfort zone.

Finally, Poppies got up the nerve to make the move. He showed up with a friend to help him acclimate to what he considered the outside world.

The transition from home to our gym was a difficult one for Poppies. His home environment had created many habits he didn't even know he had. For instance, the crime rate was so high on the reservation that he was habitually fearful and distrustful of the people around him. When he got to our gym, he immediately noticed how nonchalant we were about our personal possessions.

"Why do you guys leave your wallets lying around?" he asked.

We explained that there were no thieves on Team Alpha Male. He looked at us incredulously and said, "If we did that at home, they'd be gone in a second."

He left his four children and a volatile, off-and-on relationship with his wife to come and train with us. He was clearly dedicated to his fighting career, but after he had been with us for about three months, I told him, "Poppies, you need to go home and see your children. We'll be here whenever you decide to come back."

Poppies was an example of unconscious incompetence. When we first met, he was twenty-one years old but didn't understand how different his upbringing was from other fighters'. Reservations have long been among the most destitute areas of our country. Incidents of teen pregnancy are often ten times higher on the "rez" than outside. Alcoholism, among minors and adults, is stratospheric. School dropout rates can exceed 80 percent. This was the environment Poppies was attempting to escape, but the prospect of entering a world he perceived as far more cultured and structured than the one he'd known on the rez filled him with trepidation. He had never given much thought to anything outside his limited sphere, and he didn't fully realize how different his upbringing was until he got outside and saw a different world.

Fighting was just about the only thing in Poppies' life that made sense. It provided order amid the chaos. It didn't take him long to realize he could be good, too—good enough to break out into another entirely new world, the world of world championships instead of Native American championships. At five nine and 170 pounds, he was strong and fierce.

It was clear, however, that Poppies would only be as good as his habits, and if he committed to rounding out the blunt edges of his style, he could make a breakthrough in the fighting world. He possessed the right mentality and the right focus for the actual fighting part. He loved to spar, and he loved to grapple hard. But ancillary details needed to be addressed along the way. Because of his lack of success in school, Poppies had an idea that he was stupid, and he needed to rid himself of this belief. He had dealt with learning disabilities growing up, never having specialists to help him along the way. Learning was something that came easy to him in the MMA world and he was extremely resourceful and intelligent in a lot of different ways despite his lack of book smarts. He didn't like to run, and he didn't like to spend a lot of time drilling new techniques—both aspects of elite stamina training—but the *most* disturbing lifestyle issue was his diet.

When I asked him what his main food was, he broke into a big smile and said, "Spicy Red-Hot Cheetos." No lie—Spicy Red-Hot Cheetos. I tried to

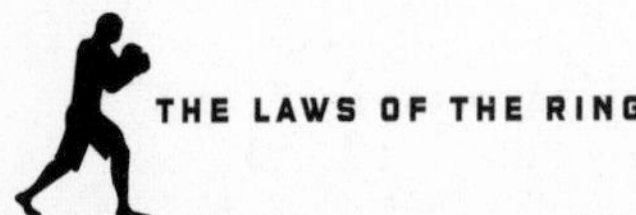

hide my disgust, but he must have noticed because he said, "Oh, and I eat at Jack in the Box, too." He had grown up eating the cheapest and least-nutritious food available. Fast-food burgers, white bread, frozen dinners, school lunches, high-carb snacks full of high-fructose corn syrup. I wasn't surprised when Poppies told me he had nearly died due to a burst appendix when was only eighteen. He had been exposed to very few fruits and vegetables. And those he had tried he wasn't interested in eating again.

I took this as a challenge. As with most every other lifestyle choice, I'm pretty fanatical about my diet, and I believe I get a lot of my strength and durability from the food I put in my body. I take diet very seriously, and seeing Poppies repeatedly toss garbage into his body made me cringe. It was a bad habit that was getting in the way of his purpose. For him to compete, change was needed.

But like many lifelong habits, this was difficult to break.

I'd give him tomatoes.

"I don't eat that, bro."

I'd give him lettuce.

"I don't eat that, bro."

This was frustrating, and the more difficult he became the more intent I was. I definitely needed to take a new approach, and one day it dawned on me: He'd turn down any fruit or vegetable he had tried in the past. The routine was almost reflexive. If he'd had apples before, he refused to eat them. If he'd had carrots before, he'd refuse to eat them.

Okay, Poppies, I thought to myself. *I think I've figured out a way to make this work.*

There are a lot of fruits and vegetables in this big wide world. I didn't have to focus on the common ones. If I brought Poppies something he'd never seen before—kale or acorn squash, say—he couldn't refuse it by telling me he didn't eat it. How would he know he didn't like it if he'd never seen it before?

It worked. I'd prepare something he hadn't seen before and—perhaps to please me—he'd eat it. I would hide stuff, too—mix zucchini into eggs or spinach into meat. In the process, Poppies discovered a taste for "unusual" vegetables. Once he did, he saw a huge difference in how he felt and performed.

Once he saw the results, the rest was easy. Something he was originally forced to do became something he *wanted* to do. The bad habit was broken and replaced with a great habit.

Changing his diet changed his life. I firmly believe what we put into our bodies is that important. Just as my brother, Ryan, has been able to maintain a more stable mental state through diet and exercise, Poppies' new diet has made him healthier, both physically and mentally.

Poppies talked about his people a lot. It was partly because our world was so different from his; he felt the need to explain those differences to us. Little things related to bigger things. Our lighthearted needling of each other always got him talking about the attitudes of his people. But I quickly learned that people and place were intrinsic to who Poppies was as a human being. To paraphrase the old saying, we could take Poppies out of the reservation, but we couldn't take the reservation out of Poppies.

He had one desire: He wanted to fight. When we first met, he couldn't really articulate why, but the more time I spent with him the more I understood that his desire linked back to his home and his people.

"Everyone in my tribe is fighting all the time, always at each other's throats," he would say. He laughed about it, but his fighting career allowed him to find a bigger purpose. He developed a following among his people and fought some big fights at the Tachi Palace. On the nights he fought, nobody else in the community did. They all got under the umbrella with Poppies.

"When I fight, everything changes," he told me. "They all come together to root for me, and I bring my people closer."

Poppies lived with us for three years and I spent a lot of time with him, most of it focused on his development as a person. He was a good fighter, and he got better under the umbrella of Team Alpha Male, but the most important improvements Poppies made were out of the cage. When I first met him, he didn't have a productive focus in his life. But during our time together, he became better all around. He even extracted himself from the abusive relationship he was in with his wife and married another woman, named Lucy, who happened to be sweet and educated. She has a great job as a pharmacist's assistant. I was the best man in their wedding and gave a

truthful speech about Poppies when I first met him. Everyone laughed at the story while Poppies kicked me under the table. Together they have eight kids—her four and his four. Today, he puts his family first, and *everyone* is better for it.

Conscious Incompetence

If you're exhibiting signs of conscious incompetence, you need a serious self-assessment. You're doing the wrong thing, you know it's the wrong thing, and yet you continue to do it.

The popularity of MMA and the UFC has decreased the number of wild-eyed guys who think they can fight. The barroom brawler mentality has diminished as people understand the varying skills needed to be good at the sport. But back in the early days of my career, every guy who'd ever dropped someone in a bar believed he was the next Randy Couture.

As I started to make a name for myself in the sport, I was contacted by a lot of guys who thought they could fight and wanted to use my connections to get into the game themselves. These were mostly old friends from high school who had wrestled with me, or discovered weight lifting or martial arts after they graduated and felt they had developed physically enough to be contenders. Now, I was more than happy to help if someone showed interest and a willingness to train, but I was less comfortable with acquaintances and old friends looking to use my status as a means of improving their luck in the bedroom or fattening their bank account. There was a pretty clear difference between the serious and the frivolous.

I'll tell you a cautionary tale about an old high school acquaintance I'll call Jack. Jack appeared at the gym one day, asking me if I remembered him and wanting to know if I could hook him up with a fight.

I remembered him. Good guy. Well meaning. But not on anybody's most-likely-to-succeed list. I recalled him being in all the remedial classes and barely managing to get through high school.

I had no idea whether Jack could fight. I had no idea *why* he wanted to fight. I asked him if he'd had any experience fighting.

"I've been training," he said.

I asked him where.

"In my garage."

Great. I didn't have much to say to that, and I'm sure Jack could sense my lack of commitment to his cause.

Admittedly, my struggle to get a fight—as a former successful Division I wrestler—was always at the forefront of my mind when I was faced with these situations. I mean, I was polite with everyone, but there was a thought nagging at the back of my mind: *How can all these guys think what I do is so easy?*

But I told Jack what I tell everybody: "Show up at the gym and start working out. We'll see what happens from there."

He came to the gym the next day, and I watched him just long enough to know it was never going to happen. When he was finished, I said, "Dude, you need a lot of work."

He looked up at me and said, "I don't care. I just want a fight. That's all I want: one fight."

"It's not that easy, Jack. There are a lot of guys with experience who have trouble rounding up fights."

This was where Jack played his ace.

"I don't really want to train to fight," he said. "I just want to fight. And if you get me a fight, I'll repay you by landscaping your backyard for free."

Much to my surprise, Jack had turned into a very successful businessman. He was working as a landscaper, and he had no problem coming right out and telling me he was making a hundred thousand dollars a year. Now, while I can honestly say that money isn't my primary motivation, this was shortly after I'd opened the gym and shortly after I'd quit my job busing tables, and I was living pretty frugally with my buddies. A hundred grand seemed like a million bucks to me.

Okay, so . . . moral dilemma? Do I seek out a fight for a guy who isn't equipped for it just for my own benefit? How much was a backyard worth to me?

Ultimately, I assessed that he was fully competent and that if it meant *that much* to him, I had enough pull to get him a low-level fight that few would ever see and nobody but Jack would remember.

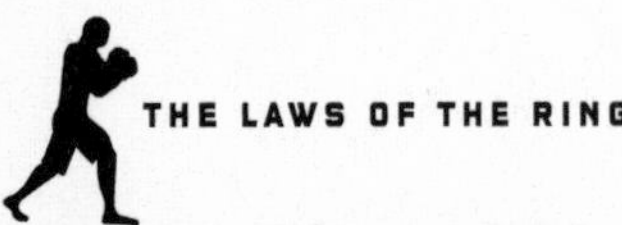

When I had it arranged, I called him and told him. He was ecstatic, but before he could thank me for the twentieth time, I said, "Jack, I got you the fight, but I really want you to come into the gym and train. You need to train."

I didn't want him to go out and get hurt. He could embarrass himself—that was *his* problem—but an injury would weigh on my conscience. But once I got him the fight, I never saw him at the gym.

I called him a second time and he said, "I'll be good. I've been training in my garage."

By then, I gave up. *Okay. Whatever. Suit yourself.*

Jack's fight was at an Indian casino called Konocti Vista, in a parking lot. When I saw him before the fight, he was shaking. I swear I've never seen a human being more scared than this guy was in the minutes leading up to this fight. It was like all his bluster and confidence leaked out of him onto the ground and he was left with nothing.

I tried to talk to him. "Hey, man, how you feeling?" He wouldn't even respond with words. He was making these guttural sounds that conveyed no information whatsoever—except that he was scared out of his mind. His face was completely white. I gave him the option of backing out, but he shook his head vehemently and said nothing. He was going to go through with it, apparently, no matter what.

Jack walked into the cage as slow as I've ever seen anyone approach a fight. It wasn't a psychological ploy either. This was like a walk to the gas chamber. It wouldn't have surprised me in the least if he'd thrown up right there on the canvas.

And it only got worse. When the ref said, "Fight," Jack came charging forward. His opponent punched him a couple of times, slammed him, beat him up a little bit more, and then choked him out. There was very little resistance. Jack's philosophy was unique: He would get in there and get his fight over as quickly as humanly possible. I stood there shaking my head, not sure whether to laugh or cry, as he got up and walked back to his corner, defeat covering him like a blanket. This was something he wanted so badly—until it was actually happening. And then there was nothing in the world he wanted less. Thankfully, he didn't get hurt.

Clearly, Jack's priorities were messed up. He was a ridiculous, fun-house-mirror example of misguided priorities and lack of planning. Not even three weeks later, he reappeared. He told me he knew what he did wrong and how to fix it. He was going to "go back into" training and work hard. And oh, by the way, he wanted me to get him another fight. At the same time I was hearing from friends back in my hometown that he was hanging out in the bars, telling everyone he was a professional fighter. That, of course, had been his motivation in the first place.

I didn't want to be involved with anything like this. I washed my hands of the operation. But Jack somehow managed to get himself another fight, and of course, he got his ass kicked again before deciding to hang it up for good. He fought twice and lost twice, simple as that, but I guarantee you he got a lot of mileage out of the stories in the bars in Lincoln. Who knows what happened in those stories. I'm guessing they bore little resemblance to the fight I watched.

I got my backyard done, though.

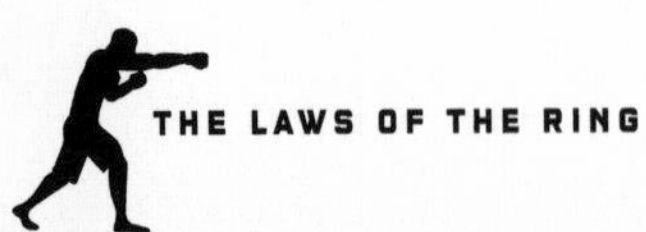

THE 10TH LAW OF POWER

USE YOUR HEAD . . . WHATEVER WAY YOU CAN

Among the many things you could do to your opponent in the old, Wild West days of MMA: head-butt, kick a guy in the head when he was down, elbow from any position. Professional fighting was a slightly more refined version of Senator McCain's "human cockfighting" by the time I arrived in 2003. You couldn't head-butt or eye-gouge, but the sport still had a ways to go before it became what you see today. I entered an ever-so-slightly modified version of those days: mean, somewhat vicious, borderline sadistic, with just a few more rules than a bar brawl. There was great demand to see these early fights, since there weren't many places to see them and there was never a scarcity of bloodthirsty, beer-soaked fans willing to pay for the right. The ticket I bought to see my friend Tyrone Glover that night in the crowded, smelly ballroom in Colusa? It cost seventy-five bucks.

Tickets that expensive meant fans wanted to be treated to a show they could say justified the cost. That led to one of the most dangerous aspects of the old MMA: referees who allowed fights to last way too long.

The changes came about for a simple reason: In order to survive, the sport had to adapt. So many organizations jumped in when they recognized the economic potential of the sport, and so many of them lost their asses because they didn't understand the market or couldn't maximize its potential. The UFC saved it. People like Dana White and the Fertitta brothers (Frank and Lorenzo) stepped in to usher it toward a more fan-friendly, mainstream sport. MMA was either going to change and become more palatable to the general public, or it was going to be a freak show of sadism with the fighters as sacrificial lambs.

The evolution of the UFC is a broad example of people who got creative with their passion (I'll describe some of the specifics of those creative beginnings later on). My personal evolution as a competitor is a more specific example. Like many MMA fighters, I came from a college-wrestling background. Despite the number of fighters who have taken that route, it's not a seamless transition. College wrestling is regimented and regulated, while MMA is a free-flowing combination of many different disciplines. Creativity is key.

Two legendary fighters in my profession are Randy Couture and Mark Coleman. Couture is renowned for having one of the most adaptive and creative minds in mixed martial arts. He spanned different generations and rules, and in the process, not only defied Father Time, but thrived until the very end of his career. Coleman, on the other hand, while a legend of the sport whose brash personality and gritty toughness likewise kept him in the sport into his late forties, didn't fare as well with the changing tide in MMA. This was evident when they met in the twilights of their careers in a historic UFC bout.

Coleman started fighting in 1996, when the sport was truly anything goes. His nickname was "The Hammer" and his tool of choice was his head. His signature move was a heat butt, which became illegal about the time Coleman hit his prime. But his career dropped off considerably when the rules changed, and by 2004, he started losing close to as many fights as he won.

I once hung out with Coleman in a Las Vegas club, long after his best days in the game were behind him. He had a group of buddies around him, and these buddies were some of his loyal friends. They were proud of him, boosting him up, doing anything for him, and eager to talk about the good old days.

They'd had quite a bit to drink, and one of Coleman's guys told me, in a wistful tone, "You know, Urijah, things really changed for Mark when they took away the head butt."

Coleman heard him, and he kind of rolled his eyes. I'm not sure he agreed, though I don't remember him disputing the claim, but it's a matter of record that he was a far more dangerous fighter before the sport changed. I'm not sure his troubles arose when the head butt was outlawed—you'd have to ask Mark to get the whole story—but as an observer, I see him as an extreme example of a guy who didn't use enough creativity to adapt to a changing environment. He had worked his whole life so diligently in the world of wrestling that he was able to compete at its highest level—and his grappling skills coupled with his infamous head-butting technique and his ground and pound were enough to compensate for his lack of mastery of all the martial arts for a time.

But in fighting and in life, you have to be able to change. Couture went on to win several world championships and was a contender well into his late forties because of his creative willpower and ability to adapt. As he aged, his hands got better and his submission game improved. He was undoubtedly smarter about how he used his body as it aged. You, like Couture, have to be flexible. You have to be able to improvise. Whether it's developing another signature move or rethinking the way you deliver pizzas, you need to have a strong-willed creativity to thrive. In a way, you need to be strongly flexible. I know that sounds like a paradox, but it's not.

No matter how well you plot out your path, things will change. You can define your sense of purpose and have the most positive attitude imaginable, but you're still going to face challenges. You're going to hit roadblocks. You're going to have to adapt.

How you adapt is key. The *how* defines the level of success you are likely to reach. If you've reached a point where you are committed to pursuing your passion, you've undoubtedly compiled a mental or written list of pros and cons (if not, you should!). But somewhere in between those two black-and-white sides of the ledger, there's a vast gray area. Once you make the decision to incorporate your passion, that area in between—every if/then scenario that forces you to think on your feet and requires compromise and flexibility—becomes the most important place in the world.

THE 11TH LAW OF POWER

YOUR FATE IS *NOT* PREDETERMINED

I was working the front counter at my Ultimate Fitness gym in Sacramento a few years ago when I looked up to see a wild-looking old guy with bright red hair and a white handlebar mustache. He was overweight but tough-looking, and I wondered for a second if he'd mistaken our building for the tattoo shop next door.

"What can I do for you?" I asked him.

"I'm here to sign up," he said with a gruff tone that fit the entire package. "I want to do some kickboxin'."

This is a little different than kickboxin', I thought. But whatever: If he wanted to join up, he could join up. I discussed the fee schedule and told him that we handled payments through electronic funds transfer.

"I don't want that," he said. "I drive a truck and I travel, so I don't want a contract."

This was a new one, too. I told him we could either do the EFT or he could pay for a year in full. I explained that I had no other way to handle it.

"I'll pay in full, then—I've got money," he said with a smirk.

And so went my introduction to Red Robinson, one of the more amazing characters ever to cross my path. Red was fifty-nine years old when he walked into the gym, ready to make a big change in his life.

And what a life it had been. As I got to know Red, he began to share his story. The short version is this: He'd done just about everything bad in the world, and he was tired of it.

The longer version is more interesting. He'd done enough cocaine to kill a small country. He worked as a collector for some bad folks and did everything a collector for bad folks is called upon to do.

So this wild guy with a crazy background came into the gym wanting to work out. He'd cleaned up his act eleven years earlier—when he was forty-eight—and he wanted to take the next step to becoming healthy and productive.

Red came in the first day. He came in the second day. He came in the third day. He came in every day after that, to the point where he was working out three hours straight. He got fit and strong and healthy. His attitude changed. His entire worldview changed. Red Robinson went from being a guy who looked like he'd done all those bad things—and more—to looking like a guy who couldn't possibly have done *any* of those things.

Red and I had nearly nothing in common at first glance. At the time he was fifty-nine; I was twenty-seven. He was gruff and unrefined, while I was easygoing and intensely disciplined. Just accept that Red's background was unlike anybody's I'd ever met, and that there was no Christian commune or child acting in his past.

But despite the differences, or maybe *because* of the differences, Red Robinson and I became good friends. He was serious about undoing all the damage he'd done to his body over the years and listened intently to the things I had to say and the suggestions I had to make. For instance, one day I started talking to him about healthy foods because he was interested in nutrition. I told him about my mother feeding us only the freshest vegetables and trying to stay away from processed foods. I told him how I'd refined that philosophy and had become even more vigilant about what I put in my body.

As it happened, Red had a farm outside of Sacramento, and before long he began bringing in tons of awesome fruits and vegetables. He started making his own juice and bringing jugs of it into the gym.

But even more than that, Red and I had some deep discussions about life and how to turn things around from a place many believed to be unredeemable. He wanted to start coming to my fights, and before long, he was part of my team. We took long drives in his old truck to appearances or fights. We'd drive from Sacramento to Fresno or some other place and I'd hear all of his wild stories. He would shake his head as he told me, "Some of the happiest times in my life were when I was beating someone up in a bar."

He had been a professional pool hustler, and he bilked people out of more money than he could count. For seven years he ran a couple of strip clubs where workers' rights weren't exactly a priority. He kicked down doors and beat people up when he went to collect money. He'd been shot twice and stabbed fifteen times and had the scars to prove it. He was, by his own estimation, "a horrible person."

So one day I asked Red: "What changed? What happened to make you leave all that bad stuff behind and change your life?"

I discovered Red's life turned on a simple question. About twenty years earlier, a live-in girlfriend who was studying psychology asked him, "Why are you so angry?"

He didn't have an answer. *Why* am *I so angry?*

Sometimes, you are something simply because you never thought you could be *something else.* It doesn't have to be anything as drastic as Red's anger, but superficial qualities tend to seep into our subconscious until they define who we are. We accept them, oftentimes because the people in our lives accept them.

(Apparently the girlfriend was doing a case study on Red for one of her classes. "She got A's all the way through," Red said with his gruff laugh.)

Just because you have embarked on the wrong course doesn't mean you have to remain on it. Every bad road has an off-ramp. The off-ramp might lead to a more winding and convoluted path to your destination, but the important thing to remember is that the off-ramps exist. They're waiting for you.

It's an intrinsic part of our nature to want to belong. Whether it's something positive (charity groups) or negative (gangs), we draw power from belonging. Being part of something bigger than ourselves creates a sense of

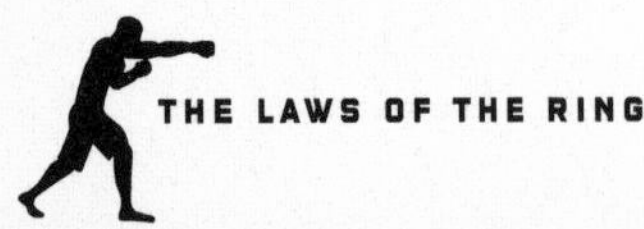

purpose; groups empower the individual, and some of the most amazing and productive achievements in history have come when good people with a strong purpose bonded together for the common good. On the other side of the coin, some of the most remarkable accomplishments in life come when people who are drawing negative energy from their group break out and change their ways.

Think of all the stories of gangsters who have abandoned the street life to pursue something positive—often something that runs directly counter to their previous lives. Shawn "Jay-Z" Carter is one of the most successful hip-hop artists in America; he is originally from the Marcy housing projects in New York City, and endured a traumatic and dysfunctional upbringing. In his music he refers to selling crack cocaine and being immersed in criminal activities. Yet today he has been actively making good. Recently, Jay-Z has used his fame to bring awareness to the battle against the global water shortage. He pledged over a million dollars in relief after Hurricane Katrina and was actively involved in the 2008 efforts to get young people to vote in America.

Many ex-gang members reject their previous ways and devote themselves to keeping others from making the same mistakes as they did. I contend there is nothing more difficult in life than changing your affiliation, because doing this requires such a deep, personal change. It's the equivalent of turning your back on your own identity. You change who you are, and there's nothing more frightening than the realization that your identity—the thing you have clung to your entire life—needs to be abandoned.

This is what happened to Red after his girlfriend asked him that simple question. *Why are you so angry?* For one of the few times in his life, he didn't lash out in anger at someone who dared question him. Maybe it was something in her tone, or the directness of the question, or the fact that most people were afraid to ask Red Robinson a question that might force him to assess himself as a human being. The bottom line is that this girlfriend was the off-ramp. Now, an off-ramp can be a girlfriend, friend, advertisement for a MMA gym, whatever, but if you're in a downward spiral, *that's* when you should be consciously looking for one. They do come along. It's a matter of whether or not we're paying attention to them.

As Red looked at her speechless, he realized it was the first time he'd been forced to ask himself that question. He was so stunned, he couldn't muster up a response, but the question bounced around in his mind for days after and he came to a couple important conclusions: (1) anger was making his life miserable; and (2) life is empty when your happiest moments come when you're being destructive to yourself and others.

The first thing Red did was stop abusing his body with drugs and alcohol, which took care of a whole bunch of his worst habits. The second thing he did was reevaluate his life to figure out how he could maximize his happiness.

Red asked himself an all-important question: "What do I like to do (other than beat people up), and how can I incorporate it into my everyday life to make myself a happier and more productive person?" His *legitimate* business, hanging drywall, wasn't the answer. He hated it. But he liked to travel. He liked the feeling of heading out on the open road to see something he'd never seen. He liked adventure. So, at forty-eight years old, Red changed his life and took a job as a truck driver.

He *loved* it. He was sober, which made his disposition better, allowing him the full opportunity to enjoy his work and his travels through America. In turn, this made him less prone to anger. Before long, he made the decision to save his money, and within three years, he bought three trucks and opened his own trucking company. To drive the other two trucks, he hired friends who were down on their luck, but far more positive influences than the characters with whom he'd previously associated.

Predictably, given Red's new outlook, the trucking business did well for many years, and as he approached the age of sixty, Red found himself in position to retire with a good chunk of money in the bank and a farm to live on. But after a few years, he became more aware of this unhealthy body he had ravaged with drugs and alcohol for so many years and for which he never accepted accountability. He was also a fiery-spirited redhead, and had always loved competition. In his youth he trained in boxing and judo and was an accomplished horseback rider, in addition to his street-fighting prowess. Red was drawn to the world of MMA, and it was something he wanted to pursue in his new quest to get his health in line. It was natural for Red to

be associated with the toughest dudes in the area; the legitimacy and growth of the Sacramento fight scene provided him with a healthy way to join some tough "peers" (even though he had a few years on most of the other fighters on Team Alpha Male).

When he first walked into the gym, Red was 217 pounds; he's now about 180. But it's not just weight loss. He has gotten in such great shape all around. He has a blast hanging out with world champions at the gym, but he also competes in jujitsu tournaments. The man is a beast.

Oh, and one other thing: As of this writing, he wants to take a fight. Seriously, at sixty-four years old, Red Robinson wants a cage fight. We're not going to let him—there *are* times when passion can lead you astray and cause you to forget yourself—but the point is that Red readily acknowledges that he's the happiest he's ever been, and his transformation started with a question. The question triggered a much-needed self-examination, and that ultimately led Red to put his passion first—the passion being *himself.*

His story makes me think back to the saying on my mom's refrigerator.

Dream impossible dreams. When those dreams come true, make the next ones more impossible.

Red's first "impossible" dream was getting sober. So much of his life was wrapped up in drugs and alcohol that quitting was more than a simple lifestyle change. His second impossible dream was to rid himself of the anger and become a happier person, which he achieved by first getting sober and then recognizing his passion and finding a way to maximize it. His third impossible dream was to get his body as healthy as his mind.

He's proof it's never too late to achieve the impossible, and never too late to evaluate and change the most fundamental part of your being, so long as you have the courage to face who you really are.

THE 12TH LAW OF POWER

FIGHT ADVERSITY WITH *PASSION*

This book has been a lot of years in the making. I first began thinking about writing a combination motivational/self-help book four or five years ago. One of the first people I consulted was my friend and neighbor Jim Peterson, a high school vice principal and a specialist in behavior modification.

Jim and his wife, Renata, had become a great part of our community. They helped to develop a series of life-skills workshops that we put on for the team over the years. I even gave Jim the nickname, "the Mind Coach," to officially add him to the staff of MMA specialists who were building our team stronger. Jim and I sat down and discussed concepts that would resonate with people who were looking to extract themselves from a personal or professional rut. A theme I believe to be one of the most important is overcoming adversity.

This is obvious, right? In order to make big changes in your life, you're going to have to work through hard times. You're going to have to lower your shoulder and surge forward when you might be the only person who truly believes in you.

It occurred to me that *overcoming adversity* is a term that's easy to dismiss. It's vague and somewhat clichéd. And so Jim and

I discussed ways to illustrate this concept, to make it real and tangible and attainable.

To take control of your life, you have to take control of expectations. The ability to overcome adversity is a valuable asset, but it avoids a major truth: So often, adversity is imagined. Much of what we expect from ourselves is a reflection of society's insistence on promoting the idea of the instant success story.

There is no such thing, but we fool ourselves into believing there is. We look at the people on television and hear their abridged stories—from nowhere to hero in no time—and miss out on all the difficulties in between. America has attached itself to so many rags-to-riches stories that we start to fool ourselves into thinking it's the norm. And if we aren't getting as much attention or money as someone in a similar field at a similar age, we tend to view ourselves as unable to measure up.

This leads to a poison known as envy.

Jealousy and envy are often used synonymously. The two words have become so interchangeable in common usage that most people think they convey the same meaning. They don't, but the confusion is understandable. Linguists, psychologists, and other deep thinkers have pondered the difference for years. Philosopher John Rawls draws the distinction this way: *Jealousy* is the desire to keep something you already have but fear losing, while *envy* is the wish to have something you don't have but someone else does.

Envy and jealousy are poison, and both are unnecessary roadblocks on your way to a more passion-filled life. We are aware that the phrase *enjoy the journey* contains wise advice, but we rarely follow it. We're in such a rush to reach some goal, and we're always looking around to see where everybody else is.

"We all start from different places," Jim said. "That's something that everybody needs to understand and accept before they can achieve any real self-improvement."

To drive the point home, Jim told me about an exercise he does with high school students. He credits this exercise to Pat Quinn, a national teacher trainer.

Jim walks into a class and asks the students to stand up. He says to them, "We're going to do an exercise for the next few minutes. I just spoke with your teacher and she's agreed that anyone who successfully completes this exercise is going to earn fifty extra-credit points."

At this point, the students usually do *something*—smile, pump their fists, cheer—that indicates they're okay with Jim's plan.

Then Jim says, "All you have to do to earn the points is touch the light switch on the wall over by the door by taking no more than one step."

He continues by saying, "All right—we'll start with the first row."

This is the row closest to the switch. The students are all easily within one step of the switch. Usually they have a look on their face that says, *Cool. We've got the hookup.*

The students just outside the reasonable-reach zone always enjoy the exercise the most. They get to show off their cleverness or athletic ability as they jump or stretch their way close to the switch. Jim makes a point of noting that most of these students are able to complete the task in the same amount of time as the first students because the first ones—those closest—never try to reach the switch quickly.

The students in the outer rows, as you might imagine, do not enjoy this exercise. A few always protest loudly, and it's not uncommon to hear someone mutter, "Man, this is bullshit." Before these students completely turn on Jim, though, he asks a question: "Is there anyone here who couldn't get to that light switch if they had to?"

The answer is always the same: "Duh?" (They are teenagers.)

Jim then shows some creative ways to get within a step of the switch: the moon walk, electric slide, bear walking. The kids then start to understand that being creative can get you within one step of the light switch.

Jim holds up a hand to quell their rising indignation and says, "All right, then. Anybody who goes over and touches the light switch is going to get the full points. Work with me, guys, I swear there's a point."

After the students dutifully walk over and touch the switch, Jim unveils the lesson.

"The purpose of the exercise is to point out to you guys that we all start from different places," he says. "But just because someone heading for the same place as you starts from closer doesn't mean we can't all get to where we want to go."

The truth is, expecting a student to touch the switch in one step is as ridiculous as you expecting yourself to meet the same sales quota as a twenty-year veteran in your first month on the job. It's not a reasonable expectation.

The more Jim and I talked, the more we realized that the only way to overcome adversity is to be *consistently persistent* with your behavior.

Persistence happens when nobody's looking. I was a successful fighter at a young age, but nobody who sees me fight in front of twenty thousand people sees the hours of training that went in to perfecting certain techniques—or even one specific move. From the outside, it looks like I sprouted whole in the middle of a UFC cage, with thousands in the stands and millions watching at home. But of course that's not true. Not true at all.

After Tyrone Glover's fight, which, by the way, he won, I asked him for the promoter's number. He was hesitant to give it to me. He stopped and started a few times and then said, "Well, it's kind of hard to get a fight. You have to go through someone to do it."

"I don't care," I said. "I'm going to do this one way or another. Just give me his number."

Tyrone shrugged and told me the guy's name was Ted Williams. He gave me the number.

Sweet. A good first step. I've got a name and a number. Time to get to work.

I called. And I called. And I called.

Finally, Ted Williams answered. After so many unanswered calls, I was a little startled and a little nervous at hearing his voice. I started talking as fast as I could, making sure I got it all out before he could respond. "Hi, Ted, this is Urijah Faber, and I want to fight. I'm a college wrestler and—"

Click.

He hung up.

I called back. No answer.

That was unexpected. From the seats at the Colusa Casino, this fight scene didn't appear to be an exclusive club. There didn't seem to be strict requirements for entry. I was a decorated Division I college wrestler, not a guy who sucker punched someone in a bar once and came away calling himself a fighter. Apparently I was unaware of some of the intricacies of the profession.

My dealings with Williams provided a valuable lesson on pursuing a passion: You will be discouraged. It might happen right away, like it did with me, or it might be down the road. But make no mistake: It will happen. You will be told "No," in no uncertain terms. You will have to fight through the negativity, and the only way to do that is to be guided by a strong sense of purpose.

As a result of being blown off, I took a different approach. I went to all the gyms in Sacramento that trained fighters. I figured if I showed what I could do against the guys who were getting the fights, I'd begin to make a name for myself. Word would spread, and Williams would be left with no choice but to take my call.

At one of the gyms, I gave one of the jujitsu instructors all he could handle. The guy who ran the gym, a fast talker named Carlos, told me, "Yeah, man, I'll get you a fight."

I had some reservations about Carlos, but who was I to argue? I wanted a fight. He said he could get me a fight. What did I do? I told him to get me a fight. He proceeded to do just that, but along the way he told Ted Williams he was my wrestling coach at UC Davis (completely untrue) and followed that with more claims of questionable veracity. I wasn't going into this blind, though. At this stage of its development, MMA was a shady business, so it shouldn't have surprised me to find shady characters running it.

And so, if you followed the bouncing ball from Tyrone Glover to Ted Williams to Carlos and back to Ted Williams, you'd discover how I came to fight Jay Valencia. When it was over, after I'd beaten Valencia and sold a lot of tickets and brought the fans to their feet, Ted Williams came up to congratulate me. I was still a little pissed at the backdoor route I'd taken to get the fight, and so I said, "Hey, Ted. *Now* are you gonna call me back?"

Unfazed, he said, "Everybody out there loved you, man. When are you going to fight again?"

"Are you gonna hang up on me again?"

"Oh, of course not. I'll call you back *now*."

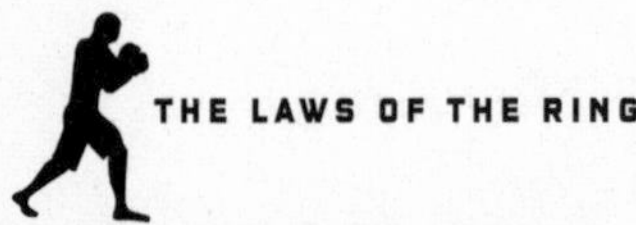

THE LAWS OF THE RING

Nobody would have blamed me if I had given up my quest to secure my first fight. I easily could have thrown up my hands and said, "Well, I tried," after my phone calls to Ted Williams had been repeatedly rebuffed and, worse, ignored. But I *knew* I could do this, and wasn't ready to fall back on the excuses about the politics of ultimate fighting, or the unfairness of the promoter, or the lack of available opportunities.

I got the feeling I was one of the few people who didn't just bow down and thank Williams for the chance. His group—*Gladiator Challenge*—was pretty much the only show out there. But as I looked at Ted Williams, a man I had associated most closely with a dial tone, I had one thought: *It won't be long before you need me more than I need you.*

Here's another exercise Pat Quinn describes in his training, which was employed by a kindergarten teacher I'll call Mrs. Andrews.

Every year on the first day of school, Mrs. Andrews takes her kindergartners—full of wild energy and first-day nervousness—into the school's gymnasium. She tells them to line up along the sidelines of the basketball court, and once they are all in some semblance of a straight line, she begins speaking.

"Kids, do you like to run?"

"Yeah!" they scream.

"Good," she says. "Because this is what I want you to do. I want you to run as fast as you can from the line you're standing on and stop at the other line at the other side of the court." With this, she points to the opposite sideline.

"Do you think you can all do that for me?"

"Yeah!"

Then Mrs. Andrews pauses, like she forgot something, and says, "Oh, before you start, there's just one thing: You all have to get there at the exact same time."

This causes serious confusion. First the kindergartners try to figure out how they can manage to pull off this trick—kindergartners aim to please, especially on the first day of school—before someone finally raises his or her hand and says, "But, Mrs. Andrews, if we all run as fast as we can, we're not going to get there at the same time."

"Why not?" she asks.

"Well, because we're not all the same."

"Exactly," Mrs. Andrews says. "And starting today, I want all of you to remember that. We're not all the same. We all go at different speeds, but we can all make it to the same place if we try hard enough. One person will get there first, one will get there last, and everybody else will be in between. But if we all understand our different speeds, we will all get there, and that's all that matters."

These two exercises are simple, elementary examples to illustrate our different aptitudes. The lessons they teach are irrefutable, and yet why do we forget them? Or, more to the point, why are we choosing to ignore them?

Comparisons can spur competition and ignite greatness, but they can also stall progress and create feelings of doubt and worthlessness. The kid who notices early in school that his classmates are finishing math problems faster than he is automatically reaches the conclusion that he's poor at math. He must be, right? I mean, the only way you would take longer is if you aren't as good at solving the problems, correct? Wrong! Just like the people sitting farther away from the light switch, he just might need to take a few more steps to get to the same place.

We can't all get there first, but we can all get there.

When these concepts are exhibited clearly and without judgment, everybody understands. We can understand that we all start from different places when the issue concerns our proximity to a light switch. We can understand that we all operate at different speeds when the issue concerns our ability to run from one line to another and arrive at the same time.

In these cases, we understand what it means to be persistently consistent. We understand that by running as hard as possible every time, we'll get better. We'll improve. We'll get to that line sooner. We have evidence on our side. It's obvious, right?

But things change when the issue is *life*. When it comes to big things, we forget the simple lessons and fall back on false premises and easy judgments. We settle for the easiest option—to let adversity overcome us—and dismiss

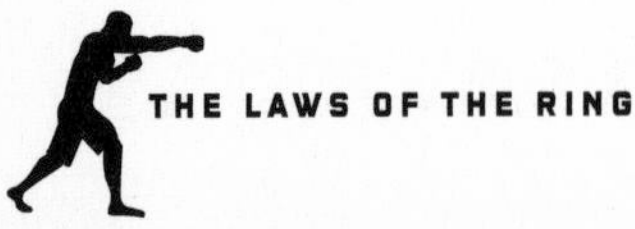

the truly worthwhile pursuits as being either too difficult or impossible. Too many of us ignore the basic principles and give up on our passions. Often it's because we lose sight of our passion. But adversity can redefine it for us.

The Inspiration and Purpose of Joseph Benavidez

When it comes to identifying and cultivating a sense of purpose, I can't think of a better example than my friend Joseph Benavidez. Let me tell you his story.

Joseph grew up in New Mexico, poor, with a dysfunctional family life and wavering focus. Although he was a state-champion high school wrestler, he started drinking early, and by the time he was seventeen or eighteen, he had a serious issue with alcohol. His father spent several years behind bars, and Joseph was the only one of three brothers to graduate high school. He was close to his mother, a strong woman who was fighting upstream against social and economic factors, but his father was unreliable and a poor role model whose other two sons followed in his footsteps.

Joseph drank, and Joseph fought. His type of fighting, as you might have already guessed, was even less sanctioned than the kind I was doing.

And then, at twenty years of age, Joseph decided to change his life. He quit drinking. He started working out. He heard about this new kind of fighting—MMA—that was mostly an underground phenomenon at the time. He thought he'd be good at it, even though he weighed only 135 pounds and—aside from his high school wrestling—had no formal training in the martial arts.

From the moment he got serious and began to train, it became evident that Joseph had a future in the sport. Of course, that prediction depended on the sport itself having a future. At the time Joseph began dedicating himself to fighting, there was no guarantee the sport would progress with him. This was early 2005, and the chance of making a living from fighting MMA was about the same as a young man in 1974 deciding he was going to make his living as a computer programmer. It took foresight and faith, and even then a lot of things outside Joseph's control had to happen for it to become a reality.

Still, Joseph persisted. He started getting some amateur fights. He loved every aspect of it—the training, the fighting, and the sense of accomplishment it gave him. He liked the distance it created between who he was and who he was in the process of becoming. When he got into that cage, he wasn't a poor kid with a troubled past and a complicated family life. He was a fighter. He had a sense of purpose in the ring, something that took him far away from his daily challenges and made people respect and, in some cases, fear him.

Joseph was motivated by everything in his life that wasn't perfect. He took all those things—his family life, his old bad habits, and society's low expectations for someone like him—and unleashed them in the cage. Once he made the commitment to the sport, his sense of purpose was profound. He fought and trained like a man determined not to let his dream die.

In a strange twist consistent with the confusion of the early days of MMA, some of Joseph's "amateur" fights were against professionals. He even got paid for some of them, even though they went on his record as amateur fights.

Regardless of semantics, Joseph went out and fought whomever they put in front of him. He fought fighters who outweighed him by twenty or more pounds, and he beat them. There were very few opportunities for fighters of any weight back then, and far fewer for a 135-pounder. No matter; Joseph fought up and Joseph fought well.

And then one day Joseph and his mother watched a documentary on MSNBC called *Warrior Nation*. It showed a young, lightweight fighter from Sacramento attempting to make this new sport his career. The show featured me, and it ignited something even stronger inside Joseph Benavidez. He'd been motivated before, but seeing someone else who shared his passion took it to another level. On his television, he saw someone close to his size who was intent on making it. It's funny how perception works: I saw myself as a struggling fighter, filled with passion and energy and hope, but also as a fighter who was short on opportunity. Joseph saw me as nothing short of a miraculous success story.

The documentary was a huge break for me in so many ways. As you will read later, it set in motion a series of events that seemed almost providential, although at first they seemed to be nothing but random. What I didn't know was how the film might affect other fighters, guys who were looking for a tangible reason to follow their passion. Never mind that I was just a couple of years removed from quitting my job busing tables at a restaurant that sat twenty paces from my rented room. Never mind that I had *no* idea whether my quest to make my passion my career would be successful. I wasn't getting paid jack shit, but for Joseph Benavidez and others, the mere fact that I was *following* my passion and being paid *anything* to fight qualified me as a success story.

And how did I know this? Well, I discovered it the day Joseph Benavidez showed up in my gym.

That's right—Joseph just showed up. Shortly after he saw the documentary, he scraped up enough money for a plane ticket from Albuquerque to Sacramento and told his buddy Daniel Moffat, who was based in Sacramento, that he was on his way and needed a place to stay.

One problem: Joseph couldn't find me. My gym wasn't quite finished yet. We had some equipment and a slim list of class offerings, but most of the folks in the gym at this point were charter members who were in the fighting community. Joseph found a couple other MMA gyms in town where he trained and asked around to see if anybody knew where he might find me. Neither of the gyms' proprietors had heard of me. The day before he was scheduled to return to New Mexico, he found a third gym, where he got an opportunity to do some sparring. And he *destroyed* people. One of the guys watching him said, "Dude, you're really good. You need to go train with Urijah."

Finally, someone who knew me, and he offered the information without Joseph's having to ask. Joseph told him he'd been trying to find me, with no luck. Joseph cursed his rotten luck; he had a flight back to New Mexico the next morning, and the surcharge to change his flight was just too much at this point. *Maybe next time,* he thought.

The next day, he arrived at the airport only to find that his flight was canceled and the airline couldn't get him on a return flight till the following day. To this day he says he doubts that anyone in the entire history of aviation was as happy to have his flight canceled as he was. The second he was booked on a flight for the next day, he went directly from the airport to my gym.

When he arrived, I was working behind the counter. At this point, trying to get the gym operational, I was doing everything: mopping the mats, working the counter, teaching classes.

He walked up and introduced himself, saying, "My name is Joseph, and I want to train with you."

It still hadn't really hit home that people might recognize me from TV, so when I looked at him a little puzzled, he told me he had seen the documentary and admired what I was doing. Of course, I was flattered, but more to the point, I was about to start a class, so I told him to jump in.

I could tell immediately that he wasn't some bum off the street. He was cut, tough, and had serious endurance. But the X factor was this mean streak I picked up on—this whiff of desperation coming off him. Here was a guy who was training for something more important than a possible paycheck. I loved his demeanor, and I loved hearing the circumstances that led him to my doorstep. Joseph was raw, but he was fierce, and I could see right away how special this guy was.

When the class ended, he told me, "I want to do this full-time. I've had seven amateur fights, but I'm ready to make a run at this."

He told me his life story. He told me about his family and his brothers. He told me about his tough times, and how he got sober. He was working in a T-shirt factory back home doing silk-screening, and although he didn't use these exact words, he had made the decision to let his passion lead him. He had drawn strength from the documentary and seeing it had made him feel a little less alone in his pursuit. None of this came with an instruction manual, but he was motivated by one thing: He wanted to do what he loved, and he was willing to get out of his comfort zone to chase it down.

Late 2005, when Joseph walked into my gym, featured only a slightly more promising landscape than *early* 2005, when Joseph started training, and every guy who wanted to fight for a living was up against the same roadblock: opportunity. There just wasn't much of it, and definitely not enough to provide sustenance for the number of guys who wanted to pursue MMA as an occupation. Adding to it was Joseph's size; there weren't many venues

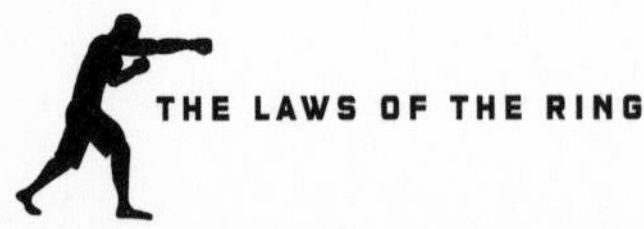

for fighters in heavier weight classes, and there were almost none for someone like Joseph, whose best fighting weight was 125. (My best fighting weight is 135, but when I started out, I took fights at 145 and even 155.)

Yet Joseph was undeterred. He knew the odds, and he didn't care. The way he saw it, he'd beaten longer odds just by overcoming his personal demons, escaping a tough past, and becoming a good enough fighter to even be *considered* as a professional. I think he already recognized that his presence in my gym alone was a personal success story and that in the face of the odds he'd already beaten, what kind of impediment could a lack of opportunities in his weight class present?

"I want to do this for a living." He must have repeated that line five or six times before he left my gym that day. I nodded along, but inside I was thinking, *Fuck, dude—I'm the guy you call your inspiration, and* I'm *not even doing this for a living.*

But every man creates his own reality, and even though this promising young fighter saw me in a way that I had not yet been able to see myself, I wasn't going to trample his dream by downplaying my position in the MMA hierarchy. And besides, not only was it clear that Joseph had exactly the right attitude for realizing his own potential, I truly believed that I could help him become a better fighter. It might not work for him—hell, it might not work for any of us—but if it was going to work for anyone, it was going to work for guys who had positive attitudes and a sense of purpose. Guys like Joseph.

As we shook hands and he told me, once again, that he wanted to fight for a living, I said, "Cool, man. Here's my number. Keep in touch."

He promised not only to keep in touch but to return. He had some matters to clear up in New Mexico—namely, a job to quit and a family to inform—and then he would be back to live with his friend in Sacramento and train full-time in my gym. *My* promise was simple: I would have a job in the gym waiting for him when he returned.

Without fail, every other week I'd receive a text: *This is Joseph. Just reminding you I'll be moving out soon.* I regularly responded by telling him to make sure to let me know his plans.

What Joseph was doing with those texts, whether consciously or not, was moving closer to his goal. He was holding himself accountable by reminding not just me but *himself* of his promise. Even if he was facing the worst possible conditions back home, he was taking the time to do that one little thing that moved him incrementally closer to his dream.

To incorporate your passion into your life, you need these kinds of triggers. You need the accountability, focus, and mentality that something as simple as a text can provide. It establishes your goal *and* puts someone else in the mix to help with accountability. Humans have an instinctual need to belong, and by texting me his desires repeatedly, Joseph found a way to make a connection—in essence, a sense of belonging—without being physically present.

Sure enough, three months after I first met Joseph, I was teaching a class when the door opened and he walked in. His packed-to-the-gills '86 Lincoln Continental was parked in the lot out front. The guy may have mentioned exactly when he was coming during one of our calls, but our conversations were just a small part of my busy life at the time and I didn't realize he was actually coming until he pulled up to the gym. I had to a admire a guy who had driven straight from New Mexico to the gym—not even stopping at his friend Moffat's house to drop off his stuff. He was so excited to get started he couldn't wait. He had uprooted himself and everything he owned (it wasn't much) to chase his passion. His sense of purpose firmly established, he was ready to go to work.

"Leave that hoopty out front," I yelled over to him, "and hop into the class."

From that moment Joseph became a part of my community. He was under the umbrella. I put him to work mopping the mats and cleaning the gym. He was a tireless worker, and he spent every spare moment of downtime taking advantage of his new environment. He'd hop on the treadmill during a fifteen-minute break. He'd do abs work during lunch. And when it was time to train, there was no guy in the gym more serious than Joseph.

It was clear from the beginning that he was going to be very good, and very soon. He was killing it. I recognized this and told him that although there wasn't even a 135-pound class at the time, he'd be an animal at 125. Always the compliant student, he trained with that mind-set, and I just hoped that the evolving state of MMA could somehow cater to a guy of his size. He was one of the toughest guys in the gym, but, predictably, it was tough to get him training partners, let alone organized fights. So, knowing his skill, I'd put bigger guys—some with actual UFC experience—up against Joseph. They'd look at him funny because he was so tiny, then he'd give them the fight of their lives. People were blown away by this guy.

Other fighters—lesser fighters—were getting far more opportunities because they were bigger, but in his weight class, Joseph was just wrecking people at *145.* Nobody wanted anything to do with him. The guys they put in against him at local contests had no chance. He won his first seven fights after he moved to Sacramento and began training with us, but he was frustrated by his inability to get a title shot, even in the lesser shows like *Gladiator Challenge* and *King of the Cage.*

Finally, Joseph's frustration boiled over.

"This is bullshit!" he said as he stormed into my office one day.

I was taken aback. "Dude—what's going on?"

"Dustin Akbari is getting six grand for his next fight and it's only his second fight. I've won seven straight since turning pro, and I can't make anything. I can't even get a title fight. When's my chance going to come?"

Joseph was angry, and he had a right to be. For some reason, Jason Georgianna, the guy he had knocked out in his previous fight, was getting a title shot as a fill-in at the Palace Fighting Championships at the Tachi Palace Casino. It wasn't fair, but the system at the time—if you could call it a system—wasn't engineered to be fair. The Indian casinos ran organizations that were both unorganized and unpredictable, which easily led to frustration and confusion. Matchups, even championship matchups, were often made for political reasons, and sometimes, seemingly, for no discernible reason whatsoever. Additionally, the people running the big shows, where real money was paid, didn't think smaller fighters could carry a card. They thought people wanted to see bigger men with the prospect of bigger knockouts. Because of this, they didn't put as much thought into the smaller weight classes.

"Joseph, I hear you, but you've got to be patient in this business," I said, trying to calm him down. "You're doing everything the right way. Your chance is going to come."

"I've *been* patient," he shot back. "I'm running out of patience."

Now, what I'm about to tell you sounds fictional, but I swear to you it is true. As Joseph was standing in my office raging about the unfairness of it all, I received an e-mail. It caught my eye in the middle of Joseph's diatribe because his name was in the subject line.

I read the message and attempted to follow Joseph's tirade at the same time, but gradually the e-mail stole all of my attention. It was from a promoter offering Joseph the opportunity to fight Kid Yamamoto, who was a national superstar in Japan and in MMA circles around the United States. The payday: thirty thousand dollars!

I held my hand up to get him to stop talking and smiled wide. His look indicated he thought I was mocking him.

"Dude, how'd you like to fight Kid Yamamoto in Japan?"

"Shut the fuck up, man. Don't mess with me like that."

I shrugged. "Suit yourself, dude." Then I angled the monitor so he could read what I had just read.

Curiosity got the better of Joseph. He leaned in close to the screen and read the e-mail. He looked at me, and then read it again. It was like an electrical current ran through him and I could feel the energy coming off him. He was shocked, looking around wondering what to say next.

"Should I do it?" he asked. "Should I do it?"

I laughed. *Should he do it?* I find when faced with a big moment, everybody experiences a brief feeling of indecision. It's the feeling I got when I drove into the parking lot of the Colusa Casino the first time for the Jay Valencia fight. It's linked with the ideas of passion and purpose, because the humility that drives you to work so hard for something you want is the same humility that makes you slightly skeptical when the goal is actually reached. Of course, Joseph knew he should take the fight, but it was inevitable that he would experience a moment of disbelief when it finally happened.

I practically leaped out from behind the desk. "Yeah, you should do it! And do you know why?" I didn't wait for an answer. "Because you're going to *fuck—him—up*."

A month later, the guy with the hoopty Lincoln—complete with a bouncing hula chick on the dash—–who had taken a flier on a trip to Sacramento to meet a guy he'd seen on a fighting documentary, was sitting next

to me on a flight to Japan to compete in one of the MMA's biggest stages against one of the most successful lightweight fighters in the sport.

But when we got to Japan, we found out that Kid Yamamoto had been suspended for the fight. We never got a clear answer why—the reason was "undisclosed"—but the promotion, Dream, replaced him with another, lesser Japanese fighter. This took a little luster off the fight, since Yamamoto was a big deal and a win over him would have given Joseph a direct path to one of the top five spots in the featherweight rankings. In short, Joseph ended up fighting a guy named Junya Kudo, and he absolutely wrecked him, submitting Kudo in the first round.

We were both a little disappointed that Yamamoto was replaced; his status in the game would have gone a long way toward fast-tracking Joseph's reputation. But the win in Japan did earn Joseph a spot on the television show *Inside MMA,* on which I stirred up some controversy when I said, "This is my guy and he's the best one thirty-five fighter in the world."

That may not sound like much, but in the MMA world, ego is everything, and star bantamweight Miguel Torres's enthusiastic camp saw it as a sign of disrespect toward *their* fighter. Whatever. I was entitled to my opinion and my opinion turned out to be justified.

See, the biggest game changer from the fight in Japan was that the people who ran World Extreme Cagefighting (WEC) immediately saw Joseph's potential and signed him to a contract, and after a string of four fights, during which he won three and gave Dominick Cruz a serious run for his money in a loss by decision, they matched him up with the recently dethroned Torres. Still, Torres had never been submitted—until Joseph made history at two minutes fifty-seven seconds of round number two.

But Joseph's story carries a far more important message than wins and losses. Joseph not only comprehends, but diligently follows, the tenets I describe in this book. The important thing to note is that despite his difficult past and negative family influence, Joseph found a purpose in his life. And the proof is in the fact that he has excelled in a field that requires discipline, sweat, and savage workouts, not to mention an equal amount of intellectual dedication to understanding the martial arts. And let's not forget that while, as I write this, the lighter weights are getting the props and attention we always knew we deserved, at the time it was expected that, like boxing, the heavyweights would be the main attractions. So not only was the sport largely illegal in the United States and almost entirely an underground enterprise, Joseph—like me—was a niche within a niche, and he consequently blazed a trail for the little guys. But his *intention* wasn't to be a pioneer. The opportunity he created was for *himself* and the passion was his own—and he followed it straight into the unknown.

There might have been times when Joseph's faith in the system wavered, but he never lost his sense of purpose. With that in mind, it's important to remember this: Stay away from people who tell you that your goals are impossible. In most cases, the people who will dismiss your ideas don't have any of their own. If you have done your homework—meaning if you've identified your purpose and have set out a plan to achieve that purpose—you shouldn't be bothered by naysayers. They are destined to remain outside the umbrella; they don't know what you know.

That's worth repeating: *They don't know what you know.*

If Joseph Benavidez had listened to the people in his life who told him he was crazy, he'd still be working as a silk-screener in a T-shirt factory in New Mexico. And you know something? He might have gone on to become the greatest silk-screener in the world, but there would always have been a hole in his heart where his passion resided. He would have spent his days wondering what might have been. And maybe he'd be the guy I tell *you* to watch out for—the one who shoots down the dreams of others whose purpose seems utterly out of step with the expectations of conventional society. Instead, Joseph does just the opposite as an integral member of the Alpha Male community, where we support our mutual purposes: to be the best mixed-martial-arts practitioners we can be, and to develop our passions inside and outside the cage.

And yes, Joseph and I have fought at the same weight, and at one point you could have seen our names next to each other near the top of the UFC bantamweight rankings. However, there's no chance we'll ever fight. We're friends and teammates, and that's the deal. Our respective journeys to

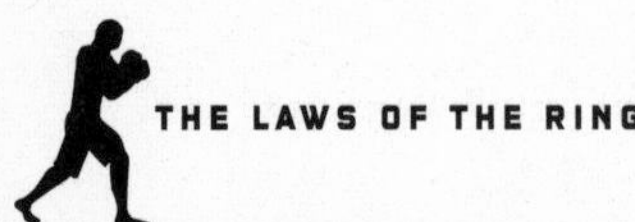

the top of our profession will continue, with Joseph in my corner and me in his.

But for the record, I think I could knock him out.

And for the record, Joseph thinks he'd do the same to me.

And that's where this argument is going to stay: in the realm of the hypothetical.

More than half a decade after Joseph's desire to jump into the fight world was sparked, his true weight class is being introduced on the largest stage of MMA. The president of the UFC, Dana White, made the announcement that the 125-pound weight class will start its life in March of 2012. When the announcement was made, there was no question in MMA circles around the world about who was going to be the number one seed in the race for the title.

I don't want to sound paternal here, but I'm proud of Joseph. His career is a revelation, and it unfolded from one Law of Power to the next. Joseph's career arc teaches one overriding lesson: You don't have to stay where you are. You don't have to defer or dismiss your dreams. Identify your passion (know what you're fighting for), develop a plan (know how to get it), and commit to a sense of purpose (know how to keep it). And if it doesn't work out perfectly, something else will. You can almost guarantee that even if your ultimate dream doesn't work out, you will be better off in the long run for attempting to pursue it. You stand a far better chance of incorporating your passion into your life if you take a big chance and see where it leads.

The message we try to send is consistent with Team Alpha Male's sense of community: It's perfectly okay to fail. It sounds corny, but it truly is about the journey. Every person who comes through our door is treated with respect regardless of skill level. Guys who have been part of the team take something away from their participation, and they leave something behind, too. No matter how long you're here or how successful you are, we hope you are a better person for having been here. Conversely, those you worked with are better for having had you here. Again, it's all about tapping into your positivity.

THE 13TH LAW OF POWER

EVERYONE NEEDS A LITTLE REASSURANCE—BUT ASK SOMEONE WHO KNOWS

Two years before I graduated from UC Davis, when I was still just a fan of MMA, I went to a party with a bunch of guys I knew from high school to watch a video of my buddy who had haphazardly taken a fight at an Indian casino. He was an offensive lineman on my high school team and was a tough kid, but he had no business fighting. We all sat down to watch the fight, but to my disappointment it only lasted forty-three seconds. It was September of 2001 and my friend Randy Halmot was up against future UFC referee Herb Dean. Herb wasn't a master in the sport, but he had at least trained in the different disciplines. The fight started and Randy came out much bigger than Herb and looking tough . . . for about three seconds. What happened next was an MMA clinic: punch to the head, kick to the body, double-leg takedown, elbow on the ground, and a finish with a rear naked choke. Herb had done just about every type of offense possible on my big buddy Randy, in less than a minute. Immediately after we watched the pathetic showing, all of my beer-saturated friends, who weren't wrestlers or boxers, martial artists or fighters of any sort, started throwing out their "expert" opinions on what went wrong. The conversation then turned into a debate, with each person making a case for why he would be great at "cage fighting."

I sat there listening, trying not to betray my disbelief. All along, I was thinking, *These guys would be* terrible *at fighting. Are they being serious right now? They would all get their ass kicked!*

While listening, I was waiting for one of the guys to chime in with a bit of reality, but the conversation continued, and I began to realize that almost every one of these guys thought he could make a run at being a professional fighter. You have to understand one thing: These guys were known mostly for their proficiency as party animals, so they were full of crap on most topics. But it stuck with me: *Every last one of them thinks he could do this.*

I was stunned that these guys were serious, and I was immediately dismissive; but then, a tiny seed of doubt crept into my mind. I was quiet at the party, but if I had spoken up and said that with serious training I *knew* I could be good at this, would those guys have walked away from the party thinking *I* was the crazy one?

I went back to wrestling at UC Davis that Monday, but the thought still nagged at me. It stuck in my head even two years later when I was confident that I was going to try my luck in the fight world. Were my sense of purpose and positive attitude combining to create a delusion? In 2003, when I made the decision to give professional fighting a try, I thought back to this night with my buddies and I approached my college wrestling coach, Lennie Zalesky, a man who knew me well.

"I know I've told you I think I could be good at this fighting thing," I said. "But the weird thing is, I remember watching my buddy get beat up one weekend when I went back home. I was with a bunch of guys who definitely would *not* be good at fighting, and all they could talk about was how good they'd be. And they were serious. I hope I'm not being delusional."

"Trust me," my coach said. "You're not being delusional. You'd be very good at it."

I like to see myself as a self-motivated self-starter, but sometimes even I need the affirmation that comes with something as simple as someone telling me what I already know. This is especially true if your chosen path, like mine, is unorthodox. But let me at least offer you partial reassurance here. If your passion is something that few people in your immediate vicinity understand, the likelihood of their succumbing to the temptation to dismiss it as impossible or impractical—which I, admittedly, did with those friends (none of whom became fighters, by the way)—is much greater than it would be if your passion were something equally ambitious, like, say, being the best life insurance salesman in the country. You don't have to work in the insurance industry to understand an insurance salesman's general business and know that he doesn't have many peers telling him that he is crazy or unrealistic in his chosen profession. So there I was, not only endeavoring to be a professional athlete, which in and of itself seems like a fantasy; I was also striving to be a professional athlete in a sport with a virtually unknown market. Anyone reading this who was designing Web sites in the early nineties must know something about this.

If you have decided to embark on an unconventional path, you have to know yourself and be secure enough in yourself to withstand the inevitable: quizzical looks, biting questions, sometimes outright mockery. That's when you have to keep people close who keep you honest. A hard-nosed wrestling coach is great; but a straight-shooting friend can be equally effective.

Virgil Moorehead is a member of the Big Lagoon tribe in Humboldt County, in the far northwest of California. Virgil is getting his Ph.D. in clinical psychology from the Wright Institute in Berkeley, California. He has two master's degrees, one in marriage and family therapy and another in clinical psychology. He comes to counseling honestly, having grown up on a reservation and struggled with sobriety for many years.

Our relationship is unique. I've joked with Virgil for years about his being the model for conscious incompetence. I dig on him about reading every book on recovery known to man, and still having to battle his demons. But that's nothing new for us—we are constantly at each other's throat, finding our darkest places and going after them.

I treasure my relationship with Virgil because it's based on an intense brand of honesty. As I become more recognizable as a public figure, there is no shortage of yes-men willing to tell me what they think I want to hear. Virgil is like my grounding wire, always there to tell me what I *need* to hear.

Virgil is a terrible loser, and that extends to my losses as well. If I lose a big fight, I might get two solid days of the silent treatment from Virgil. He even rides me when I win, as evidenced by his verbal jabs at me in Palm Springs after I couldn't finish off Rami Boukai. When I lost the Pac-10 wrestling championships my senior year at UC Davis, Virgil walked around with his hands on his throat, saying "Ch-ch-ch-ch-choke" for about two weeks. He takes the losses harder than I do, and digging on me is just the way he shows it.

Virgil has been sober for more than a year as I write this, and I'm proud to see his life coming together. His old ways of conscious incompetence are giving way to bright signs of conscious competence.

Virgil is advancing toward his doctorate and will undoubtedly be one of the greatest addiction counselors the world has ever seen. (Providing he doesn't use the same "tough love" approach he uses on me with his patients.) Anybody who can overcome the history he's faced and combine it with an incredible education is bound to be able to help others. The fact that he's overcome his background is truly epic, and he could end up quietly doing more to help others than anyone could ever imagine. It's important to have people you trust who give it to you straight, especially in a world where the easy thing to do is pat someone on the back, or say nothing at all. Sometimes a little harsh criticism can spark a self-awareness that keeps you on track, just so long as you never let it hold you back.

THE 14TH LAW OF POWER

LET PASSION LEAD (*YOU* KNOW WHAT'S BEST FOR YOU)

On the beach in Mexico, a man sells peanuts all day. He goes home at night to his family and plays the guitar and sits along the beach.

A businessman on vacation comes to the beach one day and buys some peanuts from the vendor.

"My man," the businessman says, "these are the best peanuts in the world."

"Thank you, sir."

"I'm a successful businessman, and you need to make a plan. You need to branch out. You should get a second peanut vendor to sell at the beach up the road, and then a third at the next beach, and pretty soon you'll be able to franchise your peanut-vending business."

The peanut vendor listens calmly and politely.

"Then what?" he asks.

"Then you take your franchise to the United States. You'll have peanut vendors all up and down the West Coast, and you'll sit back and collect the profits."

"And then what?" the vendor asks.

"Well, isn't it obvious? Then you'll be able to retire. You'll spend your days hanging out at the beach with your family, playing the guitar without a worry in the world."

The peanut vendor looks at the businessman and says calmly, "But that's what I do right now."

The lesson? Be careful about imposing your judgments on people whose values or talents don't mesh with yours. Relish small victories and never minimize happiness. Success, contentment, and ambition are all in the eyes of the beholder.

It's harder to let your passion lead you when your entire upbringing has been based on what I call the "scramble-for-security model." If your parents lived their lives fixated on conservative principles of working for status, saving every dollar, and planning for every negative possibility, you're going to have a harder time breaking free of that mentality.

I give motivational speeches to many groups in and around Sacramento—corporations, schools, youth sports organizations—and one topic that frequently arises is the difference between having a "job" and having a "career." This is an important distinction, and one that everybody should address. Is your work merely a job, something you do because it affords you the benefits of pay and security, or do you have a career that is both financially and emotionally fulfilling? Your answer to this question may have its roots in the environment and culture of your childhood.

I made two hundred dollars to fight Jay Valencia at the Colusa Casino, one hundred to win and another one hundred as my commission from the tickets I sold to family and friends. Those were heady times for me—first pro fight, a win, and some promising signs that I could please a crowd and make a few bucks in the process of pursuing my passion. A five-hundred-dollar night was a significant event for someone who was busing tables and earning eight grand a year from a coaching gig.

And I left the casino that night with the promise of another fight. It was really happening, and I was really pumped to keep training and keep fighting and see how far this crazy dream could take me.

But about three days after the fight, after I was finished coaching for the day and before I began busing tables, I walked in the front door of our house in midtown Sacramento to see my friends Dave and Dustin hanging in the living room, dour looks on their faces.

This was *not* what I was used to with these guys. It looked like something really bad had happened. They asked me to sit down.

"We don't think you should fight anymore," Dave started in. "It seems like it could get . . . addicting."

At first, I was relieved that the problem wasn't something more serious.

"Well, guys, I don't think that's going to happen," I said dismissively, returning to check the messages on my cell phone. But when I looked up, I realized they were dead serious. Apparently they felt my journey into professional cage fighting necessitated an intervention. I summoned a more serious tone.

"Look, this is what I've always wanted, and I'm stoked about getting ready for my next fight soon."

"We know, we know," Dustin said. "But you can't keep doing it. It's just crazy."

Were these the guys who were standing and screaming when I put Valencia away? Were these the guys I was looking at while I screamed, "Those are my dawgs!" after the ref stopped the fight? Were these the guys who . . . wanted me to stop?

I started laughing, but in a "what's really going on here?" kind of way. "Guys, you were there. You saw how cool it was."

They both pleaded guilty to having had a blast at the Valencia fight. They admitted that they got caught up in it, but they were worried I might get hurt. They said that once they had a chance to digest the event, they concluded that the sport was brutal and dangerous. And, honestly, I completely agreed. That was what I loved about it: the brutality and the edgy feeling I got putting my pride on the line.

But despite my protestations, I had to stop and acknowledge my fundamental attraction to what's essentially a violent activity. Of course, it's not like I wasn't aware of how my sincere enthusiasm for fighting could cause the slightest bit of discomfort to the people closest to me. Honestly, I didn't tell

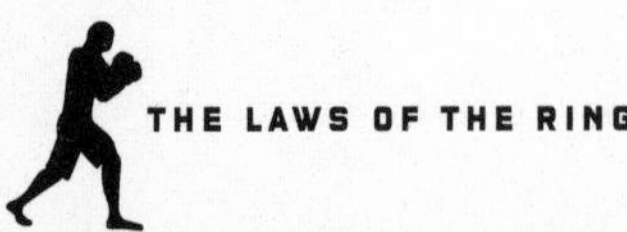

my mom about my fight until two weeks later, when I sat down and showed her the tape.

As she sat there watching, I could see her face drop and the look in her eyes change from slightly concerned to appalled. She had seen many wrestling matches, but nothing that could have prepared her for the level of violence and mayhem in which her son was now engaged. She didn't have much to say, but when the tape was finished, she was certain about one thing, and one thing only: If it was up to her, I would stop fighting. Now, remember, she was a free-spirited person who had raised a free-spirited son, but she was also the kind of mother who made her children go without Novocain at the dentist's office because she didn't believe in altering the mind with drugs, legal or not. In her mind, this sport—this brutal combat sport—was a drug that would surely damage her son.

"You need to stop this," she said with a laugh that was a little uncomfortable.

I looked at her with a crooked smile and chuckled. She wasn't amused.

At this point I was twenty-three years old and had been living on my own since I was nineteen, and while I know a parent's acceptance of a child's decisions varies from family to family, my mom had by now become accustomed to reasoning with me rather than prohibiting.

"Are you going to do that again?" she asked.

When I responded only by looking at her and giving her a sly smile, stating the obvious without saying a word, she said, "I'll pay you not to fight. How much money will it take to get you to stop?"

I pondered her proposal. I ran the Valencia payday through my mind. "Five hundred dollars every minute and a half," I said.

She looked at me and shook her head. She knew a lost cause when she saw one. Those sly smiles that probably got me into a lot of trouble that first year at Davis told her as much, and she relented. Fighting might have seemed abhorrent to her, but my happiness meant more. Always had. After all, she was the one who had filled her children with confidence in themselves. She was the one who had exposed us to modeling and acting. She was the one who suggested we could sing and dance when there was no evidence to support it. The idea that I would pursue something outside the mainstream for the sheer joy and challenge of it was nothing if not consistent with my upbringing.

In the first few minutes of this powwow with Dustin and Dave, I dismissed my friends' concerns, not because I was indifferent to what they had to say, but because while they thought what I was doing was crazy, I thought that *their desire to see me stop* was crazy. Why wouldn't you want to see your best friend happy? Then it *really* hit me. Sure my natural tendency is to be positive, but there's no doubt I was nurtured to wish for everyone to get what they themselves wished for. My parents led by example. But though Dave and Dustin were two of my best friends, their views on my pursuit of a fighting career stemmed from *their* upbringing.

Therein lies the beauty of my background: Because it was as unconventional as my decision to fight, it freed me of any of these hang-ups. My mom wasn't thrilled with what she watched on the tape of my first fight, but she wasn't going to be shamed—or worse, shame *me*—for wanting to be a fighter. Her judgment was based solely on the physical risk attached to the endeavor. A blanket condemnation would have been inconsistent with her mentality. But Dave and Dustin's view was one that was shared by the majority of society. It wasn't that they didn't want to see me happy; it was that, basically, they thought I wasn't in my right mind. The sight of my getting punched in the face wasn't their only concern. What bothered them was that they believed that a decision to make something so outrageous my livelihood would surely lead to great *un*happiness. To them, the risk and the reward didn't match up.

Not only high school students in high-achieving families but many high school students in general are often pressured to get into the best colleges. If their parents guide them through high school and support them emotionally and economically through college, there is an unspoken expectation that they will repay this investment by getting a job their parents can be proud of. When formal education ends and full-time employment begins, parents want to be able to say that their child is a productive member of society. There's nothing inherently wrong with this, of course, but "aspiring

MMA fighter" didn't exactly spring to mind as a socially acceptable and productive occupation for a recent college graduate in 2003. That is the mentality Dustin and Dave represented when they sat me down for the big talk.

To Dustin and Dave, it was more like *People like us go to college, earn a degree, and leave their childish ways behind. They get good jobs with benefits and potential for advancement. They don't fight hard-luck toughs in casino ballrooms in front of crowds of bloodthirsty, dentally challenged fans.* To *me,* though, fighting was fun—a blast, really—and it challenged me in a way that nothing had before or since.

Passion is intensely personal, and everyone has a different passion and a different definition of what expressing this passion gives them. Clearly, not everybody can be a professional athlete or have a high-profile job. That's not the point. Occupations and career paths that some of us consider mundane are absolutely perfect for others. There are no rules, and if I have a problem with the plumbing in my house, I want the most passionate plumber around to be the one who shows up at the door to fix it. But what I say is that if you have an intrinsic fascination with hand-to-hand combat, then be a fighter. If you have a penchant for repairing the infrastructure of residences, then be a plumber. Striving to get a job simply for its social acceptability is—at least in terms of reaching your potential—doomed to failure in the long run. In the short run you get comfort and stability. But then you become so entrenched in a certain way of life that it can be difficult to break out. Dreams become casualties of economic realities. Passion becomes lost. The vibrancy of life becomes an afterthought. Work becomes toil, and toil becomes misery. To me, that's sad.

Now, some people start off on this path and actually sustain this trajectory for a long time. Some actually *get* the house and the boat and the wife with the regular hair appointments and the kid with the pitching lessons and the daughter on the traveling soccer team. But then, years later, when you ask yourself if you are happy and the answer is no, it's tough to retrieve your passion. You've exposed yourself to the elements, so to speak, and there's no umbrella in sight. You're forced to continue on the unhappy path to . . . where? Retirement? When you finally get a chance to cultivate the passions you've allowed to wither and die over the previous forty years?

These words aren't meant to be harsh, but think about it: Even if you get joy out of your family and your hobbies and your remodeled kitchen, that's one hell of a tough bargain. Forty-plus years of passionless work for forty-plus hours a week, just to be comfortable and socially acceptable? Just to be *comfortable*? That equation doesn't work for me, and it never did. You shouldn't let it work for you either.

If you truly want to break free, you're going to have to do the toughest thing imaginable: escape the comfort zone. Don't let convention and comfort lead. Let *passion* lead.

There was one overriding theme about my lifestyle at the beginning of my fighting career: It had *nothing* to do with comfort and *everything* to do with passion. I did what I wanted to do with a sense of confidence that announced to the world that I believed I could do anything. But don't think I'm coming at this subject with a total lack of perspective. Practically speaking, there were moments when I thought the business of fighting might never reach the level of my passion in my lifetime. Accordingly, inside, my confidence wavered. And I confess to wondering if it would be feasible to continue to follow my passion from one Indian casino to another. But over time, with the knowledge that I gained from observing the changing landscape, I mapped out how to make this crazy vocation a *reality.*

As for Dave and Dustin, from the moment they asked me to sit down, defeat was already in their eyes. I think they knew they might as well stand out in the street and argue with the wind, that my mind was made up, but they were earnest and well meaning. There was no envy or jealousy. To be honest, there wasn't much in my life to envy back then. When I graduated from college, I had the tiniest room in our house, not much more than a closet, and I was working at the restaurant and bringing food home so I'd have enough fuel to get me through the days of long workouts. I was coaching and training and managing to remain upbeat through it all. Dave and Dustin were far more comfortable than I was—higher-paying jobs, wealthier families, less pressure to make enough money to get through the week. I honestly admired how together their lives were, especially since I was making it up as I

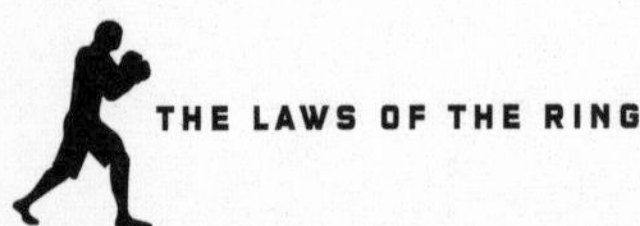

went along. But their passion wasn't my passion. That was the main reason they were sitting in front of me in the living room giving me their best undertaker faces; they had taken a good look at my experience, and it scared the hell out of them.

"Look, guys, I appreciate your concern," I said. "I know you're my friends and you've got my best interests in mind, but I'm not giving this up."

They didn't immediately accept the answer, but they came around. And as soon as they felt that "this fighting thing" made me genuinely happy, they dropped their criticisms and have been nothing but supportive since. In fact, after that conversation, the three of us would sit around and watch video of my fights over and over. Dave and Dustin would just sit there with their eyes bugging out and their jaws hanging open.

"Dude, I can't believe you're doing this shit!" Dave would say. "It blows me away!" I'd overhear them telling their other buddies on the phone, "Urijah fought this big Mexican dude, and he kicked his ass."

Dustin and Dave did what they felt was the right thing for their friend, and they didn't bring it up again. My fights became their guilty pleasure. They continue to attend . . . and they keep having a blast.

THE 15TH LAW OF POWER

EMULATE THE SUCCESSFUL

An Ohio paper-mill worker named Donald Ray Pollock, whose main contributions to society were drinking too much and doing too many drugs, decided he wanted to become a writer. He had no formal training as a writer and no means of acquiring that training, so he took a unique approach to finding his own voice.

As recounted in a profile by the *New York Times'* Charles McGrath, "[Pollock] began by retyping the stories of writers he admired—Hemingway, Cheever, Richard Yates. 'I'd type one and sort of carry it around with me for a week, reading and rereading, and then I'd pitch that one and do another. I probably did that for 18 months. I'm not a real close reader and typing those stories out gave me a chance to see . . . how you make a transition . . . how you do dialogue. You don't fill the page with blather. I knew that in the back of my head, but it still helped to see it.' "

Imagine that: This man sat down with books by his favorite authors and painstakingly typed their words verbatim as a means of getting closer to the genius that created them. Obviously, there's no one single way to give life to your passion. Everyone has a different process, but one thing is irrefutable: It starts with initiative. Whether it's researching the hiring practices of a business you love or typing famous short stories, you need a catalyst in order to begin the process.

Pollock proved that emulation is not a bad place to start. He let his passion lead and followed it wherever it took him. His rudimentary approach had some drawbacks—he admitted that his early stories read like cheap imitations of the men he admired—but eventually he discovered and developed his own voice. He went back to college and developed a style that blew away his professors first, editors and publishers later. He published two excellent books, *Knockemstiff* and *The Devil All the Time,* in his midfifties. Not surprisingly, the critics and the literary world fell in love with his stories.

Pollock merged his unique perspective with the technique of his favorite authors and his passion became his life.

We all need role models. Even the most driven and focused person draws inspiration from the success of others. Passion is a great GPS for life, but you can't just punch in an address and go flying past all the landmarks on your way to the destination. Over the course of allowing your passion to lead, you need to stop and learn a few lessons from those who have traveled the same path.

One of the most influential fighters in my early career was Bas Rutten, a Dutch kickboxer, MMA heavyweight. Rutten's eclectic style of fighting and his use of body shots to put away opponents changed the way a lot of people viewed MMA as a combat sport. He beat just about anybody who was anybody in the UFC in the early days and, no one will disagree, is one of our sport's true pioneers.

But Rutten's greatest impact on my career was his personality and style *outside* the cage. I remember sitting at home just a year into my fight career and being so excited to get Bas Rutten's "El Guapo" technique DVD. I popped it in the player and got a little taste of the Bas personality. The menu picture on the screen was Bas in a Speedo, doing his signature jump-in-the-air splits, and a catchy song that he had written and produced was playing. The song told a hilarious story about a phone conversation with a girl. Bas was explaining to the girl, in musical phone conversation, of course, how he had just finished a big fight and that he wasn't able to have sex for a few weeks before his competitions. As he put it, "It's the rules, baby!" He then proceeded to try to convince her to come over to his house. The chorus was as follows: "I want to chill . . . (Kick back y'all) I want to relax . . . (Kick back y'all) I want to chill . . . (kick back y'all) and maybe have some sex (kick back ya'll)." It was super unexpected, but had me laughing hysterically. I had to share the song and the DVD with all my training partners and learned some great techniques from Bas along the way.

When I finally met Bas for the first time, I was on set with him in Japan for an interview on the Dream fight organization. During the interview, I paid homage to my Dutch heritage on my dad's side and told Bas, "My pop is full-blood Dutch, and my grandparents were immigrants from Holland."

Bas looked at me with a big smile and said, "Uh-oh!"—then turned directly to the camera and, with a cocked eyebrow, said in a deep voice, "Party time!"

When I got home three days later, my pop picked me up at the airport; as he swung the car door open to let me in, he was smiling ear to ear and all he said was "Party time!" We both started busting up laughing and then I gave him the lowdown on the Japan/Bas Rutten experience.

Bas's charisma and easy way of dealing with people struck me as impossibly cool long before I had actually decided to pursue fighting as my sole vocation. He loved the sport and the fans, and they reciprocated his love by forming a community around him. It's no surprise that Bas's demeanor and attitude helped him become a commentator after his fighting career was finished. To me, Bas is a perfect example of someone who invested in his passion and had it pay him back many times over, even— *especially*—after he stopped fighting.

Another one of my heroes is the great Randy Couture. Randy and I had a mutual friend in Sacramento who brought Randy to my second fight. This may have been in the early days of MMA as we know it, but it was still a big deal to me, because Randy was already a major, respected talent in the fledgling fight community. To have him present at one of my early fights is something I'll never forget.

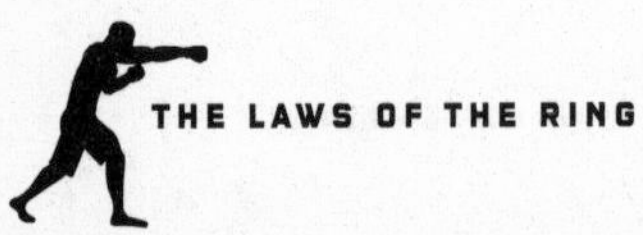

After the fight, my friend told me, "Hey, we're going with Randy to the Mandalay Bay in Las Vegas to watch the Tito Ortiz–Chuck Liddell fight. Randy says whoever wants to come is welcome—and *you're* coming."

Of course, I didn't protest. In a very short amount of time, I'd gone from someone who was begging for a chance to fight at the Colusa Casino to someone who was being invited to hang with Randy Couture before the first epic Ortiz-Liddell fight.

We ended up with eight or nine people piled into Randy's room. My high school sweetheart Michelle came out for a day and hung out with us. And here we were, hanging with not only a world champ, but *the* biggest name in the sport—in my eyes, a living legend—and simply being among the tiny posse was far and away the coolest thing ever. But it didn't stop there. Scott Smith was one of the other fighters who were on the trip. We went down to the pool at Mandalay Bay and hung out with Randy for a while. Randy was balding and wearing a Speedo, lying in his chair. Scott turned to me and said, "I'm not sure if I should feel cool because I'm hanging with Randy Couture or weird because I'm hanging with a forty-one year old in a Speedo." We both laughed hard.

Randy was so engaging and easygoing and not only took the time to answer every silly question I had, but encouraged my fighting pursuits. I picked his brain about the fight game, but what affected me most is the same thing that drew me to Bas. There wasn't any one specific piece of advice he gave me, but he was so simple and real. Randy, to my surprise, had a son who was only three years younger than I was. I remember asking him details about his son, as well as realizing that this guy who I was so happy to be hanging with was almost old enough to be my dad. Randy was so down-to-earth.

"Yeah, he wrestled for a while growing up, but it wasn't his thing like it was for me. He's just a good kid. Not sure if he's gonna fight," Randy said frankly. "Ryan [his son] just turned twenty-one not long before my fight with Tito [Ortiz] a few months ago and he came out to the fight. I get back up to my hotel room and he's passed out right in front of the door!" He laughed his hearty laugh, then went on: "I just picked him up and brought him in the room, don't think he's used to Vegas yet." It wasn't anything intense talking with Randy, he was easygoing and kind—but his willingness to simply include me meant more than I could express. For the first time I felt like my passion was being taken seriously by someone who was in a position to know. My presence in Vegas, in Couture's suite, was all the validation I needed at the time. I hadn't *arrived,* per se, but I felt I belonged to a brotherhood that understood where I'd been and where I wanted to go.

I was becoming more observant. By being around successful people who shared my passion, I was able to gain a better sense of myself. In any profession, you learn things along the way. You take the best qualities from people and try to emulate them. You forget the rest. And I remember looking at Randy Couture and thinking at the time, *If I ever get anywhere near that level in the sport, I'm going to be as supportive and cool as this guy.*

I was determined not to take the opportunity for granted. I had a good time hanging with Randy, but I considered it work to an extent; I had the unique opportunity to observe how someone in the upper heights of the sport handled himself, and to learn from the experience. This wasn't about telling people about an awesome evening with Randy Couture; it was about learning through observation from one of the top performers and best role models my profession has ever known. The main lesson that I took from Randy was that he was just himself. His image as public figure was consistent with who he really was.

Find people who inspire you in everyday life and learn more about them. It could be a teacher or a family member, even someone you have never met. You can always search the Internet, buy a book, or simply introduce yourself. Be creative when you are pursuing your passion and relentless in your pursuit.

THE 16TH LAW OF POWER

EYES FORWARD

You can't be timid if you're going to put yourself in position to allow passion to run your life. Big changes demand big thoughts and big actions. But this doesn't mean you should quit your job immediately to pursue your passion of raising goats; you can't begin to do this until you're ready to move toward that goal on a creative, consistent basis. You should at least know how much goats cost, and how much land it will take to raise them. There are practical aspects to living the life you dream.

We've all heard countless stories of professional athletes who have made a ton of money, saved none of it, and ended up with very little to show for their careers. The disease is easy to diagnose: Athletes consider themselves invincible, and they never foresee a day when the money is going to stop flowing and the cheers are going to stop ringing in their ears. Even those who understand how fleeting success is in the profession often believe the fame will continue. These are the ones whose plan for the future is something vague like "become a movie star." They don't bother with acting classes, of course, because their athletic fame will automatically compel directors to cast them in important, lucrative roles in big-budget films.

How often does this actually happen? Seldom enough to qualify as never.

It's no different with nonfamous people. Stuck in careers that pay well and provide all-important security, many people live for the promise of a comfortable retirement. They prepare financially but ignore everything else. With nothing but years of soul-crushing work on their résumés, they mistakenly believe they can be rid of the job and suddenly find themselves content and fulfilled. Their passions are either gone or buried under layers and layers of neglect, and by the time they realize this, it's too late. They might try to take up golf or another of the traditional leisure activities, but they find they don't have the patience or the physical ability to pick it up at a late age.

In a sense, they didn't take the acting classes either.

When I started fighting, I knew I would never have the earning power of someone like Mike Tyson, but I always had my future in mind. I wanted to maximize whatever opportunities were available to me, and the exposure I would get fighting would simply be a means to another end. I wanted to set myself up for a future career while I was competing in my present one.

With that as background, it might be easier to understand why I started a clothing line after my second professional fight. Very few people knew who I was, but that didn't stop me. I got the idea for a line of clothing called Alpha Male Clothing and I set about trying to make it work. I didn't know the first thing about starting a clothing line. I was a guy in a pair of mesh shorts that I put ALPHA MALE on the front because I thought the name was cool. Once I saw that people liked it, I figured it might be a fun and relatively easy way to make a few extra bucks.

Getting back to self-knowledge: I wasn't trying to compete with Nike. I didn't envision a multinational conglomerate. But I did think I could start small, create some small-scale buzz, and see where it would take me.

My first investor was my buddy Dustin Soderman. I convinced him to plunk down $250 to help me get started making T-shirts. Because of my coaching gig at UC Davis, almost immediately everyone on the wrestling team was sporting Alpha Male T-shirts. They were walking billboards for me, the best kind of free advertising, and then one of my friends on the UC Davis football team, Marc Manfredda, asked me how he could get one. I made it a point to learn the ins and outs of the clothing business, so when

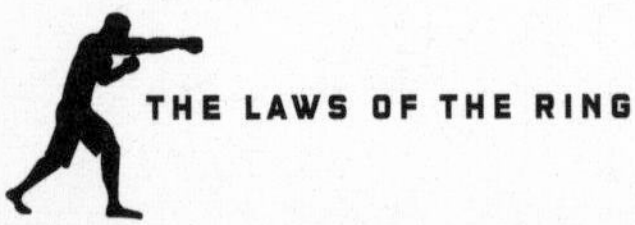

Marc asked for the license to produce the T-shirts and take a cut for himself, I saw an opportunity and obliged. It wasn't long before most of the football team was wearing them.

There wasn't a lot of money in those T-shirts by Nike standards, but there was enough to make a difference in my life at the time. I was busing tables at Ink, making eight grand a year as an assistant coach at UC Davis, and training for fights that were never guaranteed. So anything extra to help pay my $220-a-month rent was valued.

More than that, the experience taught me that I could be successful with an offshoot of my chosen profession. Later, I developed FORM Athletics with an incredible businessman named Mark Miller. We quickly sold it to K-Swiss for a significant amount of money. But without the baby steps I took with the built-in customer base for Alpha Male, the idea of FORM Athletics might have seemed daunting. Instead, I had the knowledge and experience of putting together a product and marketing it with minimal risk. Perhaps more important, I had the knowledge to partner with someone who had the business savvy to make it happen. But more on networks later.

THE 17TH LAW OF POWER

YOU NEVER KNOW WHO'S WATCHING: THE POWER OF PERSONAL CREDIT

By now, you at least know there are two things you must do to live your passion (after adopting a positive attitude, of course): (1) identify your strengths; and (2) be brutally honest with yourself about your weaknesses. Once you come to terms with the results of your personal inventory, you will come to a conclusion: You can't do everything yourself.

When I first started fighting professionally, I didn't have an area of expertise, but there was one thing I knew that I loved and that was fighting. Surprised? I didn't think so. I wasn't much of an expert on anything else, but I knew wrestling and had a love for all forms of martial arts. When I wasn't training, it's what I read about and thought about. Then I started to have business ideas that required not just a set of skills to implement, but money I didn't have. The only thing I had to fall back on was a fanatically positive mentality that anything was possible, and, *just as* important, a willingness to *learn* from people who knew more than I did.

The $250 investment from my friend Dustin for Alpha Male clothing was the first step toward broadening my horizons and making my community a part of my profession. We started something, and it worked in a small-scale way. It planted a seed in my mind that I needed to be open to opportunities that would help me achieve my goals. At this time that meant finding ways to make outside income so I could keep fighting. I was heading into uncharted waters; there was no union for guys who fought in Indian casino ballrooms, no salary scale that told me what I'd be making in five years if I reached a certain level or won a certain belt.

That's why I was intrigued when I came into contact with Jeremy and Sidney Dunmore, two brothers who owned a construction company called Dunmore Communities. The Dunmores had taken a unique path to wealth, and they took a unique path into my life. Their father and grandfather were immensely successful homebuilders in the Sacramento area. Jeremy and Sidney split from their father's company, Dunmore Homes, and started Dunmore Communities with a piece of property and funding from their grandfather. They put a subdivision on that piece of land at a time when Sacramento was growing and the housing market was booming. It was low risk, high reward, and they got filthy rich in a big hurry.

Part of being rich, in the Dunmores' world, was *enjoying* it. Jeremy, the more flamboyant of the two, bought a stretch Suburban and hired a driver named Claude to drive him around. One of the Dunmores' financial advisers was Coach Dave, the head wrestling coach at Sierra College, a community college near Sacramento where I had trained in the past. I was two fights into my pro career when Claude was driving Jeremy around with the financial adviser, and my name came up around the topic of the fight game. Coach Dave said, "I remember Urijah: hardest-working kid I ever saw."

Claude, who by coincidence was friends with one of my UC Davis teammates, Adrian Garcia, chimed in.

"Urijah's the man," he said, looking in the rearview mirror. "You should look him up."

Jeremy, who was a fan of combat sports and a fitness buff, was intrigued.

"Good enough for me. Ask Urijah if he wants to meet up for dinner."

Jeremy was pitched to me as this young, hip multimillionaire, interested in the fight game, by my buddy Adrian Garcia, so when the Suburban pulled up on the day of our lunch, I wasn't terribly surprised. Claude stepped out of the driver's side and led me into the backseat of the long black machine. There was Jeremy, with a welcoming grin on his face.

"What's up? I'm Jeremy." We shook hands. "Let me see your abs," he said just as soon as Claude shut the door. Okay, this was a little weird. I complied unenthusiastically, keeping a sharp eye on him, making sure he meant no funny business.

"Nice," he said, in a way that suggested I'd just showed him a shiny watch he was thinking of buying. I breathed easy. Apparently he was just assessing a potential investment.

Then he lifted his shirt. "Here, check mine out," he said, like he was showing off a new toy. But something in his tone suggested that, for him, this really was just part of casual banter.

"That's not bad, dude," I said, a bit weirded out by the exchange. Satisfied with my reply, he engaged me in a discussion about fighting and my "career" (which, again, had spanned a whole two fights).

"Your name keeps coming up from different people," he told me. "People we trust. And I just wanted to meet with you to see if there's any way we can help you out."

I learned over lunch at a local Davis restaurant called Fuzio's that Jeremy was a former competitive Jet Skier. He was now *way* into working out and wanted to be around the fight scene.

Jeremy was rich, living big, and he was looking for different ways to use his money to open doors, particularly for his peers. He was only four years older than me and, despite the obvious financial discrepancy, made it perfectly clear that I *was* a peer.

Despite my initial reservations sparked by the abs show, Jeremy and I built a friendship over the following weeks. I was struggling financially and, with just two fights under my belt, not exactly established professionally, and because of Jeremy's guidance and generosity, I got to have a glimpse into a far more luxurious lifestyle. We were establishing a rapport that suggested to me that he was indeed interested in supporting my endeavors, but the subject of *money* had not yet come up.

You're Always Selling Yourself

One day, during one of our meetings, I offhandedly mentioned my Alpha Male clothing line, which was really nothing more than a handful

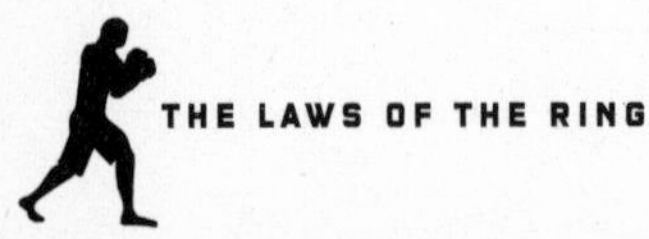

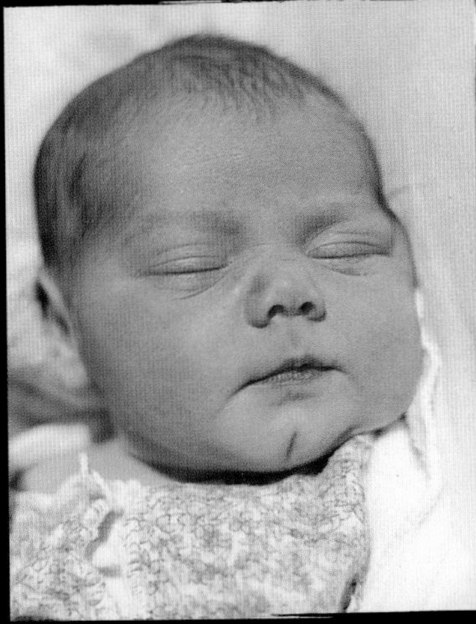

Signature chin.

Peace, love, and happiness!
My parents, Theo and Suzanne.

Playing dress-up with the neighborhood girls.

Mom and me, always drawn to the ocean.

With Ryan in a hammock during the early Christian commune days.

Modeling event. I was pretty used to being in front of a camera.

After the J.C. Penney state fair fashion show, where my mom modeled each year.

Lincoln Colts, seventh and eighth grade. We moved from downtown Sacramento to the small town of Lincoln when I was in seventh grade.

I always looked up to Ryan. He beat me in the muscle category when I was in eighth grade.

Eighth-grade graduation with a hand-me-down shirt.

Happy to have our new baby sister, Michaella.

One of many bloody lips.

The Faber boys at Ryan's high school graduation.

Senior year in high school.

Senior year in college.
RANDY MARTIN,
MARTIN PHOTOGRAPHY

Senior year in college with Ryan, my longtime girlfriend Michelle, and Michaella.

With Michelle, the day after my first loss to Tyson Griffin.

At the afterparty with my mom, after the first Pulver fight. She has never been to a live event, but she will hang out afterward.

After a BBQ on the block with some of the top dogs on the team. *(From left to right:)* Joseph; Chad; my business partner, Matt Fisher; my first training partner, Dustin; the wild man from Thailand, Master Thong; UFC fighter and childhood friend Danny Castillo. MT's shirt is something else.
TRACY LEE

Private workout at UFC 139 in San Jose. Skinny and still seven pounds over but feeling good.
JAMES LAW

Cruising the streets of Sacramento after my victory over Jens. UFC fighter Clay Guida decided to join me on the roof. Joseph, Dustin, and Master Thong were along as well. TRACY LEE

With Jens Pulver and his wife, after I fought him at Arco Arena. Big point in my career. First hometown fight in front of a big crowd. Jens was always one of my favorite fighters. TRACY LEE

Street-legal dune buggy. I'd always wanted one of these. Best impulse buy yet. TRACY LEE

Matt Sanchez borrowing my head (which a fan had airbrushed). We were having fun at the gym before Sanchez was a businessman, Chad was a contender, and Danny was a staple in the UFC. That's me with the Alpha Male hat covering my face.

Taking good care of the infamous cleft chin. Getting greased up.
JEFF HUTCHENS

Out back of the Colusa Casino, trying to stay warm. Rough bunch of peers.
JEFF HUTCHENS

Shadowboxing in my room. I still have a habit of doing that. Photos of my family and friends on the wall as well as some funny pictures.
JEFF HUTCHENS

Just felt right. Coming into the cage for the first time. Mark Munoz, my buddy Virgil, and Cassio Werneck were in my corner. JEFF HUTCHENS

I was so pumped after the big win over Jay Valencia. I was the only one in the arena that knew for sure that I was going to win. JEFF HUTCHENS

In the coaches' locker room at UC Davis. I'm sure it had been a long day, since I was working three jobs and training in between.
JEFF HUTCHENS

Back when shoes were allowed in fights, as well as knees to a grounded opponent. Times have changed in MMA.
JEFF HUTCHENS

Walking in the ring before my first fight. I found the Santa Cruz beanie while working in the grounds department at UC Davis.
JEFF HUTCHENS

Working up a sweat in my tiny apartment. Seems like I was always visualizing my first fight. JEFF HUTCHENS

Escorting Michaella, who was homecoming princess, during her senior year at Santa Barbara High School. My stepdad, Tom, was out of the country at the time and I was happy to step in. DAN LINDSAY

Red Robinson, the street-smart version of Einstein. He's a hustler!

The Team on the Block: Poppies is proud of his new physique. My brother, Ryan, is flexing in the back. Tommy and two of Alaska's finest, Justin Buchholz and Eddie Hoch.

Joseph getting used to the media. He was still driving his 1986 Lincoln Continental, his prized possession. He loved that car.

Some of Poppies's hometown buddies with Team Alpha Male at his wedding.

Best man at Poppies's wedding. I was honored since he had twenty-eight groomsmen.

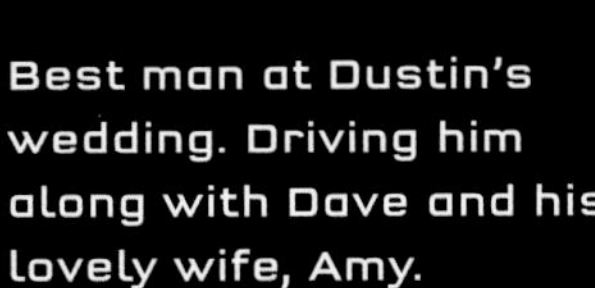

Best man at Dustin's wedding. Driving him along with Dave and his lovely wife, Amy.

About to hit the town. Virgil, Sanchez, Poppies, Lance, Chad, Justin, Joseph, and the Team.

After a big win against Rafael Ascuncao. Three of my best friends ringside: Tommy on the left, Dustin on the right, and giving Dave a big hug. Long road from my first fight at Colusa Casino.

of T-shirts and workout shorts at the time. But I was serious about moving this forward and let Jeremy know it. It wasn't just something to which I was lending my name—which at that point wouldn't have really helped anyway. I had a sharp vision for the art and the community that would buy it.

And Jeremy loved it. The name, the idea, the market analysis, everything. After my pitch (I'm not even sure I realized it was a pitch at the time) he proposed paying me eighteen hundred dollars a month to train and, at the same time, to run the clothing line.

I really wasn't mentioning the clothing line to show off how well rounded I was, but apparently Jeremy was looking for that added spark in order to sponsor me—something that separated me from other athletes. The clothing line provided him with the opportunity to do just that.

I struggled to keep my eyes from popping out of my head. Not counting the money I'd earned in my two fights, I was killing myself working three jobs—coaching, busing, and fighting—to make slightly less than that. The whole world opened up in front of me at the prospect of being paid eighteen hundred bucks a month to do what I was currently doing in my spare time anyway (of course I didn't see my fighting career and fashion ambitions as such a frivolous hobby, but that was the reality before meeting Jeremy).

In return, I agreed to wear a henna tattoo—DUNMORE COMMUNITIES—across my back for my upcoming fights. "It's not like you're going to be selling a lot of houses for me," he said, "but it's just another way for me to market."

Jeremy's investment in me worked for both of us. The more we hung out, the more Jeremy saw that I was enthusiastic and passionate about training and fighting. But he also saw the way I saw my career giving birth to other enterprises. I wasn't obsessed with just the act of fighting, but with the culture it bred and the passionate community it engendered. I wasn't concerned just with winning, but with participating and contributing to this movement. Jeremy had a lot of money and wasn't afraid to spend it—private jets, wild vacations, out-of-control shopping sprees. Now he wanted to give back. But he didn't just want to donate to an organization that would spend the money as they saw fit. He wanted to see where his money was going. And in me he saw a struggling fighter with big dreams and a practical way to implement them. More important, he could attach himself to me and my goals.

Unfortunately, my career took off just as the housing market crashed to earth, and Dunmore Communities was one of many casualties of the housing-foreclosure crisis. The sponsorship was cut short, but make no mistake about it: Jeremy's contribution had a major impact on my career. Not just logistically, but morally. It was the first time I was able to look at the fight game and think, *I really might be able to make a living at this.*

Perhaps because she and my dad struggled financially for so long, my mom always preached to Ryan and me that our financial credit was second only to our health. She wanted us to be aware of how a person's credit follows him, and what it says about him as a responsible and dependable adult. As I got older, I adapted her thoughts into one of my own: The most important thing a person can have—and it's worth capitalizing—is *personal* credit.

By my definition, personal credit is a combination of your word, your personality, and your trustworthiness. In other words, personal credit is a summary of your identity—nothing short of *who you are*. There was no way for me to know it at the time, but I was building personal credit with Jeremy Dunmore every time I walked into the gym at Sierra College as an eighteen-year-old fresh out of high school, and every time I sold a T-shirt or treated a fan with respect.

You need to remember you're doing the same thing, too—every time you speak to a business associate or encounter a stranger or order a meal at a restaurant. The image you convey and the decency you show will determine how you will be judged—today, tomorrow, and perhaps many years from now.

And it started with idle talk and a dubious abdominal display in a stretch Suburban. A wrestling coach and a chauffeur who I knew only casually vouched for my credibility to a wealthy entrepreneur, and it went from there.

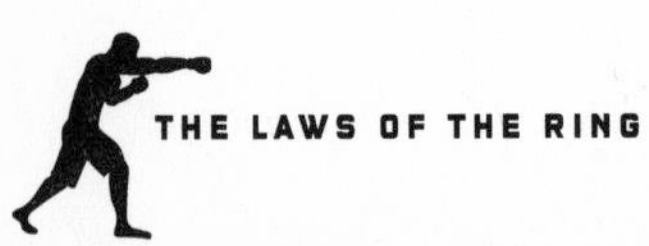

THE 18TH LAW OF POWER

OPINIONS DON'T DRIVE REALITY

After the second time I fought Mike Brown—which I'll discuss in more detail later—a guy came up to me in Sacramento and said, "I never really was much of a fan of yours because of that whole 'pretty boy' thing, but I really became a fan after that fight."

I clenched my jaw a little tighter and, withholding some choice words, said, "I appreciate it."

I thought by the Mike Brown fights I would've accepted the "pretty boy" label that had been affixed to my résumé, but I'd be lying if I said I'd shaken it off by the time of this backhanded compliment. I had never seen the whole "pretty boy" thing, because I don't fit into my own description of a pretty boy. I don't fake tan. I don't pluck my eyebrows. I don't shave my chest. I almost never comb my hair. That makes me 0-for-four on my personal "Pretty Boy Checklist." And, oh yeah, I train every day and fight for a living.

My third professional fight was against a tough dude named David Velasquez. He was the *Gladiator Challenge* champion at 145 pounds, and this fight was for his belt. He was a thirty-seven-year-old man with missing teeth and scars across his body that looked to me like stab wounds. He wore shorts that had "5150" across the belt and the back. If you don't know, "5150" is the California penal code number for putting someone in a seventy-two-hour psychiatric hold. Colloquially, it means someone who has been identified as a threat to himself or others.

A week or so before the fight, Velasquez was in the locker room of a health club in his hometown of Yuba City, about forty miles north of Sacramento and about twenty-five miles from my hometown of Lincoln.

He was talking to a buddy about his upcoming fight in Colusa. He told his buddy, "You gotta come watch this fight, man. I'm going to destroy this pretty-boy college kid."

His buddy said, "Oh yeah, what's his name?"

"Guy named Urijah Faber," Velasquez told him.

Velasquez didn't know one important piece of information: The guy who was getting dressed on the bench next to him and his buddy was my girlfriend Michelle's father. He owned a Kawasaki shop in Yuba City and worked out in the same gym as Velasquez. Thanks to the connection, I heard about the episode immediately after David left the club.

To be fair, it was a safe bet that Velasquez and I came from different backgrounds. He didn't give the impression of being someone who spent part of his youth in a free-range Christian commune. And the only "statement" I was making was on my back: a henna tattoo that read DUNMORE COMMUNITIES.

But fighting is one of the purest ways to observe the power dynamic between two people. It is about as primal as human interaction can get. For whatever reason, this has always been something I felt a compulsion to explore. The first time I saw fighting, I said, "I'd be really good at that. No one would be able to beat me up." I felt that even before it was true, and much of it had to do with the social aspect of the interaction.

There was a part of me that viewed the entire enterprise as a sociological experiment. Just like my first fight with Jay Valencia, everything society puts forward indicates that I should have been deathly afraid of David Velasquez. Judging by appearances, the things he'd done and the things he'd seen, the

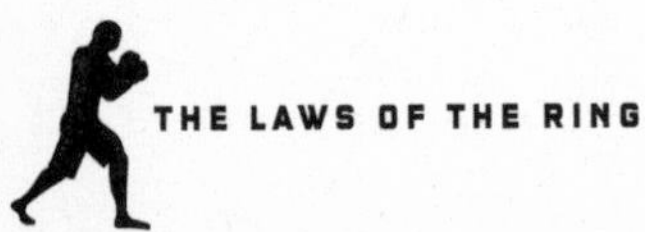

5150 shorts and the loud mouth, vile fans who supported him . . . it should have scared me right out of the cage before the first bell.

The first lesson I was taught in an entry-level political science course was this: The most dangerous people are those with the least to lose. The guy with the least to lose—the guy who has suffered the most and just figures the hell with it—is the guy who has the advantage. Because of that, the guy with the least to lose will do the most to win. I'm not trying to compare what happens in a cage fight with actions of historical importance, but the man-to-man battle inside a cage can be seen through the same lens as the Middle East uprising in the spring of 2011. The people in countries like Egypt and Libya decided they couldn't continue to live under the oppressive regimes that ruled them. They got tired of being trod upon, subjugated, and ignored. They looked at their situation and decided it would be worth risking their lives to change it, simply because they would rather be dead than continue living under the dictatorial, dream-killing systems. They had nothing to lose, so they rose up and fought for their lives.

And David Velasquez should have had the least to lose. On top of everything, he was a good fighter; with eleven fights to his name, he was a former teammate of the legendary Frank Shamrock and had lost a tough fight to Jens Pulver in the UFC years prior. There was nothing I could do to this man that someone else hadn't already done to him. I had a college degree and a marketable face and a sponsorship that paid me to train. How much did I really need this? How much would I gain by beating him, compared to how much he would gain by beating me?

What did he have to fear? After all, he was facing someone who would ultimately be tagged as the "pretty boy" of MMA. And yet, I felt absolutely no fear.

The Velasquez fight was like something out of a movie. I stood in the back corner of the amphitheater, waiting for my walk-up music to start, and from across the corridor I could see and hear Velasquez, who—as the champion—would enter the cage second.

"This is my house!" he screamed. "This is my house!" Over and over, as if those were the only four words he knew. He was alternately shadowboxing and punching himself in the head as he glared across at me.

From above me, a chubby dude in the stands looked down on me and my guys. He was yelling, too: "Mess this pretty boy up, Dave! Mess this pretty boy up!" He was wobbly, the beer inside his plastic cup sloshing and spilling onto the floor, misting us. A female version of him—tattooed, drinking, fat, loud—stood by his side.

My music started, a roar shook the small arena, and it felt like every hair on my body was standing at attention.

Velasquez came into the cage screaming. He paced around yelling. Then he got nose to nose with me and popped his mouthpiece out so I could see his missing teeth. "I'm gonna whoop your ass, boy, and teach you some respect," he said. Inside I was calm and composed. I had prepared well for this fight, and I was confident in both my planning and my ability. Velasquez was attempting to intimidate me, but I refused to give him the satisfaction of a response.

I *wanted* him to scream and yell and waste his energy. I knew it was a show. I knew he was acting tough because he couldn't figure me out. I had him worried, and his insecurities were on display every time he opened his big mouth. He was trying to sell me on the idea that he could intimidate me with his looks and his words.

The only emotion I was feeling was impatience. He was pissing me off with all his jumping around and his stupid proclamations, and I couldn't wait to punch him in the mouth. I'm a relatively calm guy in the cage, before and during the fight. I get antsy, but I'm not going to make a big scene or break out into some tribal dance just for the show of it. The anticipation gets me fired up inside, though. There's a part of me that instinctually strives to correct whatever it is that's pissing me off. In this case, David Velasquez was pissing me off. *Pretty boy?!* Outwardly you couldn't tell—I think I appeared composed—at least that's what those who watched the fight tell me—but inside I was thinking a wide variety of words you wouldn't use at Sunday school.

Finally, as he jumped around in my face one more time, I clenched my jaw and looked at him very calmly. "I'm going to knock the rest of your teeth out," I said. Pretty calmly, I think. The look on his face indicated that he expected me to back down, or at least respond to his wild histrionics

with some of my own. He didn't expect the calm confidence. I think it gave him pause.

The fight started. I took control right from the beginning and started beating him up. His demeanor changed completely. "5150" or no, on this night, *I* was the one who was a danger to others, and the "others" was one David Velasquez. There were no more threats coming out of him. I didn't hear "pretty boy" again.

We were on the ground when the bell rang to end the first round. He jumped up to head to his corner, but before he did this, a most amazing thing happened: He reached out and shook my hand.

His mouth had been muted, but the handshake spoke volumes. All he did was nod, but it told me he went to his corner thinking, *Okay, this guy's for real.* I had already earned more than his respect. I had taken the best he had to offer and topped it. His gesture of sportsmanship was the acknowledgment.

It was a good fight. He fought to the end. He was motivated. He saw that I could fight, and that I was not going to fall victim to his posturing, so he decided to give me the respect he thought I deserved and keep fighting his best. He knew it wasn't going to be enough, but that didn't stop him.

In the third round, I did a bad setup to a shot and got kicked in the face. He got me square, and a curtain of black flashed in my eyes. In the moment it barely registered. There was no fear that I had suffered some damage, or that I might be knocked unconscious and lose the fight. I was only tangentially aware of it happening, like a shooting star that flashes in your peripheral vision. David Velasquez couldn't beat me. I couldn't let it happen. I shook it off and doubled into him with a takedown. I used that moment to recover my wits, and then I shot after him and pounded him to leave no doubt.

When I first started hearing "pretty boy," I recoiled some. It wasn't who I was, and it wasn't how I wanted to be perceived. But then I got honest with myself. As I looked across the cage at David Velasquez, it was pretty obvious. I don't look like the *public perception* of a fighter. The marketers of the sport have done a good job imprinting on the minds of the public that a fighter is the ultimate warrior, a serious, machinelike beast with scars and tattoos and a shelflike brow. Consequently, detractors see mixed martial artists as brutes and bullies. But this is where the perception and reality diverge. People who open their minds and take the time to research MMA discover that the nature of the sport requires us to be extremely critical and intelligent, possessing the same attributes of champions in any other sport. The most successful guys have it all—intelligence, discipline, fitness, dedication.

And then there's me. The so-called pretty boy. Not an enviable moniker in my line of work. But I learned, over time, that I couldn't control every external force. I must admit, the perception has worked to my advantage. Opportunities for endorsements and high-profile fights grew in part because I was marketable and could serve as a likable spokesman. In this case, I learned to live with it and take advantage of it. I never considered slapping tattoos all over my body or cutting my hair or doing something crazy to change my image. In fact, I guess I was able to debunk the idea that a so-called pretty boy couldn't compete in the vicious sport of mixed martial arts.

After the fight Velasquez was respectful. It was my third fight and my first title fight, and he said, "I'm ready to pass the torch. You deserve it."

My favorite photo from that fight is me holding his head late in the fight, and every bit of his head is covered in blood. I'm looking into the crowd, smiling. It reminds me of why I started in this sport, and the attitude that I try to keep in my world. Life can be brutal and messy, but it's about the experience. There is no doubt in my mind that Dave Velasquez sees that picture and holds his head high. Our battle that night is something he can be proud of, a feather in his cap, a part of the journey of his life, and a great story for both of us to tell.

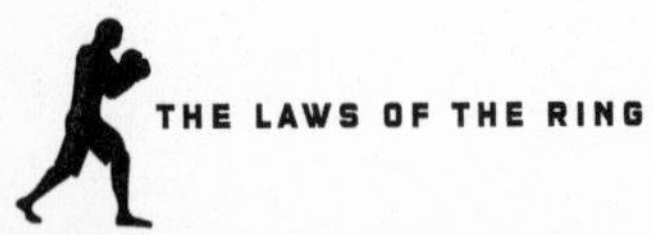

THE 19TH LAW OF POWER

KEEP IT REAL: BUILD YOUR NAME BY BEING YOU

Right after the Velasquez fight, a big African-American guy came up to me and introduced himself. He really didn't need to, though, because I was a big fan of Quinton "Rampage" Jackson. It was June of 2004, before he had become a big name in the UFC or made any movies in Hollywood.

"My name's Quinton," he said. "I fight for Pride; it's like the UFC in Japan."

"I know who you are," I said. "I watch all your fights."

He was actually surprised, because at the time he was relatively unknown in the United States. Rampage made his name in Japan, where he was loved for his fighting, his big slams, and his sense of humor. I had seen a ton of the interviews he'd given while fighting for Pride in Japan, and I thought they were hilarious. I loved his gamesmanship and how he managed to be both incredibly intense and funny at the same time. The idea of him coming to the Colusa Casino and watching me fight was a big deal to me.

"I'm going to be a big fan of yours," he told me. "I don't know what it is about you, but I usually get jealous of up-and-coming guys. I'm not jealous of you. When I saw you get kicked in the face and get right back up, I said, 'I like this dude!' "

At the time I didn't have a nickname, and was just getting a hold on the whole idea of marketing yourself and the business of the fight game. Well, Rampage was there to help.

"Play up the whole surfer thing," he told me. "You know, do the 'hang loose, cowabunga, dude' thing. You gotta market yourself, you gotta stand out. Your fighting is badass! I'll be rooting for you man, I'm your fan." This was a cool experience for me, encouraging, to say the least. I had one of my favorite fighters saying that I was "badass." I kept Quinton's advice in mind over the next year of competing, at the end of which I still didn't have a nickname in the sport. It took a hint from another peer before I finally sniffed out my "California Kid" ring name.

The next year I had heard that there was a competition for grappling where you could make up to ten thousand dollars competing in a no-gi Brazilian Jiu-Jitsu competition. I looked up the tournament online, saw that it was only two weeks away, and sent an e-mail to the guy who was in charge, Kid Peligro. It read, "Hi, my name is Urijah Faber. I am a former Division I wrestler from UC Davis; I was top 12 in the nation in 2002 and a runner-up in the University Nationals for freestyle wrestling the same year. I also currently have world titles in both the *Gladiator Challenge* and *King of the Cage* MMA leagues. I've been training jujitsu for two years under BJJ world champion Cassio Werneck, and I'd like to compete in the ADCC this year. Is it true that I can win $10,000? Please let me know, thank you. Urijah Faber." That same day I got a message back that said they would love to have me.

So I woke up the next morning and went about my day, coaching wrestling two times, once at 6 A.M., then again from 3 to 5 P.M. After that I showered up and drove to Carmichael, about thirty minutes away, to train jujitsu at six-thirty. I walked into the school and popped my head into my instructor Cassio's office.

"Hey, Cass, I think I'm gonna do that no-gi tournament called Abu Dhabi. I heard you can win like ten Gs."

He looked at me briefly then looked back at his computer and said in broken English-Portuguese, "Oh no, you can't do that tournament. That's the world championship, that's the biggest tournament in BJJ. They only allow ten people in each weight in the whole world. And it's in two weeks."

I was a little confused, so I explained, "Well, I sent an e-mail, I'm pretty sure that I can." Cassio explained again that this was an elite tournament. There were qualifying tournaments and representatives from around the world, the most difficult tournament to get into; he wasn't even allowed to go because he didn't live in Brazil anymore.

"Maybe try out next time Urijah, it's every other year." I explained again that I had sent an e-mail and they told me that same day that I could compete. I walked over to Cassio's computer and pulled up the e-mail. It hadn't occurred to him that I had some serious credentials.

"See, they said I'm good to go." I had never seen him so excited, nor did I have any idea that it was such a big deal; to me it wasn't. It would be my first jujitsu competition ever and I only had two weeks to learn the rules and regulations of official ADCC world championships.

Two weeks later I was in Southern California ready to compete. It was pretty shocking when I got to the Host Hotel. I had brought my two buddies Virgil and TJ with me on the trip, as usual, and found out that although the rooms were paid for, each competitor was matched up as roommates with another competitor. I got my room assignment and it turned out I was supposed to be rooming with one of the brightest up-and-coming stars of the UFC, Georges St-Pierre. With Virg and TJ at my side, I tracked down Georges to explain to him that I had screwed up and brought my friends to stay in our room.

"St-Pierre, St-Pierre!" I yelled down the hall. When I approached him, he thought that I was some kind of eager fan and treated me as such, turning to me quickly and extending his hand to shake.

"Hello, how are you? Georges," he said with a big smile and a funny French Canadian accent.

I could tell he had no idea that I was his roommate, so I started the conversation with, "Congrats on your last win! You did awesome." He answered quickly, trying to get the small talk out of the way, and move on.

"Did you want a picture?" he asked sincerely.

"Oh, I don't have a camera, man. I'm supposed to be rooming with you but I brought my two friends. Sorry, man, I just didn't realize that we were sharing." A lightbulb went off in his head.

"Oh!" He laughed. "It's okay, I'm gonna get my own room. Good luck tomorrow."

I said, "Cool, man. Yeah, you, too, and I'm a fan of yours. I fight, too, in *King of the Cage.* My name's Urijah."

It was starting to sink in that this tournament was a big deal.

The next day I came to the tournament and everyone was there. I started looking around and saw one of my early favorites, MMA superstar Tito "The Huntington Beach Bad Boy" Ortiz, warming up to my left. To my right was former UFC champion Ricco "Suave" Rodriguez and UFC welterweight contender Frank "Twinkle Toes" Trigg. I walked to the edge of the mat and said hello to my fellow Northern Californian competitors Gilbert "El Niño" Melendez and Jake Shields. Gilbert and I were in the same weight class and knew each other from college wrestling. We had also done some cross-training that Nick and Nate Diaz had put together. Jake and I had been in the same small school subsection together in high school in neighboring towns, and knew each other pretty well.

"What's up, Gil, you got Japan first? I've got Parrumpinha from Brazil [one of American Top Team's BJJ coaches]. Let's get it done for the USA, baby! Good luck."

Gil gave me a big smile and said, "Forget that, let's do it for Cali!" I laughed and we gave each other the standard California handshake.

"Yup, let's do it for Cali!" I smiled with a little extra pride. I continued to walk around the arena and saw a small crowd around a big dude with a huge chain hung on his neck. It was Quinton "Rampage" Jackson. A friend . . . and a fan of mine. He caught a glimpse of me walking up the concourse and yelled out, giving me his big signature smile.

"What's up, California Kid!"

I gave him a head nod and shot him a smile then went on my way. But that name bounced around my head. Gilbert's comment about doing it for "Cali" was there, too. I remember thinking, *California is a cool place.* I made my way back to the warm-up mats and was soon approached by none other

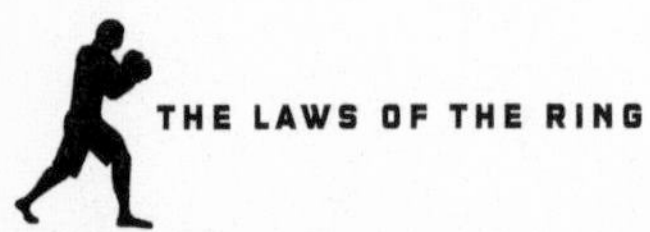

than UFC's ring announcer Bruce Buffer. It was my first time meeting him and I was a fan. He had been hired to announce the event and was looking to get my name perfect for the announcements.

"You're Uri-Jah right? I'm going to be announcing you today." He didn't get the name right, so I corrected him.

"It's actually pronounced U-*ri*-ah, the *j* is silent. I'm sure it's hard to get all the names right, you have to say a ton of them." He was quick to correct me.

"Actually, I rarely have trouble with names. It won't happen again," he said with confidence, making it very apparent that he wasn't the type to make errors in his area of expertise. "Do you have a nickname?"

I quickly told him that I didn't. "No, just my name."

He said, "Okay, nice to meet you," and turned to walk away. I stopped him after a few steps and got his attention.

"Hey, Bruce, actually I do have a nickname. Put down 'The California Kid.'" He looked at me and quickly jotted it on his notepad.

"Got it!"

The tournament was tough. I won the first match against the Brazilian black belt Parrumpinha and then lost a hard-fought battle with multiple time BJJ and ADCC world champion Marcos Feitosa in the only submission loss of my life in competition. But some more important things happened that day. I was a peer with some of the biggest names in MMA and had competed at the highest level in a discipline that I had only trained in for two years, and I felt in my heart that with a few adjustments I could have been a world champion that year. My new nickname was established and I was excited for the future of my career, knowing there was a place for a happy, friendly, blond, and bronzed kid from California.

It's obvious that certain areas in life are filled with stereotypes and status quos, but it's always best to stay true to yourself and carve your own niche in this world. Even when you may seemingly not fit the mold.

THE 20TH LAW OF POWER

BUILD A COMMUNITY OF POTENTIAL

Here's what I've learned: If you surround yourself with positive, like-minded people, success will follow. The power of community is vital for physical, mental, and financial health. As I sat down to write this book, I came to understand some deep-seated values that I held, values that trace back to my family's time in the Christian commune. Many of the tenets that have guided my life, I now realize, were not from specific teachings and lessons of the Christian commune but the positive energy and combination of the great people that made up the group.

The question is: How do you go about forming or joining the kind of community—a community of potential—that brings out the best in both the individual and the whole? My experience with the Dunmores, despite being relatively short-lived, taught me to seek potential in others. I don't look for people who *have* achieved great things; I look for people who *will* achieve great things.

After my third fight, right after I got the Dunmore sponsorship, I decided I wanted to buy a house. I didn't know anything about real estate, but I knew I wanted a house and I knew my meager income made the prospect unlikely. I had a college friend, Michael Yosef, who was in the mortgage industry, and he said, “I can get you a loan.”

“Dude, my income was only ten thousand bucks last year.”

“Don’t worry about it,” he said. “We’ll figure it out.”

With that vague commitment providing motivation, I went house-hunting. I was so ignorant of the process that I refused to speak with real estate agents because I didn’t want to have to pay them. I didn’t know they showed houses for free, which is why I turned away ten or twelve agents who expressed an interest in helping me. So I drove around on my own, looking through neighborhoods I liked that contained houses I could afford (that was a rare combination), picking up flyers, and hitting some open houses.

At an open house in an older part of Sacramento, I met an agent named Dana. She was filling in for her friend, who was supposed to be showing the house, and I liked her immediately. Dana was a tough, smart woman and gave me a quick crash course to educate me on the real estate process, which relieved any worries I had about paying an agent to show me homes. I told her I knew I could afford a monthly house payment, because my plan was to move my buddies into the house and split up the cost. She believed me and agreed to help me find something.

Looking back, I see that I was a real estate agent’s worst nightmare, spending the first month with Dana tossing out lowball offers on all these shitty houses. But I loved her straightforward and honest approach; she would look at the houses I was targeting and say, “You don’t want to buy this house” or “What are you looking at *this* for?” She was more supportive than perhaps was reasonable, but I guess that’s why I trusted her.

Then we found a pocket of nice homes tucked in between Interstate 80 and a busy industrial street I didn’t know existed. It wasn’t a prestigious address, but it was superquiet, with big trees and huge backyards. It was perfect.

I found a house that was kind of a piece of shit, but it was a nicer piece of shit than any of the others I had considered. It had a huge mess of a backyard, with old trees and junk everywhere. I could see the potential in it right away. I didn’t see the disaster it was; I saw what it would become. The houses in the rest of the neighborhood were all well kept and unique. Most of my neighbors were in their eighties and many had them built years ago. A fireplace sat in the middle of the living room and there were old beat-up hardwood floors that I thought looked kind of cool. There was a big detached garage and huge trees in both the front and the backyard. I could envision a big pool in the back (when I earned enough money) and the neighborhood was quiet—at least before I got there. The house was a metaphor for the way I saw the world: raw but promising.

So after lowballing all these houses for weeks, I told Dana, "I love this house. Offer full price." There were two other full-price offers, from people I imagine were far more qualified to own a home, but Dana went to work. She told the old lady who owned the house my story. I don't know what version she told her, but I ended up getting the house. I moved in a couple of my best friends, Dustin Soderman and Virgil Moorehead, to help pay the mortgage.

Dustin soon got serious with his future wife, Maggie, and moved in with her. Shortly after, my buddy from college Tommy was making the move from a nearby town and was looking for a house. I showed him my neighborhood and the house next to mine, which happened to be for sale. Virgil and Tommy decided to partner up and buy the place. I moved in a young aspiring fighter from Hawaii named TJ Kuahine who I had met at a wrestling camp, and then my college wrestling rival, Matt Sanchez, who had taken my spot as a coach at UC Davis moved onto the block (more on him and our rivalry later). The place was always jam-packed. Guys would drop in and stay on the couch for a few weeks, get some training, then head home or find a way to stay. Tommy and Virgil had five rooms in their house and kept filling them up with renters: old college friends, wrestling buddies, aspiring fighters. My friends would get married or otherwise head off on their own and someone new would snatch up their spot.

Flash ahead, pretty soon I owned three houses on the street and my friends owned two. The houses have been filled with guys from every part of the United States and many parts of the world: Thailand, Brazil, Australia, Japan, Canada, Alaska, Florida, Idaho, Hawaii, and of course California (from San Diego to the edge of the Oregon border). Today, we have what amounts to a fighters' commune. This is my network. We're all huddled

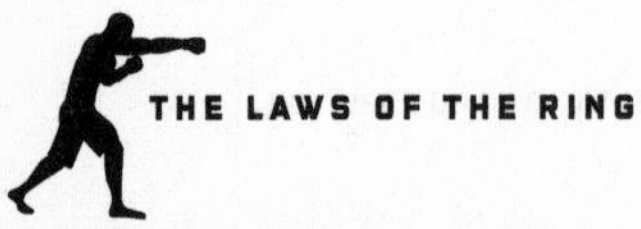

under the umbrella, including Pop and Ryan next door. Tommy handles the business side of things (you'll read about him shortly), I handle the fighting, and many others fill the gaps in between. I guess you could call it a nonreligious rebuild of the Isla Vista Christian commune. We call them "friendly houses" and it all started with a tough-minded real estate agent who saw something in a young guy with a limited job history, very little money, and a penchant for fumbling around with more passion than knowledge.

THE 21ST LAW OF POWER

GO THE EXTRA MILE

You don't catch people's eye by doing the bare minimum. You don't advance in a profession if you're willing to do something only when there's a price tag attached to it. Proving your passion often means pursuing it for the sheer love of it. To use the example of my fighting career, you'll do it hoping it pays dividends down the line, but you won't do it *knowing* or even *expecting* it. You do it, as I did, locked in the moment. If you find something you're passionate about, you have to go the extra mile to be noticed.

Sounds good, right? But how do you get noticed? How do you transform your sense of purpose, your tireless work ethic, and your personal credit into the ability to impress other human beings? A lot of motivational speakers and self-help books preach the importance of having people skills. It's a standard, almost commonplace aspect of the genre. Think about it: How many job interviews include the prospective job applicant boasting of being a "real people person"? How many HR directors die a little inside every time they hear someone trot out the "people person" answer as a reason they should be hired? Seriously, what does it even mean?

It seems to me the terms *people skills* and *people person* have been misused and overused into meaninglessness. Is a people person someone who can carry on a credible conversation? Is it someone who can make other people feel good about themselves? Is it someone who can defuse a potentially volatile situation with a coworker or client?

Here's my definition of a people person: someone who enjoys interacting with people, has a knack for building friendships, and can use these characteristics in order to communicate and succeed. The communication may or may not be verbal. From the time I stepped into the cage, I was told I had a magnetism that drew people to my fights. It was completely unconscious; I didn't even know it existed until I felt the crowd's excitement that first night in the Colusa Casino. The idea is not only to convey your passion but to share it. This is a pretty broad category, and it includes things like communication, motivation, and charisma. It includes more tangible qualities such as organization and work ethic, and less tangible ones such as empathy and trust.

Put simply: You need to be able to communicate well enough to bring like-minded, strong-willed, successful people along with you.

Tommy Schurkamp is one of my best friends. He is also my closest and most trusted business associate. We wrestled together at UC Davis after being rivals in high school. He's from a small town called Escalon in the foothills above the San Joaquin Valley, and our teams competed against each other in the higher-level high school tournaments.

As I said before, when I bought my first house, Tommy and Virgil bought the house next door. Tommy soon became the guy I trusted and leaned on for everything from business advice to my daily schedule. When he left college, Tommy worked as a surveyor for an engineering company. He would leave the house at four-thirty in the morning, spend eight to ten hours at his surveying job, and then come home and help me organize my affairs.

Tommy would pay my bills, schedule my calendar, and organize my mail. I used to have to sell tickets to all my fights, and Tommy took charge of that. By my third fight, we were selling three hundred tickets to all our friends and their friends. It's not as easy as just leaving three hundred tickets at "will call." The ticket purchasers didn't all know each other, and everyone had a preference for where they wanted to sit and with whom. Tommy had to make a seating chart and collect the money. Tommy became the guy who handled all the overflow in my life: getting specific food I might need, scheduling doctors' appointments, helping organize the team when it first got started. A lot of small things added up in a huge way.

And for his trouble, I paid him absolutely nothing. We were friends. I would do it for him, and he did it for me. It was never an issue, which was good because I didn't have the money to pay him, anyway. But when things got rolling with my career and our team, I offered Tommy a job as chief operating officer of Faber Enterprises. He dropped the surveying gig, no questions asked.

He was working for next to nothing, but the quality of life, by his own account, was far better than it had been. As I made my way into the limelight as a fighter, the parties grew more lavish and the people more attractive, and Tommy and I were traveling together to places as close as Canada and as far away as Japan and Brazil, having a great time along the way. But it's also important to note that jealousy and envy were never issues in our relationship. Our relationship was based on mutual respect, and we treated each other as equals. I have never felt like Tommy's boss, and I don't believe Tommy has ever felt like he is subservient to me. I trust him implicitly to make good decisions on Team Alpha Male's behalf.

Tommy's investment in the team didn't start with a financial investment. It started with a spiritual and intellectual one. As a former wrestler himself, he loves the team concept and missed it immediately after leaving UC Davis. He continued to do some martial-arts training but never pursued MMA. Instead, he became sort of a "team mom"—and I use the term lovingly—for Team Alpha Male. He started out putting together a media side to my career that allowed people to see me with viral videos (that helped lead to the Kenny Powers commercials) and created content that allowed people to get attached to my brand. Then he helped turn our team into a group that not only trained together but served as a family, complete with team dinners, golf tournaments, and an end-of-the-year banquet. Today, he's the heart of Team Alpha Male.

Flash-forward to when I started FORM Athletics with Mark Miller.

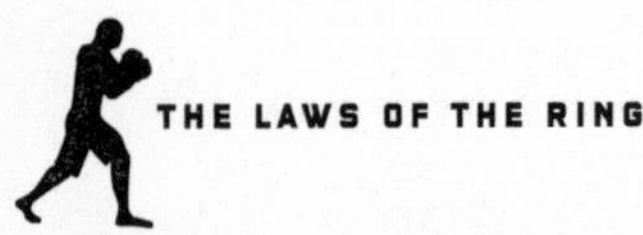

Tommy was the point man for my side of the operation, which meant handling just about every aspect of the business with aplomb—most of it for little or no pay—and when we sold the company to K-Swiss for a large profit, K-Swiss recognized Tommy's hard work, business savvy, and brains and hired him to help run the team side of the brand.

At the same time Tommy continued doing a lot of the behind-the-scenes work for me and the guys on Team Alpha Male. He was helping with fight promotions and some management stuff, and he was always tossing out great ideas that always advanced our cause. His financial reward was always secondary, but Tommy's work in this regard caught the eye of Jeff Meyer and MMA Incorporated, my fight management company (the formation of which is a great story, I'll share later). It didn't take long for them to hire Tommy and put him on *that* payroll.

So yeah, Tommy's a "people person." He could articulate our shared passion and produce real results. He's a positive person with a creative mind and an ability to converse with a wide variety of people. He's smart and he understands how to handle different types of personalities. I have no doubt he could walk back into the engineering world and make the climb up the corporate ladder in that profession if he wanted.

The bottom line is the guy who was working as a surveyor for an engineering company for little pay—and gave up the profession to work for even less as my support system—is today being paid—and paid well. He just kept working and enjoying his life, and before long, it became lucrative.

There's power in doing more than you're asked, and more than people expect of you. It's a "people skill" because it gets you noticed, and appreciated, and rewarded. It's a measure of your personal credit, the biggest people skill of all, and it ties in nicely with my desire to look for people with potential to do great things.

Tommy took a chance. He made a lifestyle out of his passion. Conventional thinking would call for him to stick it out with the engineering company, make the best of the surveying job, and wait for the inevitable promotion. And for people who are passionate about building roads, levees, and airport runways—people who are extremely valuable to society—that's the perfect approach. Go the extra mile in that profession and be noticed and rewarded the same way. This isn't to suggest that ditching a traditional profession for something as unusual as Tommy's is the only way to go. It is, however, suggesting that there are definite traits that are shared among successful people—in every profession.

And going the extra mile is one of them.

THE 22ND LAW OF POWER

CREATE YOUR OWN OPPORTUNITIES: THINK OUTSIDE THE BOX

Sometimes potential is obvious. When Joseph Benavidez showed up at the gym, anyone with a rudimentary knowledge of MMA could tell he was special. But I don't want to give the impression that everyone who walks through the door ends up being a success. As the profile of our team has grown, so has the number of guys wanting to show up and train with us. They come from all over the world, and many of them don't realize their dreams in the cage. The training is difficult and the competition is fierce, and you have to have a unique combination of talent and discipline to thrive. But some guys show up wanting to be fighters and end up showing potential in a completely different field. Maybe it turns out that they love the culture more than the act of fighting itself. We have a place for those people, too.

Dustin Akbari is a good example of this. He is my longest-standing training partner. He was fourteen when I started my training in Brazilian Jiu-Jitsu and he had already been on home studies for a year studying MMA full-time. Dustin was born in Texas, but raised in Iran until the age of ten, when his family came back to America. Dustin was intrigued by my mentality when I first showed up at the gym because of my intensity, and confidence about becoming a fighter. At fourteen, Dustin was still smaller than I was, but he had grit. His training was mostly in the traditional martial arts like tae kwon do, but he had recently dedicated all of his focus on BJJ and on becoming a world champion. He would train all day, and was always picking other people's brains about techniques and ways to get ahead. So every time that I came to the gym, Dustin was the first to greet me. He would ask me every day if I would teach him a new wrestling move after practice was over. I would always agree to it. Dustin told me that he wanted to fight when he grew up and wanted to learn all aspects of MMA. As time went on, he grew, and he got better and better. Before long he was my main training partner. He would come with me to kickboxing and boxing at other gyms. Dustin had a key to the jujitsu academy and taught the kids classes there. We would open the gym during off-hours, with Cassio's permission, and we would drill wrestling for an hour with me leading the way, then Dustin would lead us through an hour of BJJ.

By the time Dustin was seventeen, I was seven fights into my career and I asked him to be my cornerman for my upcoming fight. Cassio was unable to make it, and I needed someone I felt comfortable with. Dustin was more than happy to stand in the corner, ane he did a great job.

Dustin's first pro fight was less than a year later, shortly after his eighteenth birthday, and he has had several more fights over the years, but it turned out that his heart wasn't into being a fighter like he'd once thought it was. He enjoys the lifestyle and the discipline but has stopped competing in MMA at the age of twenty-three. His résumé is thick, though. He has been in twenty fights for me as a cornerman, with seventeen of those for some form of title (UFC, WEC, *Gladiator Challenge*, and *King of the Cage*). His grappling is world-class and he has world championships under his belt. Dustin has seen Team Alpha Male grow from the two of us swapping technique after hours at the BJJ gym to one of the most dominant camps in the world. Dustin is a black belt under Cassio Werneck and is the head instructor at my Ultimate Fitness Gym in downtown Sacramento. As a professional MMA fighter, he has stopped competing with a pro record of 5–1, and now

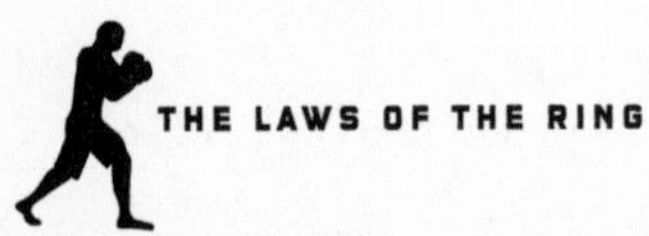

spends his time training and mentoring future champions. I know in my heart that Dustin is one of the most well-rounded mixed martial artists in the world, but his goals don't involve letting the world know it.

This is a good place to talk about the gray area of a community, which comes between the buyer and the artist—or in the case of fighting, the fan and the fighter. Maybe what makes me different from others is that I have ambitions that are linked to, but that expand beyond, the scope of the cage. But even fighters whose sole focus is their fight careers need guys to train them, manage them, promote them, etc. The point is that there are roles in the fighting community that are *not* the equivalent of being a fighter and that vary in visibility, but are just as important as the guy throwing the punches.

Let's say MMA is your passion. You got into martial arts as a kid and found it to be a great outlet. It helped you overcome some issues in life by providing discipline and self-confidence. When the MMA craze hit, you never considered fighting as a career, but finally you had a sport you could identify with and follow. You work every day to pay the bills, but MMA has become your passion. You read all the magazines, you buy all the big fights, you continue to practice karate or jujitsu at a local gym. In short, you know your stuff, but the demands of everyday life—job, family—have conspired to keep your passion for MMA on the sidelines.

In short, life has relegated MMA to the status of a hobby. Does that mean it's no longer your passion? I say no, not if MMA is what you do to escape the stresses of your nine-to-five (or more) existence. Not if the gym is the place you go where none of that can touch you.

Wouldn't it be great to increase those hours of escape? Wouldn't it be fun to let your passion lead you to some unexpected place? It doesn't mean quitting your job, but it might mean looking into the possibility of working in the industry. You have to ask yourself a question: What are the different ways people are making a living off this sport, and what would be the best fit for me?

You might be surprised at how many different types of occupations have been created by the rise of MMA and UFC. There are folks who design and make the gloves we wear. There are guys who travel the country assembling the cages we fight in. There are judges and photographers, writers and referees, promoters and public relations people. Not only are there ring girls, but there is a person at every event who *takes care of* the ring girls.

Once you decide where your talents fit best, do some research and find out who is doing the job well, and why. Here's where emulation comes in. How did he, or she, get there? What unique talents are required? Emulate those people. Talk to them. You'd be amazed at how many people at the tops of their professions are flattered to receive a call or an e-mail from someone who recognizes their success.

Mike Roberts is a great example of someone who staked out his passion and made it work around his profession. After high school, he was headed to college to play baseball, but his plans changed and his dreams were put on hold when his father had a heart attack. While his dad recovered, Mike was needed to run the family tire business. The business was very successful, but the current circumstances could have changed that drastically if Mike didn't step it up. Turned out that even at that young age, Mike had every bit as much business acumen as his father, Rich, had, and the business continued to thrive.

But secretly, his passion was combat sports. He loved fighting from its early days, and while committed to the family business, he desperately wanted to find a way to incorporate his passion into his day job. So he got creative, and managed to make Rich's Tire Barn one of the first businesses to sponsor fighters. Starting around 2002, Mike used his business to reach out to the heaviest hitters of the time—Randy Couture, Tim Sylvia, Matt Hughes, and Tito Ortiz. This was back when a relatively little guy with a relatively small business could sponsor top talent without bankrupting himself. There simply wasn't a big line to sponsor UFC fighters at the time, so Mike got a bunch of top guys to splash RICH'S TIRE BARN across the butts of their shorts.

But Mike sought to take his passion even further. He wanted to *manage* fighters. So he intelligently sought out Monty Cox, one of the early fight managers, and picked his brain about how to get deeper into the field.

Through Cox, Mike learned how to build relationships with fighters and make connections with organizations. He began scouting local fighters in and around Sacramento, and this brought him into contact with me, Scott Smith, and James Irvin. Mike called us together and mapped out a plan for becoming our manager. When we met, I remember being impressed that he had T-shirts made for each one of us. At the time that felt big-time.

Mike introduced us to a trainer and told us he wanted us to begin training together. This was before I had my own gym, and training was a dizzying schedule of different gyms and teachers. I trained at five different gyms to learn all the disciplines, including an abandoned church in a tiny town called Sheridan, where a few of the local MMA fighters were learning BJJ from a purple belt named Chuck. The idea of a central location sounded great.

Because Mike stepped it up and helped his family business to flourish, he was given enough of a leash to incorporate his passion into it. In the end, he spent far more money than he brought in, but to his credit, he never complained. He wanted to make sure we had what we needed, and his generosity reflected that passion.

Your life doesn't have to be compartmentalized: work in one box, MMA in the other. It can be a little of both. Maybe you're not going to be able to quit your job and support yourself on the money you earn as an MMA referee, but you will have more fulfillment in your life, and who knows what opportunities will come from the new involvement with your passion.

Pick somebody out. Find an MMA referee who makes the right decisions and controls his fights in a way that shows he knows both the sport and the mentality of its fighters. Watch his fights and see what separates him from the average referee. Call him up. Find out how he got to where he is. Don't be shy. What's the worst he can say? No? If he says no, you move on. Simple as that. But you know what? He's not going to say no. He's going to be so flattered you contacted him that he's going to help you out. It gets back to the power of positivity: People like to be complimented. A compliment is the most disarming "rhetorical device" in any language.

If you were able to go through your workweek knowing you were going to referee a fight at the end of it, I'm guessing you would be a better employee than you are right now. I'm guessing your boss is going to see an increase in productivity because you're a happier person thanks to the refereeing gig. You're going to be less grudging of all the petty, mundane matters in your work because it's no longer your sole focus. Even without the okay of the bosses in your world, there is a way to add your passion to your day, make your days longer. Remember how Tommy went from a 4:30 A.M. departure time to his surveying job to a full night of helping me with my action-packed hustles. Find a way and make some time because you only live once.

You might not be all the way free, but you're on your way.

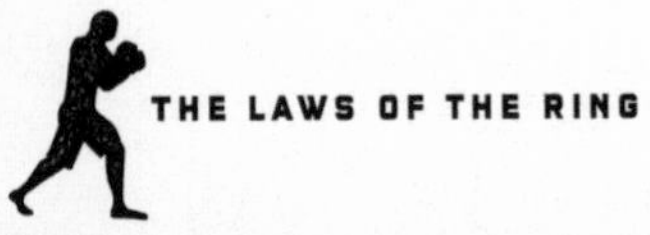

THE 23RD LAW OF POWER

CONNECT THE PEOPLE YOU TRUST

Shortly after Dana helped me buy my first house, she told me I needed to meet her chiropractor friend Matt Fisher. Matt was an ex-wrestler who followed my wrestling career through UC Davis before becoming a fan of my MMA career.

Initially, I was flattered. Not many people follow college wrestling, and my MMA career was pretty new and definitely under the radar. But I lost Matt's number just as quickly as Dana gave it to me. It was nice to have a fan, and while, of course, I didn't have any contempt for the suggestion, I was pretty content with my community as it stood.

A week later, Dana called and asked if I had gotten in touch with Matt. The tone of her voice told me she knew I hadn't. I started rifling through my brain for my list of lame excuses, but before I could summon one, she continued: "What are you waiting for?"

"It was just crazy busy this week," I replied guiltily.

"You guys will *really* hit it off," she interjected. "Worst thing that can happen, you might get some free chiropractic work out of it. People in your line of work probably need it."

I knew from my experience with Dana that she wouldn't push like this if she didn't see the potential for something special.

When I finally got around to calling Matt, I found out why Dana had been so intent on brokering a conversation. We hit it off immediately. He had been following my career because he had graduated from Lincoln High School ten years before I did and was a wrestler, too.

After about fifteen minutes on the phone, Matt said, "Hey, have you ever thought about opening a gym?"

The timing of this question was uncanny. I *had* been thinking about it for a couple years, but I never mentioned anything about it to Dana—actually, I had barely mentioned it to anyone at all. I dreamed of a place of my own, where I could grow my team and combine all my training under one roof, but the amount of work and funding needed to get it off the ground seemed daunting.

"I want to do it eventually," I said. "Right now I don't think I have the time or the money to pull it off."

Matt said he thought he could help me get this going faster than I had planned, and he wanted to meet in person to talk more about it. My sense that we were both spur-of-the-moment, do-it-now-or-regret-it-forever people was confirmed when he suggested we meet at seven-thirty the next morning— about twelve hours after our first conversation.

So the next morning I gave Matt the short version of my vision. I told him my gym would be a place where I could have all the MMA disciplines under one roof. It would be a place where I could bring fighters in to train and develop the camaraderie that would lead to the success of an Alpha Male team. It would be a place to sweat, learn, teach, inspire, and grow. I came into the meeting with Matt having crunched some rough numbers the night before. I knew it was a good business opportunity. There were enough people doing what I was doing—wandering from gym to gym to get the proper training—that I knew we could put together a solid customer base quickly. But I did have a big reservation. Having recently read Robert Kiyosaki's *Rich Dad, Poor Dad,* I was adamantly opposed to becoming a slave to my own business. Basically, I didn't want to own a gym that worked only when I was there. I needed a network of people around me—*other* teachers and *other*

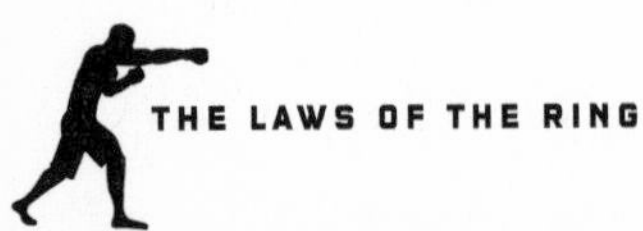

administrators who would allow me to continue to train and focus on becoming one of the world's best fighters.

"This is a good idea," I told Matt. "And when I come across a good idea, I'll do anything to make it happen. But I know what I can and can't do, and I don't want to get in over my head and feel like the place can't run without me standing in it."

Matt didn't seem fazed by this concern and said he would provide the initial funding for the gym and handle the business side of the operation (payroll, insurance, etc.), allowing me to provide the sweat equity (teaching, etc.) and the talent. I would teach all the classes to start, and I would be responsible for hiring other instructors and trainers.

I got a good feeling about Matt's intentions, and from our conversation, it was apparent to me that he was not only smart, but serious about his side of the bargain. So we shook hands and agreed to pursue it immediately. We had a partnership drawn up—Faber/Fisher LLC—that defined our responsibilities.

We then set out to find a building, and after seeing a few places that were either too big or too small, too expensive or too run-down, we found an empty building on Seventeenth and I Streets in midtown Sacramento. We couldn't ask for a more centralized location. The building was rough around the edges, but it was warehouse-style, large, open. I definitely saw what it could become—what it is today.

I leaned on my sense of community to see the solutions to the structural problems. My father is a general contractor, my uncle is a plumbing contractor, my stepdad Tom is a handyman, and Matt and I were more than willing to dig in and do as much as we could ourselves. I had all the tools I needed at my disposal, and I knew that if we all banded together, this shell could be something great.

The bureaucratic process was an enormous eye-opener: a barrage of neighborhood meetings, city hearings, construction inspections, and heavy-duty planning sessions, but after a year of unrelenting persistence and incredibly long hours extending beyond our already demanding lives, our gym—Ultimate Fitness—was up and running. Matt had his chiropractic office set up inside, and I was teaching classes and signing up members at a rate that exceeded my predictions. We took a chance, had a plan, executed it with persistence, and made it happen.

The opening of my own gym—the end result of Matt's and my mutual credibility—changed my career. It gave me a one-stop shop for my training, brought in money to assist my thrifty lifestyle, and offered me the opportunity to help others pursue their dreams.

But let's not forget that none of this would've happened had I not ultimately heeded Dana's suggestion. The big lesson here is that if you trust someone enough to let her into your network, she presumably has enough personal credit that you should listen to her when she makes a suggestion.

Connecting people is something that has helped me to do more in my own life. Don't be afraid to connect the people you trust.

THE 24TH LAW OF POWER

IT *IS* WHO YOU KNOW—AND MORE

To put a finer point on the idea of personal credit, consider this expression: *It's not* what *you know, it's* who *you know.* This is superficially accurate—and seemingly cynical—but there's more to it than meets the eye. It's not only who you know; it's what those people think about you, how deeply they want to be involved with you, and if they believe you are a credible person.

You build this credit by utilizing the Laws of Power. The network of people surrounding you is not meant to simply improve a business or maximize profits; it's a means of growing as a person and helping those around you to do the same.

When everyone contributes to the success of the whole, the individual grows along with it. The power derived from the network creates a system where people catapult each other to greater heights, which is why rigid hierarchies are often impediments to success. Cooperative hierarchies open opportunities to employ the Laws of Power to gain the kind of credibility needed to make "who you know" count.

In late 2005, my career was still new. I'd been fighting for two years, but the only people who knew who I was were a handful of die-hard fight fans. One person who had been watching from a distance was my old friend Jaimal Yogis, who had continued his journey through life at Columbia University in New York, where he was studying for a master's degree in journalism.

My upbringing was focused on education for education's sake, not education for a future salary's sake. My brother and I were taught to set our sights high, but there was no decree about what those sights should be. If we were happy and productive, we were successful.

Not coincidentally, I attracted people who had similar backgrounds. My best friend growing up was a kid named Jaimal Yogis. After my family moved from the commune and before we moved to Lincoln, Jaimal and I were outliers in the mostly conservative Sacramento suburb of Carmichael. His upbringing was similar to mine, which means his refrigerator was also filled with tofu and soy milk and his parents grew their own vegetables. He was taller than me (not surprisingly) with curly brown hair and a big smile. The hippie mentality he'd always been surrounded by was evident in his demeanor.

From fourth through sixth grades, Jaimal and I were inseparable. I was a permanent fixture in his house. Until the seventh grade, when my mom moved to Lincoln. But even though our lives physically drifted apart, our perspectives and philosophies were too similar for the friendship to dissolve and we stayed in touch as best as we could.

During his junior year in high school, Jaimal got mixed up with the wrong crowd and got himself in trouble. He got a DUI, and he was so disgusted with the social scene he had become a part of that he decided to run away. He had saved quite a bit of money from a part-time job, and he fortified that with an unauthorized cash advance from his mother's credit card and hopped a plane for Hawaii. His idea was to escape his problems by living on the beach, surfing, and studying Buddhism.

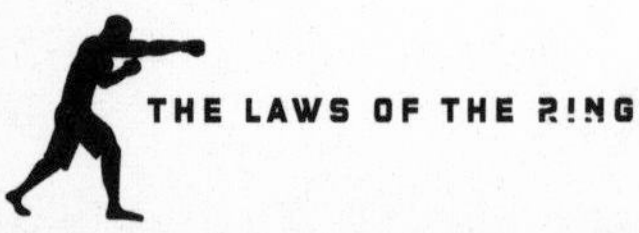

You might think that this is the place where I impose my limits on my philosophy of following your passion. That I'm going to say that running away is a bad idea. But you know what? For Jaimal, the entire experience didn't turn out so bad.

Perhaps without even knowing it, Jaimal was running away in order to inject some discipline and order into his life. He was pretty resourceful, too. He found a place to stay and was doing everything he set out to do. He sent a letter to his parents, telling them where he was, apologizing for taking the money, and letting them know they didn't have to worry about him. He had a job and was getting his head straight.

After reading the letter, Jaimal's father devised a plan of his own. He flew to Hawaii, checked into a hotel, and found Jaimal on the beach. Instead of demanding that his son come home, his father hung out with him. He surfed with him and took the time to understand where his son was coming from and what was going through his mind. They spent countless hours discussing Jaimal's future, and they reached a consensus: Jaimal could spend his senior year of high school as an exchange student abroad if he agreed to come home. This allowed him to escape the high school environment he had grown to dislike, and it enabled his parents to impose some level of structure in his life. And so Jaimal spent his senior year of high school in France, where he was able to satisfy his wanderlust and leave the bad influences behind.

Clearly, this is a great example of love, patience, and compromise, similar to the way my family has treated Ryan's illness. Jaimal's ability to follow his passion is an inspiration to me, and the story of his brief stint as a runaway pops into my head whenever I think about sticking my head in the sand and ignoring a problem I know won't go away. Jaimal made the wrong choice for the right reason, and his father was there with the guidance and wisdom that was needed in order to find a solution. Jaimal went on to get a master's degree in journalism from Columbia University, one of the most prestigious programs in the country, while still retaining his individuality. It's hard to imagine his career following a similar route had he been allowed to stay in Hawaii and carve his own path.

It had been a few years since Jaimal and I had talked, but we picked up right where we left off. He had been following my fighting career and was intrigued enough to want to write an article about me for one of his class assignments. It was good enough to be published in a major paper in New York, and that's when my relationship with Jaimal—a like-minded, passionate individual—transformed into something more.

The article caught the eye of Morgan Hertzan, a producer with MTV. He called the wrestling coach at UC Davis, Lennie Zalesky, who put him in touch with me. Morgan was impressed with the article and felt I had some marketability as a young, good-looking, well-spoken fighter with a passion for his work. Even though I recoiled at the notion of being considered the pretty boy of MMA, I wasn't blind to the benefits that such an impression provided. If I could be a championship-level fighter *and* be in demand as a role model/spokesman for the sport, I could create more opportunities for myself and use my passion to explore different avenues.

Morgan had an idea for a reality show: *Say Uncle* would find guys who were jerks, roaming through life picking on people for their own amusement. Over the course of the program, we would show their personalities, and at the end I would fight them in a challenge match.

Morgan pitched the show a few times and got no takers. (The same concept mysteriously ended up being the basis for a popular show called *Bully Beatdown.*) Morgan wasn't discouraged enough to drop it entirely, though. Instead, he turned his idea into a documentary that depicted me as an up-and-coming fighter in a sport that was beginning to gain traction.

This hour-long documentary, *Warrior Nation,* was filmed in September 2006 and was quickly sold to MSNBC. The documentary brought further credibility to me and the sport. It came during a busy and important time in my career. The gym had recently opened, my management team was in place to capitalize on the publicity, and my skill level was getting better and better. The documentary brought all of this into wider focus, and my career was ready to explode.

The catalyst for this was my long-standing friendship with a like-minded person who saw the potential in me and was interested enough to share my story with the world. Jaimal's writing, and the documentary that arose from it, changed my life. That's not an exaggeration.

Over the course of these pages, we've looked at how business relationships can become personal relationships, and in this case the reverse was true: A personal relationship became a business relationship. Jaimal was pursuing his passion and I was pursuing mine. We were both doing what we wanted to do, and our lives converged.

The positive energy that flowed from that documentary had far-reaching impact. In the year before *Warrior Nation,* I was a free agent. I was competing in a number of up-and-coming shows, getting belts in a number of organizations, and attempting to establish myself as the best featherweight fighter in the world. One of those organizations was World Extreme Cagefighting (WEC), which allowed me to fight for a title belt without locking me into an exclusive contract.

The UFC was not an option for me; they had yet to offer fights in my weight class. I was gaining notoriety, slowly but surely, through the small following of the pay-per-view *King of the Cage* fights, the coverage of WEC on HDNet Television, and MMA Web sites like Sherdog.com. My management team was still looking for the best way to capitalize on this growing attention to position me for long-term success.

At about this time along came an organization called WFA. It was the brainchild of a former fight manager named Jeremy Lappen, who believed he could create a competitor to the UFC. I liked his approach: He was paying three times what any other organization was offering, and he had already signed up big-time talents such as Rampage Jackson, Matt "The Law" Lindland, and Bas Rutten. Lappen had Hollywood connections he was determined to use to promote the sport. It sounded promising.

My negotiations with Lappen occurred at the time Hertzan was pitching *Say Uncle.* I enthusiastically sold myself to Lappen, telling him I was going to do my part to blow up in the sport.

"My plan is to build stars by highlighting personality in addition to fighting skills," he said. "I want to be the first organization to highlight the lighter-weight classes, and you have the star power to push those lower weights to new prominence."

I couldn't have said it better myself. The contract he put in front of me called for fifty thousand dollars a year—double if I won all my fights. This was the huge opportunity I was waiting for, and I eagerly signed.

All that promise, all that buildup, and then . . . the WFA tanked after just one show. Gone, poof—just like that. Their live gate was minuscule compared to their projections. Their pay-per-view attempt completely flopped. There were a lot of great fighters in the show, but they couldn't make it work. The rumor was that they had lost thirty million dollars and that all their investors had bailed, never to invest again.

The quick demise of the WFA taught me the importance of brands. The brand wasn't established, and they tried to do too much too soon, so the entire operation flopped.

This development had unexpected consequences, though. The UFC swooped in and quickly moved to continue its quest to corner the MMA market. Dana White and Lorenzo Fertitta bought both the WEC, for which I had two nonexclusive fights remaining, and my liquidated contract from the WFA.

Eventually, I got what the WFA promised: I became the face of the lightweight divisions, but it happened under the WEC and the leadership of Dana White and the Fertitta brothers. Jaimal's story and the *Warrior Nation* documentary provided me with an avenue to exhibit my personality and marketability to a wider audience.

The evolution of my friendship with Jaimal, from childhood buddies to aspiring authors, shows that relationships don't always fit in tidy boxes. Your personal credit defies categorization and compartmentalization. It seeps into every aspect of your life, for better or worse, like ink through cotton.

On Christmas Day 2008, I received one of Jaimal's sporadic phone calls. Like most old friends who don't live in the same area, we've managed to remain close without frequent conversations. This time he was in town for a few days and wanted to get together.

Jaimal came over to my house, and even though we hadn't seen each other for a while, I could tell he was eager to relay some important news. He said, "I'm writing a book on Buddhism and surfing. I've got a publisher and I'm really stoked about making this happen." When I asked him to describe the message of his book, he said, "It's about following my heart."

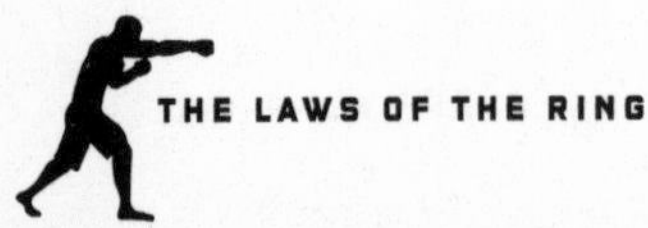

I was really excited for him, but my mind couldn't shake the irony of the situation. "You're not going to believe this," I said, "but I'm writing a book about passion and my path to fighting."

From there, we started discussing where we'd been and how we'd reached this place. We reminisced about our days in Carmichael and the freedom we'd had to explore life mentally and physically—benefits not many kids today are given in the culture of helicopter parents, playdates, and over-scheduled lives. What started as a random coincidence—two old friends writing books—became less random the more we talked. Jaimal's book—*Saltwater Buddha*—is a wonderful and well-reviewed look into his philosophy and soul. And it is my humble hope that the book you hold in your hands—although it comes from a far different place—achieves the same goal.

THE 25TH LAW OF POWER

EVERYONE HAS STRENGTHS: LET THEM COMPLEMENT EACH OTHER

It's clear by now how a chance encounter with a real estate agent extended far beyond real estate, and I think it's worth describing just how far-reaching this turned out to be. Within two years of our first meeting, Dana helped me purchase two more homes, which helped turn the neighborhood into a fighters' commune. Dana also introduced me to Matt, who helped me start the gym. Matt introduced me to Jeff Meyer, a contracts lawyer and businessman who was looking for a way to escape the rat race and develop a lifestyle more suited to a family man with a loving wife and two young daughters.

Jeff had recently left a small family winery that he helped become a flourishing business and opened his own law firm—doing work he disliked, for hours that were unreasonable. There's that bargain people make. Anyway, Jeff was tired of living for that *uncertain* future. He and Matt had become friends after sharing office space years earlier, and Jeff entered my life when Matt asked him to write up a contract for our gym partnership. Jeff's passion had always been sports, and he had become an avid fan of mixed martial arts. When Matt approached him with the contract, Jeff's mind began to reel with possibilities. *This could give me an avenue to combine my professional talents and my passion!*

Matt spoke highly of Jeff, both as an attorney and, more important, as *a person*. I saw a promising pattern developing here with regard to my network, and knew that this time around, I shouldn't hesitate. Dana → Matt → Jeff? In short, Jeff was great. Savvy. Highly professional. Looking to be inspired. I definitely saw the value in adding him to my team.

My relationship with my manager, Mike Roberts, was an informal one—no contracts or obligations. He asked only that if he came up with something—an endorsement, a sponsorship—that he get 10 percent. But when my career took off, I saw a need for more refined management. Mike had ideas, but he lacked the plan to put them into action. Although it may seem like I was making it up as I went along, going with the flow of a growing sport, I was always aware of the bigger picture. If the sport blew up—*when* the sport blew up—I wanted to be positioned to take full advantage of the opportunity. Before I met Jeff, I approached Mike with the idea of starting a management company and formalizing our relationship, but he was lukewarm on the idea. The tire business removed any financial considerations from the equation—he wasn't hurting on cash—and he enjoyed the freelance aspects of his MMA work.

I saw my connection with Jeff as an opportunity to change the dynamic. But it didn't involve cutting Mike out. On the contrary. Right away I saw the seeds of a great combination: a savvy lawyer who could complement Mike's hustle, passion, and knowledge of the sport. Obviously, I wasn't in a sport where the best athletes made the kind of earnings that other pro-athletes were making, so I needed to maximize whatever came my way. Jeff represented the professionalism that I felt I needed in order to expand my earning opportunities. If I was going to be able to get significant sponsorships and endorsements, I needed someone who could write up the contracts and represent me in negotiations. Mike's skills were more grassroots but just as necessary. I needed to convince both of them to get under my umbrella. I saw great potential in a Jeff-Mike team; now I needed to persuade them to see it, too.

I was stoked about making this work. These two guys, different as they were, could become a killer team, but they had vastly different styles. Mike was a handshake guy—no suits, no contracts, laid-back negotiations that were known to include a beer or two. Jeff was more detail-oriented, and his corporate background brought legitimacy to *any* meeting.

Even though Mike had dismissed my earlier suggestions regarding a formal arrangement, I felt a partnership might change his mind. But I had to "massage" it the right way.

I make no bones about the fact that I was anxious about brokering this collaboration. I thought about avoiding the possibility of confrontation altogether: by telling Jeff I already had management in place and calling it a day. This would remove the possibility of hard feelings between Mike and me. But that would have compromised the potential I saw in working with Jeff, who, I was sure, was a missing link in my quest to get to the top of the fight game.

So I decided to take the first step by forming an LLC with Jeff before breaking the news to Mike that I wanted him and Jeff to work together as my management team. I gave it to Mike straight, over a beer.

"This guy has great credibility, and his talents mesh with yours perfectly," I said. "He's a detail guy and you're a big-picture guy. He's got the plan you've been looking for, and he'll free you up to do what you love to do. Trust me, I know both of you, and this will work."

Over the course of our meeting, as Mike sat mostly stone-faced, I testified to Jeff's credibility and outlined his strengths in detail and in relation to our long-term goals.

As I feared might happen, Mike wasn't very receptive. Either to a formal agreement *or* to allowing someone to compromise the way he was used to doing business. But I boiled it down by simply saying, "Mike, you and Jeff are both people I need in my career."

With that, Mike agreed to give it a shot. Half of my work done, I next met with Jeff.

I reversed the conversation I had with Mike by emphasizing Mike's relationship with fighters and organizations and his knowledge of the ins and outs of MMA negotiations. I made it clear that I was by no means minimiz-

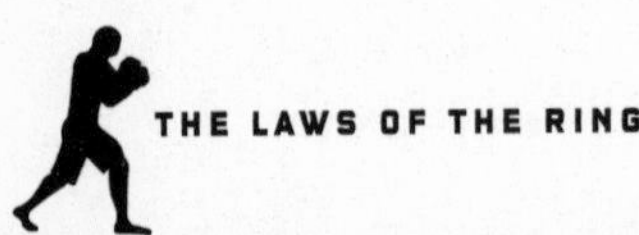

ing the abilities of either of them by asking them to work together. Quite the opposite, I thought putting them together would have a synergistic effect on all of our careers. But Jeff wasn't seeing it.

"C'mon, Jeff," I pleaded. "Just give it a shot, let's set up a meeting."

"All right," he said, relenting. "But it seems to me like too many cooks in the kitchen."

Mike's and Jeff's claims on territorial rights melted as we sat at a table in a midtown Sacramento restaurant. It was replaced by mutual—although maybe a little grudging—admiration.

I laid out my plan for them to merge into a single company, combining Jeff's knowledge of the law with Mike's management connections. In dealing with this potentially volatile situation, I had to use my positivity and creativity to sell each man on a mutual sense of purpose. They had to see the endless possibilities available if this worked the way I envisioned it.

In June 2006, three months after I first met Jeff Meyer, MMA Incorporated was formed. It took no time at all for the perfect complementarity of the partnership of Mike and Jeff to begin guiding and building the careers of our fighters. The original group of fighters consisted of me, Scott Smith, James Irvin, Scott Jorgensen, Charlie Valencia, and Joseph Benavidez. MMA Inc. remains my management team to this day, and it is a great business success story in the world of MMA.

THE 26TH LAW OF POWER

TALK THE TALK—WALK THE WALK

We all know this guy: spoiled, lazy, entitled, thinks he can talk his way into—or out of—anything. When you first meet him, he comes across well. He's friendly, seems to have his stuff together, knows a lot of people, and talks a good game. But then he says something that sets off your bullshit detector. It doesn't have to be a big deal; it's just something that hits you wrong.

You start to listen a little closer. Something else doesn't add up. It could be a boast you don't believe or an alleged fact you know to be false. These tiny things grow in your mind until they become something big enough to permanently alter your opinion of that person. Maybe you end up calling him on something and making it clear that you're onto his game. More likely, you just let all the evidence pile up at his feet and decide not to have anything else to do with him.

These people are in every profession. They are the people who inflate their résumés and exhibit questionable ethics. They believe words can substitute for actions, and they're constantly seeking shortcuts to short-term pleasure. Any personal credit they might have established is destroyed by their inability to accept who they are and work with a purpose toward a goal.

As we've discussed, it is important to associate with people whose potential and passion can help you—and them—reach significant goals. But it's ignorant to believe that *who you know* by itself is some magical passport to a better life. It's equally important for you to be able to identify people who are attempting to use your passion to help themselves and only themselves. You can't just parlay a connection, especially a loose one, into personal credit, but some people believe that's all it takes.

It's not just who you know, but what those people think about you and whether or not they think you're a credible person. *Who you are* dictates *who you know.* Everything positive flows from there.

Any benefit derived from an association with someone powerful or influential is purely a result of your personal credit. Name-dropping—a staple of the all-talk, no-action crowd—diminishes both the name and the dropper if there is no personal credit attached to it.

Our Alpha Male community is centered on a united belief that together we are better. We are equals, and we are there for each other. There is always an open bed or an open couch in our community, and there's always a job for you if you're willing to work hard and subsume your personal desires to the betterment of the whole. Come in, get under the umbrella, and work toward a common goal. These are lofty concepts, but we try to uphold them.

There's a kid named Lance Palmer who is a rookie fighter with a lot of promise at 145 pounds. If you show up at my house right now in the middle of the night, you might find him curled up on the couch in the living room. Six months from now there might be another good young fighter on that same couch, and Lance might have graduated to a bed in a house across the street.

Positive, confident people establish their own personal credit. It can't be acquired through association. In the fighting community, the guy who talks a good game but can't back it up is a fixture, but when every fight from the *Gladiator Challenge* at the Colusa Casino to *UFC 132* in Vegas is verifiable online, it's tougher to be a good liar. The popularity of MMA and the power of twenty-first-century media and technology have weeded out a lot of these guys, simply because the posers can't fake it very long before someone wises up and finds a fight record on Sherdog.com or calls a gym and discovers the truth.

A big part of all-talk, no-action is fear—a fear of putting yourself out there, which is linked to a fear of failure. It's easier to talk about something and pretend that it exists than it is to try and fail. And it's often the case that all-talk, no-action people devise elaborate and often-entertaining excuses when they're called on their falsely created persona.

But the person who constantly exaggerates wealth, or physical gifts, or sexual prowess, or intelligence is a little more sinister. He—or she—preys on others' gullibility and overall good nature. No matter how we classify ourselves, I genuinely believe that we want to believe the best in people, and that our first inclination is to accept what they say at face value. For that reason, as I will explain in a moment, ironically, the all-talk, no-action crowd only ends up accelerating its personal *dis*credit faster than anybody.

So, yeah, I have a serious problem with people who are constantly trying to enrich themselves by using someone else's status as collateral. Since I have made a name for myself in my sport, I've had to deal with more and more people who believe they can profit either financially or socially from their proximity to me. I don't like to be wary and skeptical of people's motives, but as your success increases, it becomes necessary to more carefully scrutinize those people who want access to your circle.

I'm not trying to sound boastful. This phenomenon is not limited to people in high-profile professions; most hierarchical organizations or groups invite the type of jockeying for position that all-talk, no-action folks thrive on. Some people can even rise to the top by relying on this tactic, but it is an ascent without passion, and sooner or later, a fall is inevitable. Here are a couple cautionary tales for you to chew on.

The Strange Case of Internet Steve

A guy I'll call Steve came to the gym as a big talker. He was a high-school-football star. He came from a wealthy family. He had connections that, it seemed, would take him wherever he wanted to go.

And for now, he wanted to be a fighter.

A lot of what he said was true. He *was* a good football player, but he went to three high schools and used steroids to gain an unfair advantage over the other players. He was also wealthy. Steve's father was a businessman; I believe he was in some sort of real estate. But whatever the case, Steve grew up with a lot of advantages and was never held accountable for much of anything. If he had a problem with a football coach, he transferred to another school. He bounced through life acting as if he were bulletproof. If something bad happened, his dad—more to the point, his dad's *money*—would bail him out.

From the beginning, Steve operated under the principle that people would believe what they perceived. If he put up a good front, created a good story, and stuck with it, people would have no choice but to buy into it. The image he put forward was that of a cocky, successful guy who was an accomplished fighter from the start.

To further this image, he built himself an Internet page after he had his first pro fight, which I had asked him not to take; he lost the fight but edited highlight video on it to look like he had won. This, to him, provided verification for all the truth-stretching he did to make girls like him and guys fear him. The page brought him instant recognition at the gym, but probably not the kind he was seeking. Guys immediately tagged him with the nickname "Internet Steve."

Steve didn't stop with the Web page. He was active on social-networking sites, especially MySpace and Facebook, where he exaggerated his relationship with me and inflated his abilities and his performance in the gym. In truth, I *thought* I understood how misguided he was and could help him access the kernel of goodness that I believed lay within him. He was spoiled, obviously, but I didn't hold that against him. In fact, I understood it to be one of the reasons why he was redeemable. I saw through the bluster, even when the bluster was all anybody could see.

And the truth is that Internet Steve had some talent. He was a good athlete. He was even enthusiastic and went through stretches where he appeared to be eager to learn and train.

However, his good qualities were overwhelmed by his almost pathological need to perpetuate a false image. He repeatedly dropped my name at bars and used his connection to our gym—which was full of hardworking, modest guys—to build his unearned reputation. I have no problem with my friends—people who have credit with me—talking about our relationship, but whenever someone brought up Steve's name, I couldn't vouch for him.

It was not uncommon for someone to come up to me and say, "Oh, you must know Steve. He says he's one of your top fighters." No, he wasn't, and his insistence on using the credible reputation of our gym to create a false persona didn't sit well with me or anybody else at Team Alpha Male. And so Steve quickly developed a reputation as a poser, someone whose gift for exaggeration far exceeded his gift for fighting. But this opinion I kept to myself. *If you don't have anything nice to say . . .* is what I told myself whenever Steve's name came up.

But instead of giving up on Steve and kicking him out of the gym, I repeatedly gave him chances to prove that all of his talk, self-promotion, and hype were going to turn into a lifestyle that supported them. There were times when he realized he had gone too far, and he would immediately reel himself in for a short time and dedicate himself not just to the task at hand, but to toning down his bravado. And it was my sincere hope that this ethic would prevail. To my disappointment and Steve's detriment, it never happened.

Finally, after months of what I considered second chances, I confronted Steve about the blatant lies he was telling people—mostly girls, not surprisingly—and the misinformation he was disseminating on his social-networking sites. I was also tired of trying to motivate him to practice consistently and forsake the bluster. "That stuff's not necessary," I told him. "The fact that you're lying to people about your accomplishments, and really training with the guys that are doing what you're claiming to do, is pissing the rest of the guys off."

Our conversation ended when he came to the realization that he was no longer going to be able to stick around the gym without being held accountable for his words and actions. Rather than accepting the constructive criticism in the manner in which it had been offered, Internet Steve took his exaggerations and went home. Quitting.

I wish the story of Internet Steve had a happier ending. I would love to report that he eventually took all the advice he'd been given to heart and turned it around to become a credible person and a good fighter. But this wasn't to be.

His case underscores the difficulty of self-assessment and the risk of being open to allowing anyone to have access to your life. The essence of community is to be welcoming, but at some point tough decisions need to be made. Internet Steve made it easy on me by refusing to accept my last-gasp effort to open his eyes to his behavior. Had he not done this, and had he continued to act in a fashion that was detrimental to the group, I would have had to kick him off the team. But Internet Steve's decision to quit was in keeping with his personality. Rather than face his shortcomings and vow to work on overcoming them, he took the easy way out. The commitment that is necessary for someone to look inward and face the harsh reality of his inadequacies and psychological flaws is brutally difficult. It's much easier for someone like Steve to pick up and move on to the next gym, where he undoubtedly found a new group to pitch his fantasies to.

Obviously, I learned something about myself while dealing with Internet Steve. It was a harsh lesson, too. As I said above, my inclination—and I think it's the inclination of most people—is to be accepting, to see the best in others and believe that even the worst qualities can be overcome and transformed into good ones. Understanding Steve's background, I attempted to provide him with a stable place to train and role models he could learn from. None of it, unfortunately, got inside Internet Steve and forced a change.

"What the Fuck Are You Doing in My Room?"

Joey (not his real name) is a local Sacramento guy I've known for quite some time. He came into my life after a friend told me Joey could possibly help me take advantage of some marketing opportunities. This didn't prove to be accurate, but to this day, Joey continues trying to pitch me on something or other that he claims will benefit both of us. It didn't take long for me to realize any benefit was going to be his, and his alone.

The most ridiculous example of his gall had nothing to do with money or opportunity. A couple of years ago, I took a USO tour of Afghanistan. I returned on a Saturday, and I had a bunch of messages saying that Joey was throwing himself a big birthday bash. I didn't respond to them, and I had no intention of going to his birthday party. I was totally exhausted from the traveling and my brain was screwed up from the time change.

So I went to bed at around eight that night.

At two-thirty in the morning, there was a commotion in my room. I woke up to find Joey postparty drunk, standing there with a couple of guys and a couple of girls at the foot of my bed.

"There he is, right there," he said, like I was a zoo animal or something.

Joey knew we never lock the doors in any of our friendly houses, and he saw this as an opportunity to boost his credibility with these people—most notably the girls—by proving to them that he knew me.

"Urijah, what's up?" he said, like waking me up in the middle of the night to introduce me to a bunch of people I didn't know was the most normal thing in the world.

"What the fuck are you doing in my room?" I asked, confused as all hell.

"I'm a huge fan," said one of the chicks.

"Well, uh, thank you," I replied, trying as hard as I could to be polite under the circumstances. "Now can you please leave so I can get some sleep?"

The girl told me that her boyfriend was outside—at least *he* had some sense—and then she leaned over the bed, kissed me on the stomach, and ran outside.

One of the stranger moments in my life, and it underscored a point: In order to remain consistently dedicated to your passion, you have to limit negative forces. It can be hard, but sometimes it's best to distance yourself from people who make you compromise your positive attitude by being quintessential hangers-on.

Ask yourself these questions: Are "Internet Steve" and "Joey" the kinds of people you would want as part of your network? Is there room for them under your umbrella?

These seem like easy questions, right? Well, sometimes they're not. The above stories might be entertaining, but sometimes the wrong folks can be enticing. Living in a state of paranoia isn't helpful, but awareness is. For the benefit and *happiness* of everyone.

If you recognize anything about yourself in Internet Steve—or in someone like Joey—you need to start thinking about the image you are projecting to the outside world. Employers, coworkers, friends, and family—everybody draws strength from positivity, creativity, and good habits. Think about it. Work on it. Escape the cage, build your personal credit, and become one of the people who benefits from a who's-who network rather than one of the people who begrudges others their networks.

THE 27TH LAW OF POWER

TOUGH LOVE IS AN ART

I would like you to do a little exercise. Think about the people in your life who most often complain about the "politics" of their job or dismiss others' achievements as favoritism. They might use these excuses to explain away anything from being passed over for a promotion to their son's being benched on a Little League team. They constantly feel slighted and talk about their lives as if there is an unseen force out there conspiring to hold them down and keep them from achieving their goals.

Everyone has people like this in their lives. Family members, friends, and even coworkers who, while we may care deeply about them, are, when we stop to think about it, negative forces in our lives. I'm not suggesting you cut these people out of your life, but there are ways to keep them close and still minimize their impact on your dreams and goals.

Ask yourself this question: Are those people the kinds of people you would want as part of your network? Is there room for them under your umbrella? Are they vibrant, positive, creative people who contribute to the betterment of their group? Are they free of jealousy and petty bickering?

Those are easy questions, right?

There are going to be people in your life who you can't do without, but who you can't stand to be around at times. This doesn't necessitate you leaving them in the dust, but it may mean you do some research on what it is about them you can't stand. You can actively adjust the degree of their involvement in your life. If your brother is always shooting down your ideas or your mom is never satisfied with your appearance, you may need to have an honest discussion about the things that are bothering you. You would be surprised at how many people are eager to change their ways once they are aware of the problem they're causing. If this doesn't work, then be proactive; it may mean not sharing your big ideas with your negative brother or spending a little less time with your critical mother. Replace the time you spend with them with time spent with people who get excited about your big ideas or who accept the way you look.

THE 28TH LAW OF POWER

MONEY IS A NAGGING REALITY

Charlie Valencia and I are good friends.

Charlie Valencia and I climbed into a cage at the Apache Gold Casino in Globe, Arizona, on May 13, 2006, and tried to tear each other limb from limb.

Contrary to what you might think, these two sentences are not mutually exclusive.

Charlie was the reigning *King of the Cage* champion at 145 pounds when he retired. After I took over that title in late '05, he came out of retirement to fight me and try to get his belt back. Our matchup was part of a ridiculous string of fights for me—seven in twelve months.

Charlie was a big name in the business back then, as big as a lighter-weight fighter could be, back in the days when the sport was illegal everywhere in California but on Indian reservations. He was thirty-one years old, and he'd seen just about everything the game had to offer.

So much of life is timing. In my case, I was fortunate to get into the business at a time when the people who ran the UFC came on the scene to legitimize the sport and bring guys my size out of the shadows. If that hadn't happened, and if the UFC hadn't established the WEC to spotlight the lighter weights, who knows how my career would have turned out? It wasn't always easy to foresee those events taking place, but my passion for fighting and my persistence in believing the tide would eventually turn kept me at it.

Charlie was one of the older fighters who wasn't nearly so fortunate. He was a good college wrestler at Fresno State, but the fighting opportunities weren't available when he was in his prime—at least not as we know them now.

In the mid-1990s, when Charlie was in his early twenties, he made money by fighting in bars. This type of activity was common if you knew where to find it, and Charlie did. At some point in the night, after everyone had had a few beers, the people who ran the bar would start lining up willing patrons and you'd fight the guy closest to you in size. The rest of the bar would bet on each fight, and the winner would get a share of the pot.

Charlie loved to fight, absolutely loved it, and the poor bastards who ended up being matched against him had no earthly idea what they were getting into with this five-foot-three-inch 135-pounder. Most of those guys were far bigger than him, but he'd destroy them and have a blast doing it. The few bucks he'd make doing it were a bonus.

You might remember I met Charlie on the night of my first fight. He coached *Jay* Valencia. Not many people in the wider world knew who Charlie was, but as a student of the fight game, I certainly did, and seeing him across the cage in Jay's corner was a big deal for me. Granted, I was an MMA junkie—an MMA nerd, even—but Charlie was the first guy I met in person who I had also watched fight on television before I made the decision to pursue the sport.

Charlie was an inspiration to me. He'd come up the hard way, through the early days of anything-goes "human cockfighting," and he persisted long enough to become known to early fight fans as MMA started to become popular.

The fight with Charlie was not something either of us wanted. Charlie needed money, and so he decided to come out of retirement. The organization (KOTC) told him he would have to fight me, so he reluctantly agreed. "Reluctantly" because he wasn't necessarily trying get right back to the top, and he wasn't looking to fight a rowdy youngster like me. But at roughly five grand, it was by far the best payday he could find.

Charlie dug deep and showed flashes of his former brilliance, but he had serious ring rust and I finished him off with a choke in the first round. The fight itself was immaterial. More important was the lesson I learned: Regardless of status, we're all the same. We're all just people, doing the best we can, and nobody should be jealous or envious of status. Status is temporary, and fleeting. Charlie Valencia was a big name at the wrong time, and when he fought me it was partly out of desperation. I might have been starstruck at the idea of fighting Charlie, simply because he was a face and a name that went back to the days when MMA became my obsession, but once we got into the cage, we were two guys trying to win a fight.

Money is a nagging reality, but it's a reality that, contrary to my seemingly carefree attitude, I fully grasp.

From as early as I can remember until I was about five or six, the highlight of Pop's day was coming home after work, plopping into his chair, and holding his feet up for his boys to pull off his work boots.

That's my pop: cheerful, happy, with a devil-may-care approach to life.

He's a hardworking contractor and an honest businessman. He's just not a very *good* businessman. There's no shame in that, but it has limited him. He never planned for a time when his body wouldn't allow him to do the physical labor he's done all his life. If he had a job that day, he was good. On Monday, his idea of the future is Tuesday.

He has his family—Ryan, Pop, and I have a unique relationship—and his faith, and everything else can take care of itself in its own good time. He's kind of a dreamer in that sense. This type of short-term thinking has had an effect on his life, though. There are things he wants to do with his family, but he's getting close to sixty and he doesn't have the means to do them. Years of "stumbling" means he never developed a far-reaching plan that would provide him with some comfort and security later in life.

It's important to draw a distinction between *scrambling* for security and *planning* for security. We might like to say money is not the most important

factor in happiness, but it is a reality. You need to plan for your financial needs as much as for your emotional needs. I'm not big on striving for some magic retirement number, the way some commercials for financial institutions would have you believe, but you have to assess your situation and determine how much money you need to be secure.

My pop is a perfect example of someone who didn't focus on the bigger picture. Circumstances, such as Ryan's mental illness, have made it tougher for him to see beyond the immediate. The small picture was always rosy and fun; the big picture was never a concern. As I got older and realized the short-term nature of my profession, I realized I needed to plan for the future better than Pop did. The growth of MMA has made my gym a far more profitable business than I could have imagined. Bigger purses for my fights and more outside opportunities, especially endorsements, have made it easier for me to sock a few bucks away.

Money is something that can be either overemphasized or underemphasized. In the context of your life, and your passion, here's an easy way of putting it: You need enough money to fund your passion. And if you achieve that, and follow your passion with diligence and intelligence, it will ultimately fund you.

After our fight, Charlie and I started a conversation. It immediately became clear that he and I had a lot of the same life philosophies. In fact, he and his wife, Cris, hung out with me in Arizona in the days immediately following the match. After a couple days of hanging out in Arizona, we exchanged numbers and went our separate ways—me to Indonesia for the fateful trip I describe in the next chapter, Charlie and Cris back to California.

I kept tabs on Charlie's career, but we hadn't spoken for a couple years when, out of the blue, he gave me a call. We caught up for a bit, and then the reason for the call emerged. He was having trouble finding a fight and was looking for some advice—and maybe even a little compassion. Now, as a reminder, among lighter weights in the sport's early days, Charlie was a leader. A guy who didn't just fight for sport, but for pride. He'd scrap with anyone. He wasn't just an athlete, he was a legendary fighter. In the meantime, I had risen to a level that made Charlie think I could help him. Obviously, this was a humbling experience for both of us. So we continued talking, which I felt was providing him with some much-needed release, but it was clear he wanted to come away from the phone call feeling like he was a step closer to getting a fight—a fight with a payday and a worthy opponent.

"Dude, I've gotta introduce you to my managers, Mike and Jeff," I said.

"Oh, man, that would be awesome. I'd appreciate it."

"Of course, bro," I said, still jarred by the fact that Charlie Valencia was coming to *me* for advice. "You're Charlie Valencia!"

Mike and Jeff got to work kick-starting his career, and Charlie and I rekindled our friendship. He became part of our community. We spent a few Christmases and Thanksgivings together. He helped me through some rough patches in my career, and I helped him through some tough times with his family. Charlie had a good run, too, fighting until 2011, his last fight being in the UFC. Sadly he lost by TKO in the first round, but I felt good that I had been able to help him get back on track after some tough times. More than that, though, I was proud that a man I had admired years earlier had been brought into our community.

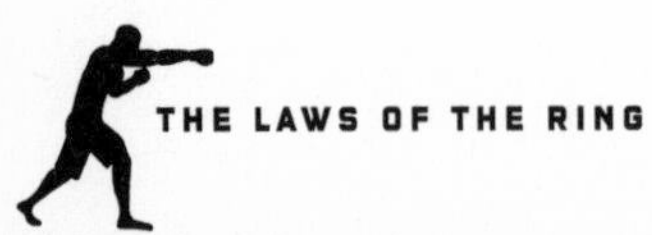

THE 29TH LAW OF POWER

BE THE BIGGER MAN

After my fight with Charlie, I took a trip to Bali, Indonesia, with two of my best buddies, Tommy Schurkamp and Virgil Moorehead. Toward the end of the trip, I went out with Virgil to a bar. Tommy had flown home the day before because he had to work, and Virgil left the bar early in the night because he was fighting to stay sober and wasn't handling the bar scene very well.

I had met some chubby European girls, and we were having a good time dancing and talking. The scene was mellow, the girls were friendly, so I stuck around by myself.

A short time after Virgil left, I was dancing with these girls when one of the sturdy local Balinese walked past and shoulder-bumped me. I ignored him initially, but then I caught him looking at me from about five feet away in a menacing fashion. It became clear he wasn't going to stop.

At this point in my career, I was a world champion in smaller shows, which meant there was almost no chance that anybody here knew who I was. This guy definitely didn't know, and he didn't care. This bigger, tough-looking guy just saw a small American who was attracting the attention of some girls—apparently he considered that an infraction that needed to be punished.

He kept at it, getting closer to me and gesturing that he wanted to fight. I generally keep my wits about me, but it's just not my nature to back down, and eventually I'd had enough. I came back at him with the international language for "You want to step outside?"

Stupid, right? World champion or not, I'm all by myself in a bar in a foreign country, and I'm agreeing to fight a local guy with whom I can't communicate. I don't know what rules he follows when he fights, but I've got a couple drinks in me and I know there's no way to avoid this altercation.

We walked out to an alley behind the bar. It was almost completely dark, and this guy *had* to be wondering about this crazy American—five five and a half, around 150 pounds, wearing flip-flops and a baseball cap—who's decided to take him into an alley all by himself. Guys don't do that unless they've got skills, or a death wish.

Or, perhaps, both.

I saw a little doubt creep into his mind. It was in his eyes. He'd expected me to either run or continue to ignore him. Now, as we're outside, I could see him thinking, *What have I gotten myself into?*

At that moment I felt the dynamic change. Just a few minutes before he had been the one holding the power, on his own turf, with his friends, toying with me. But the moment I called his bluff, the (unofficial) laws of power shifted. I let him know I not only wasn't intimidated by the challenge, but I welcomed it, and upped the ante by dictating the terms. We were going outside, and it was dark.

We squared off in the alley, and I said, "Let's do it, motherfucker." I kicked off my sandals and tossed my hat to the ground. He started screaming what sounded like gibberish to me but was clearly a call to his buddies who were in and around the bar. He had come to the conclusion that he had asked for something he didn't really want.

A few of these guys—I recall about three or four, but I wasn't counting—materialized near us. One of them spoke broken English and asked what was going on. Finding myself outnumbered, I became a little alarmed, so I addressed him. "This guy wanted to fight me," I said. "It's got to be one-on-one."

I kept making the point. "ONE-ON-ONE."

They moved us to an elevated area that was just a few steps away from the alley, where they all stood to watch the show. I remember there was a fountain and some kind of monument inscribed with a couple hundred names of Australians who were killed in a terrorist bombing at one of the clubs a few years back. We squared off and I attacked. It was obvious that I had the upper hand, I was beating the guy up handily, but he put up a pretty decent fight for a random guy in a bar. (Remember, I'd had a few drinks, and he was obviously no stranger to third-world-country street fights.) The fight ended when I picked him up in a bear hug and brought him down onto a cement planter. I could hear the thud of him landing. I'm pretty sure his collarbone broke right before he let out a horrific scream.

So there I was, standing with these locals around me and their buddy pulling himself from the ground holding his shoulder. One of them was motioning to me to get out of there. "You won," the English-speaking one said. I knew I had to get out of there, but I wanted to grab my sandals and my hat first. I was walking around for a minute or two, just catching my breath, when I got cheap-shotted in the back of the head with brass knuckles.

The pain was vicious. It reverberated in my head, like a gong. I knew immediately it wasn't a fist. I turn around and see a Balinese man staring at me, smiling, holding up the hand with the brass knuckles, saying "One by one" in broken English.

I hesitated for a second and said, "What the hell is that?"—pointing to the brass knuckles on his clenched fist. Apparently he didn't care that I had realized he was breaking my proper street-fight rules. "Okay, let's do it," I told him, because I was pissed off and half drunk and not thinking real clearly. Besides, I didn't think I had much choice.

I tried to decide how I was going to attack a guy who, with the brass knuckles, was wearing the equivalent of a weapon on his hand, when two other guys showed up. One of them was holding a glass bottle. The other reached down and picked up a rock.

Oh, shit. I already felt the blood trickling down the back of my head from the cheap shot I took, and now there were two more guys standing there, grinning and laughing and saying, "One by one."

I quickly came up with the most basic plan I could muster: Attack them first. I addressed the bottle guy with a right and a kick, knocking him back. I grabbed the guy with the rock in his hands and tried to pull it from him. The whole time I was getting rabbit-punched in the back of the head with the brass knuckles. I'm guessing not many people reading this have been punched with brass knuckles, but that shit hurts. Every time he hit me it felt like he was tearing the back of my head open.

The bottle guy came back and I threw him over a moped and started running. The brass-knuckle guy didn't react fast enough, so I managed to get away momentarily. I ran around the corner and did a dive-roll over these metal railings to get back into the club. I figured that was where civilization was, so that's where I should be.

It turned out that the bouncers at the club were part of the group that was after me. Of all the shitty luck, right? I discovered later that the bouncers in these clubs are the closest thing to organized crime in Bali—and I was their target for the night.

I darted through the dance floor of the club, gushing blood from my head and drawing attention. My attempt to find people to help me resulted in the discovery of more enemies. There were now twelve guys after me, each one focused on doing damage to me. We ended up on the dance floor, where I was shucking and jiving and trying to free myself from these guys. I got knocked down and ended up kicking up at my attackers.

They were coming at me from all angles. Feet, bottles, and fists. At this point some of the Europeans on the dance floor came to my rescue; they started pulling people off me and shoving guys out of the way so I could make a run for it.

I got up and headed for the door. I had to shoulder-shrug through the people, jump over the base of a staircase, and get through the seated area of the bar before I could take on the guy at the front door who was trying to keep me from leaving. I took care of him with a hard elbow shiver and headed out onto the street. I felt like I was on the set of a Jackie Chan movie, or one of the Bruce Lee movies I'd loved as a kid. Except there was no glory in this.

As I made my way to the street I realized the situation had shifted. It was no longer a bar fight. *This is crazy,* I thought, *but I think these guys are trying*

to kill me. This was unlike anything I'd ever experienced, inside or out of the cage. There's danger every time you fight, but this was all-out mayhem, and the worst part was I couldn't predict who or what might turn on me next, and I didn't know where it might come from.

I needed to be strong, and even though I was used to pushing myself beyond limits, this wasn't a workout in a gym, where I could stop if I needed. This time I *couldn't* stop. Stopping meant dying.

I headed out onto the street, covered in blood, barefoot, panicked, not knowing where I was going. Most of the stores along the street were closed, but this being a third-world country, the shopkeepers hire people to sit in front of the stores overnight to keep people out and safeguard the merchandise.

I spied a Billabong shop ahead and to my right, and in my exhausted state I created a logical equation in my mind: *Billabong . . . America . . . civilization.* I jumped into the store, and the guys guarding it were trying to get me out. I'd lost my shirt by this time. I was barefoot. I was wearing board shorts with no underwear. I was covered in blood, and I was sure they were worried about losing their jobs because some crazy American was bleeding all over the merchandise.

I started begging them: "Please, help me, these people are trying to kill me."

They couldn't understand me. They didn't know the dynamic of the situation. They didn't know if I was chasing someone or if I was the one being chased. They just wanted me out of there.

At this point the guys with the bottles and the brass knuckles ran in. They were with another guy who stood in front of me holding a small hammer, which looked to me like something one of the shoemakers on the street would use. They stood there, furious.

A buzz ran through my body. *I might fucking die here.*

I thought fast. I pleaded with them.

"Please don't kill me. Please don't kill me."

They had me surrounded. I was trying to sound defeated, to make them believe I'd surrendered. They were mocking me. *"One by one." "One by one."* It had become a taunt. More bodies piled into the shop. There were now five or six of them with me in the dead of night on a dark street in Bali. They were all chanting.

They had no intention of fighting me "one by one," they weren't playing by any rules and had already seen what happened to their buddy, the one who started all this in the first place. He was the one who first decided *one by one* might be a good idea.

The gang members paused in confusion as they figured out what to do. They weren't finished, but my apparent resignation caused them to rethink their plan. The guy with the shoe hammer, who I identified as the ringleader, was doing a lot of talking and waving. It seemed clear he was going to be the one who took the next step, which they undoubtedly saw as the first step toward finishing me off. He held the hammer up and started walking toward me.

As he got closer, I had to think quickly. I was beyond the point of trying to reason with these guys. I truly believed they were going to kill me for sport. But I couldn't give up, and I had to think of something that would extricate me from this situation. Something . . . creative.

My decision was like something out of a movie script: I'd continue to pretend I'd given up. The shoe hammer got closer, and I began fake-begging him to leave me alone. "No, no, no," I said. He got closer, smiling, and I put my hands up on either side of my face as if I were ready to simply take my beating.

His devious little smile vanished. He jumped at me and attempted to swing the hammer. But before he could hit me, I drilled him with an overhand right. I felt him crumple to the floor as I raced out the front door.

It took the other guys a second to respond, but they did—loudly and quickly. Any hope I had for mercy—and I had very little—evaporated in the thick tropical air. I ran, thankful for my training, and heard them running behind me. Their chatter had gone from mocking to angry. I was faced with another decision: If I ran to my right, away from the club, there was darkness—homes, maybe, but definitely less civilization. If I ran left, back toward the club, I would be more likely to find people who might be willing to help.

Of course, running back toward people meant running the risk of being met by more people who wanted me dead.

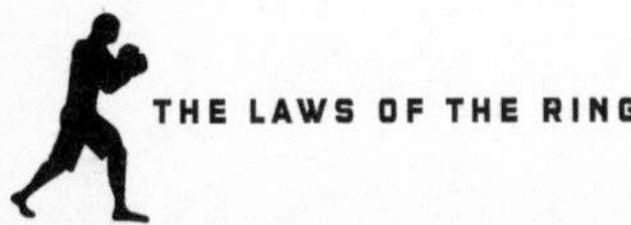

I was exhausted, barely thinking clearly. Blood was streaming down my face. I was shirtless, barefoot, bloody. It seemed impossible to me at this moment to be more exposed. Or more afraid.

I chose to run left, back toward the club. I had to keep running, but I'd never been so tired. I ran down the street as fast as my legs would allow. As I neared the spot where all my troubles began, I saw a van on the side of the street and a taxi behind it. There was a driver in the taxi, but otherwise it was empty.

I had put close to fifty yards between me and my pursuers, and I was thinking the gap—and this taxi up ahead—is what I needed to survive. All of my positive thinking culminated in this moment.

If I could only get into the passenger seat of the taxi, I would be okay.

I started to run toward the right side of the car, and then I remembered I was in Indonesia. The passenger side was on the left. I took this as a good sign; it showed I was thinking clearly. It might not seem like much, but after having the back of my head bashed in by brass knuckles, the realization lifted my spirits. My sole focus was on that left front door. It was my finish line, my lifeline.

I jumped into the cab and the driver recoiled at the sight of me. He was freaking out. I was covered in blood. He didn't see the guys running up the street. He had no idea about any of this, but I didn't have time to explain. "Go go go!" I yelled. He looked at me, eyes as wide as dinner plates. "Money, I have money . . . Go go go!"

Before he could get the car in gear, they attacked it. They were wild, enraged. This had become something more than a pursuit; their honor was at stake. They continued to be outwitted and outfought by a crazy little American, and they were furious.

I scrambled to find the lock for the door. I was fumbling, clawing at the door like a crab in a pot. Their faces were at the window, their teeth flashed, their fists pounded.

I couldn't maneuver the lock. The door swung open.

It was like they were all trying to get into the car at the same time. I thought I was dead. This was the first time my positive attitude began to waver. There was little room for creativity left. How could I get out of this? I was trapped, like a turtle on its back. They were shoving and angling to get at me. I wasn't going to give up, but I was down to my final option.

But now the driver became a concern. Where was he? Whose side was he on? I felt a shift in the car and saw the driver get out on his side. This was not good. One of the attackers reached in and started pounding me on the head and pulling me by the hair. There were open wounds on my head, and the hair pulling made the pain very nearly unbearable.

That's it, I thought. *The driver bailed and I'm done. I'm the Rodney King of Indonesia. I'm never getting out of this cab.*

Just then, the driver yanked the hair puller away from the car and hopped in. The driver was on my side! He was helping! He leaned outside of the car and yelled at the attackers. He told the onlookers to call for help. This backed them down some. I was now part of a huge public scene, and that worked to my advantage. At this point the crowd of helpers far outnumbered the attackers.

I leaned back, my head nearly in the driver's lap, and started kicking. My experienced feet were like pistons: too quick for them to grab, too strong for them to overpower, and I was fighting them off. The only question that remained was how much longer I could keep this up. While I was repeatedly kicking—I must have been on my back for twenty or thirty seconds, but it felt like ten minutes—I noticed the other attackers were involved in some kind of commotion outside the car.

Finally, there was no one left to kick. I glanced outside the car and saw another group of people—foreigners, like me—prying my attackers away. Finally, some help. The door slammed closed. The driver started the car and floored it onto the street.

My attackers, or what remained of them, stood in the street behind me waving their weapons and shouting their chatter. I didn't think the combination of happiness and relief I was feeling was possible. I was nearly crying, and I couldn't stop thanking the driver. I was bloody, sore, and beyond exhausted, but I was alive.

I told the driver to take me to the hospital. I counted seven open gashes on the top and back of my head. Just as I began to calm down, I noticed a guy following us on a motorcycle. He took one turn with us, then two. There were very few cars on the road.

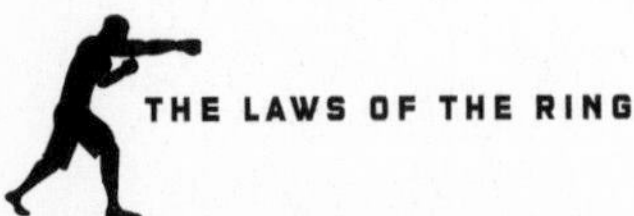

I had no idea who he was, but I wanted to find out why he was following me. I told the driver to pull over so I could get out and confront him. There was no fear in me at this point and I wanted to make sure I wasn't being followed. I had no idea if the motorcycle guy was friendly or not, but I wanted him out of my life either way.

"What's up?"

He was a local who spoke decent English. "Are you okay?" he asked. He wanted to know where I was staying and if he could help. The adrenaline was still rushing inside me, and I didn't tell him anything. I couldn't trust anyone.

"Don't worry about it, I don't want you following me," I said, and told the driver to continue.

He took me to a hospital; my hair was thick with dried blood. The first thing they did, given my bloody and battered condition, was make me take a shower to make it easier for them to examine my head. My shorts were soaking wet and bloody, and I wasn't wearing underwear, so a hospital-issue towel became my only clothing. They thought I had a skull fracture, so they sent me to another hospital for an X-ray. My feet and legs were swollen, cut, and bruised. They sutured seven different spots on my head and put cotton balls over each. The X-ray, thank goodness, was negative.

While I was in the hospital, Virgil and Bobby, the local we had hired to be our tour guide, came to visit me. The guide was furious and said he had connections with the police. For fifty dollars, he told me he would get, as he put it, "justice." I was forced to go to the police station to file a report, by Bobby, who insisted that we get "justice." I was still sporting the towel from the hospital as they lined up a bunch of guys and told me to identify my attackers from the group in front of me. I looked at them and had no idea if I'd seen any of them before. They insisted that I just choose one, but really I couldn't have cared less at this point and wasn't interested in blind justice.

I sat with a police officer to tell him my story. What followed was one of the strangest scenes of my life. I was exhausted, lying on a table in the police chief's office, wearing nothing but that hospital towel, talking to a cop who was typing on an old computer. How weird is that? It was ten in the morning and I hadn't slept at all. I was so tired from the night's ordeal that I barely wanted to stand up, let alone recount the story. I started out by sitting in a chair, and then I moved to the table. I was accompanied by a local witness who was telling his version of what happened to me. He said he first assumed that I was a crazy person, running around the club bleeding and causing trouble, then realized I was being attacked.

The officer was looking at me kind of funny, but I was too freaking exhausted to even care. When the officer left the room, the witness told me he couldn't believe I had the nerve to lie on the chief's table nearly naked. He would look up occasionally and laugh. Just another example of the crazy American, I guess.

Every couple of minutes, the power would inexplicably go out. When it did, I had to start my story over from the beginning. Finally, I asked for a pen and paper to write it all down.

My guide kept telling me, "For fifty bucks my buddy will get these guys." Nobody could believe I wasn't interested in their form of justice. "I don't care if they get these guys," I said. "I just want to sleep."

The funny part of the story was my concern about the hospital bill: How was I going to pay? I didn't have much money with me by this point in the trip. I had no health insurance. I had no idea what they would charge or how they would handle my situation. Would they send a bill to my house in Sacramento? Unlikely.

When the hospital released me, I was gritting my teeth wondering how I was going to pay for my stay. I knew what a night in the emergency room would cost in America. I was probably more nervous at this moment than I'd been at any time during the fight. Then they told me what I owed. It was the equivalent of thirty-five dollars U.S. I nearly laughed with relief. I gave the taxi driver a hundred-dollar bill and thanked him for saving my life. He was so grateful for the money, but not nearly as grateful as I was for the lift.

I was in Bali for two more days, in the house we had rented, recuperating for the flight home. I was supposed to corner Olaf Alfonso in Japan three days after the attack. The fighting organization, called Dream, wouldn't book me a flight from Indonesia to Japan, so I flew from Indonesia to Sacramento and spent twelve hours on the ground before flying another fifteen hours to Japan, in order to keep my word to my buddy Olaf Alfonso. I wore

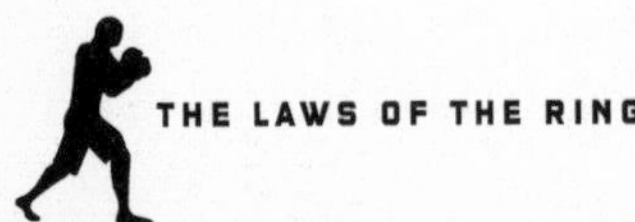

a hat over the six cotton swabs that were threaded to my head. I'm sure I was quite a sight.

Would I do it all over again given the option? No. Not a chance. My escape from the murderous thugs in Bali makes for a good story, but I wouldn't do it over again on a bet. I learned many lessons from that episode, none more important than this: Sometimes, the bigger man is the one who walks away.

There's a temptation to think you're invincible when you're a successful twenty-five-year-old fighter with a nice buzz going. I gave in to that temptation, and it was a huge mistake. I took the challenge based on principle. *You can't pick on me.* That's all it was: false machismo. I failed to take into consideration that not everybody fights by the same rules. And not everybody values life in the same way.

Context is everything. In the aftermath of this experience, I learned a lot about the people I was dealing with—their situation and their motivation. I visited Indonesia during a time when the economy was in bad shape. For the most part, the people were extremely friendly and welcoming to us, but there were times when their desperation showed. Many of them sat on the streets attempting to sell jewelry or other trinkets, and occasionally they would flash anger when they couldn't close a sale.

Young men in Bali—like my attackers—had precious few options in these tough economic times. I later learned that one of those options was to serve as "escorts" for female tourists. These guys were good-looking locals, and they would hang around bars and restaurants showering women—most from Australia or Europe—with attention. The women, in turn, would wine and dine these young guys and, if things went well, pay them for *additional attention.* I have no reason to think that the European girls with whom I was dancing knew anything about this, but it's possible the Balinese men thought I was standing in the way of their finding out.

So I unknowingly violated several local customs. For a group that is downtrodden and already working for peanuts, it's humiliating to have one of your own beat up by someone, an American, who was already viewed as a guy who was "stealing" potential customers in the bar. Their subsequent actions validated one of life's basic truths: The less you have to lose, the more willing you are to lose it.

So, no, I wouldn't do it again. I would do anything to avoid that situation. I would allow my pride to be hurt, and I would have let the instigator stare and scowl. And I would have been content to receive my satisfaction by looking at the guy and thinking to myself, *I know I can kick your ass, but I'm not going to do it.*

THE 30TH LAW OF POWER

THE POWER OF FRIENDSHIP

Here's a quick story that comes from a place about as far removed from the MMA scene as you can imagine, but illustrates how fun together with friendship can be a great ingredient for success.

Leonard B. Stern and his friend, Roger Price, were screenwriters in the early days of television. One day they were working on a script for *The Honeymooners* when Stern found himself at a loss for words. He was stuck, and so he asked his friend Price to give him an adjective.

Price gave him his choice of two: clumsy or naked.

Both of those words were hilarious to Stern, because he was searching for the right word to describe Jackie Gleason/Ralph Kramden's nose. Price, of course, had no idea what Stern was attempting to describe, and when he found out, he laughed, too.

It dawned on them immediately: They could make some money on this. Imagine if you could give someone the framework of a story and they could ask their friends or family members to fill in words based solely on parts of speech. It could be a lot of fun for those who played, and highly profitable for the two friends who invented it.

Somewhere along the line, one of them came up with the name "Mad Libs." Stern and Price figured this was an easy sell, but they quickly found that no publisher would touch it. They went from publishing house to publishing house, and each time they heard the same things.

It's childish.

It will never sell.

Why would someone buy it when they could just make it up themselves?

It would have been very easy for Stern and Price to abandon the idea. After all, how could so many people in the publishing industry be wrong? They wanted to make money, too, and they'd publish the book if they believed it had merit, right?

Stern and Price didn't give up. They didn't say, "Oh, well, we gave it a shot," before going back to their day jobs. Instead, they persisted. When it became clear that they weren't going to be handed an advance and a publishing contract, they didn't discard their passion and assume that other people knew more than they did.

Instead, they published it themselves. The first run of fourteen thousand copies had to be warehoused somewhere, so Stern decided the best available space was in the dining room of his Manhattan apartment. Part of the lore of the early days of *Mad Libs* is that Stern had to eat standing up for several months before they sold enough books to clear some space.

The result, of course, is a ridiculous success story. Stern and Price knew far more than the publishers. They sold more than 150 million copies of the various editions of *Mad Libs* and the word game has also become a huge seller as an app for the iPhone and iPad.

In fact, *Mad Libs* got so big so fast that Stern and Price opened their own publishing *house* to keep up with the demand. Just a couple of friends, doing their thing.

When I joined the WEC, which was the UFC's organization for lighter weights, I was invited to have dinner with Dana White and Lorenzo Fertitta at the Hard Rock Casino in Las Vegas.

"We have big plans for you," White said. "Keep on doing what you're doing, do the PR we have set up for you, and continue to take the sport seriously. We want to make you one of our go-to guys."

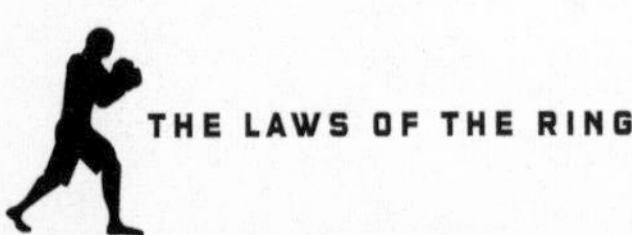

I noticed right away that Lorenzo and Dana had an easy camaraderie, and over our meals I asked them how they came together to start the UFC and bring MMA out of the dark alleys of professional sports.

And that's when I learned that one of the most successful sports corporations in the world started as a conversation between childhood friends. Dana was a guy with the foresight to see that MMA, to be successful, needed to be revamped for public consumption. He was one of the sport's first managers, repping some of the biggest names in the early days, like Tito Ortiz and Chuck Liddell. Lorenzo was running his family business, which included the Station Casinos, and was a member of the Nevada Boxing Commission. Their love of combat sports was a bond that kept their friendship strong through the years.

Dana was running a couple of cardio/kickboxing gyms in Las Vegas, and he reconnected with Lorenzo after inviting him to come in and work out. But Dana had something greater in mind for this reunion. One day, he approached Lorenzo with a business proposition: buy the UFC. Dana's plan was well considered, including the all-important steps to clean up the sport and its image in order to market it to a more general audience. Lorenzo and his brother Frank saw the potential in the UFC *and* in Dana, and in January 2001, they bought the UFC for two million dollars.

Most of you are probably familiar with the story of all the money that was initially lost, how it was recovered and compounded, and how the reality show *Ultimate Fighter* was integral to the rebirth of the UFC, so I'll spare you the hundredth iteration. The short version is they came, they saw, they didn't quite conquer, they got creative, they launched a successful reality show on SPIKE—introducing the sport to anyone with a cable box—and that investment has paid for itself many times over.

Anyway, listening to them tell the story, I said, "I just think it's so cool that you guys were friends who ended up putting your minds and your passions together." Then I got to thinking about the widespread impact of that friendship. It has created jobs for writers, referees, commentators, equipment manufacturers, gym owners, arena workers, trainers, managers. It created a system that allows fighters to work hard and create their own breaks. And it all sprouted when one friend (White) had an idea and the other (Fertitta) had the means to bring that idea to fruition.

THE 31ST LAW OF POWER

BLOCK OUT FEAR

There are only two things that you have to do in life: You have to die, and you have to live until you die. The rest is up to you. (A word on fear.)

I have not experienced fear in the cage. Many people have a hard time believing this, since they expect fear to be an inevitable part of my job. They believe I can overcome it, but never experiencing it is too much for them to grasp. It's true, though. Fighters who fear the fight have short, rough careers, and my fears are offset by my persistent mind-set and positive attitude.

The fears of a fighter are the same as those of most people in the world, except the physical risk a fighter faces is obviously greater. I fear not having financial security in my old age, or for the health and well-being of loved ones around me. On a more mundane level, I fear turbulence when I'm flying in a plane. I absolutely hate it. I don't know whether it's a control issue or what, but I hate nothing more than sitting in an airplane that's bouncing through the sky.

On a deeper level, I fear that my ability to enjoy life in my later years will be compromised by the physical toll fighting is taking on my body. This, I guess, is where my fears veer from those of most people. There is a paradox in my life: I eat healthy foods, live a healthy lifestyle, but then I willingly engage in one of the riskiest behaviors known to man. I build my body up between fights only to break it down again, and then repeat the process. As I head toward my midthirties, I can't help but see the irony of my situation. By all rights, I should live to be a hundred years old with what I choose to put into my body and the ridiculous amount of training I put in. But then, on the other side, there is the elephant in the room: the pounding and punishment necessary to make a living as an MMA fighter. It's difficult to reconcile the two, but I believe the ability to push themselves past the pain and the possibility of serious health problems in the future is a quality unique to fighters and football players and others who put themselves at physical risk. We get past these realities because we know they come with the business. It helps that the people I'm talking about do not fear the unknown. Part of the reason I don't fear getting hurt in the cage is precisely because I have *been* hurt in the cage. I've gone from consciousness to unconsciousness in my life—it's not that bad.

Fear is the biggest roadblock to creating a life that revolves around your passion. The fear can be of failure or of the unknown. It can manifest itself as procrastination or self-doubt. When you're looking to make a bold move and change your life, fear can be paralyzing.

On the other hand, the loss of fear can be motivating, even intoxicating. Some of history's most successful people—artists, inventors, political figures—have achieved greatness only after throwing caution to the wind. They've sacrificed short-term security for something far more important. Their fierce passion can also be seen as a bold stand against fear.

Again, the most dangerous people are those with the least to lose.

Obviously we're dealing here with fear and its consequences on a much smaller scale than the Middle Eastern insurgents who sacrificed their lives for a greater cause dealt with in the spring of 2011, but the truth is, you have to ask yourself, What do I have to lose? I don't mean to make light of desperate situations, but if your life is miserable and lacking in passion, your risk might be less than you think. Financial security is important, sure, but at what cost? Again, it all comes back to the saying that runs through my head whenever I'm faced with a big decision:

There are only two things that you have to do in life: You have to die, and you have to live until you die. The rest is up to you.

Think about the last line: *The rest is up to you.* Not your parents or your boss or your social group. Your decisions should not be influenced by what society dictates as "normal" or "prestigious." Live for you. If you live in fear and your mind is constantly hounded by worst-case scenarios that keep you from making the changes you need to make, then you're just living the life of quiet desperation that Thoreau wrote about. To get out and live—to really live—you need to *control* fear.

You begin to control fear by having confidence. Now, I understand that some people are naturally confident, but those people perhaps have an even greater dilemma in that they have to guard against overconfidence. (It's also important to note that bragging and blustering are often signs of insecurity and *a lack of* confidence.) If you lack confidence, a far more widespread affliction, you need to find ways to build it up. This is actually not as difficult as it sounds. I have a few simple methods I use to help build an inner confidence in those who need it. But even those who *don't think* they need help in building confidence should take note of the following.

My first step is to remind myself that I won't go without.

I have a favorite training run that takes me out the door of my Ultimate Fitness Gym in downtown Sacramento and northwest about twelve blocks toward the American River. I run until the road—Twenty-first Street—dead-ends in the silt-soft riverbed. From there, I run along the railroad tracks and through a homeless encampment that sits under a railroad bridge. It's a small-scale tent city, home to approximately fifty people.

I choose this route during times that are particularly hectic or stressful. The river provides solace and beauty, but following this path is about more than peace and scenery: The people who live in the tent city, people who have been pushed to society's margins, serve as an inspiration to me.

Don't misunderstand; I'm not reveling in their misfortune. Quite the opposite. From the first time I ran into their "neighborhood," I was taken by the adaptability and positive attitudes the residents manifest.

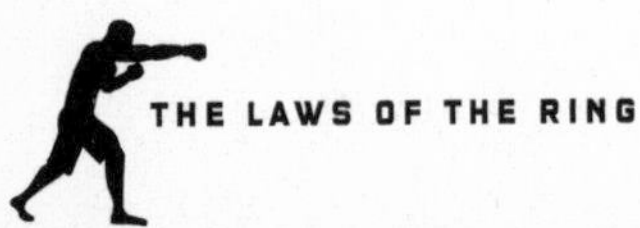

The first time I took this run was during the days when I was training for my first fight with Jens Pulver, in June of 2008. With my mind preoccupied by a thousand things on a sunny day in late spring, I ran through the dead end and out to the railroad tracks. When I noticed the tents, my first thought was that I was running into a sad and desolate place. But the more I looked, the more vibrant I noticed the place was.

I slowed, then stopped. I watched a guy, probably in his early forties, emerge hunched from one of the tents, stand up tall, and begin to stretch in the sun. He stretched for about a minute and then dropped down and did about twenty push-ups. When he finished that task, he sat on a log next to his tent and poured himself a drink from a thermos.

I wondered about what his life was like before he lived here. Were the push-ups part of his routine? How did this fit in with his personality? Was he a driven guy who lost everything and ended up out here with nothing but his tent, his thermos, and the clothes on his back? And would that drive to better himself—that small kernel of drive that still lived inside him—dry up and disappear if he stayed out here long enough? Or would it ultimately save him?

I ended up sitting out there and watching these people from a distance for quite some time. There were about five people standing in a group near Push-up Man. They were pretty ragged and dirty, but they were laughing and having a good time. I couldn't see the devastation that the life of each of them had left in its wake, the broken homes and worried parents, the forgotten children and lost promises. But I could see hope. They had lost everything, and yet they were clearly enjoying a sunny day along the river. When all is lost, there's still something left.

It sounds so simple, perhaps, but as I sat there on a beautiful, early-spring day, watching these people interact, I felt as if a weight had lifted off of my shoulders. It was a hopeful scene, and it brought me some much-needed perspective.

The world around me was moving too fast. I had to train my ass off for the biggest fight of my career against a guy I idolized—an MMA legend and one of the most formidable opponents in MMA history—a guy who once beat B. J. Penn for a UFC title (which was a *huge* deal back then). The buildup to the fight, which marked my first real media push, included a promotional tour for the WEC and a *Countdown* television show. I had to please the sponsors and promoters. But the training and the upcoming fight were not my only concerns. My gym business was just getting off the ground. I was in the process of buying a new house. And on top of all that, I was dealing with some upheaval in my personal life.

Michelle and I had been together since we were in high school, with a few breaks in between. She went to UC Davis with me, and we stayed together through four years of college. She sat down with me and helped me with college applications when I had no idea what I wanted to do or where I wanted to go. She was my best friend. Our families were close. She was the one who hung out in Las Vegas with me and Randy Couture at the start of my career. We were together for nine years, and took it on faith that we might eventually get married and start a family.

And during this time, as I was preparing to fight Pulver and running along the river, it was clear that Michelle was ready to put that plan into action. She was ready for a bigger commitment . . . and I wasn't. It seemed that over the last few years our relationship had been growing more strained. Plans for a family were getting further and further from my focus. Michelle was ready years before this time even. As my career gained momentum and MMA became more popular and profitable, I just couldn't pull the trigger. And as a result, I lost Michelle.

My uncertainty and unwillingness to commit became too much for her to handle. She wanted more control, and I was giving her less. I had to commit one way or another—either *to* her or *away from* her. And since my selfishness wouldn't allow me to commit to her, I felt the just thing to do for her sake was to call it off.

This scared me. When we broke up, I told her, "I feel like I'm giving up the one person I could spend the rest of my life with." She couldn't understand my reasoning, and she couldn't stand around waiting for something that might never happen.

This was six weeks before the Pulver fight. On those runs down to the river the questions would repeat themselves in my head over and over: *Am I making the worst mistake of my life? If I want to have a family and I believe she's*

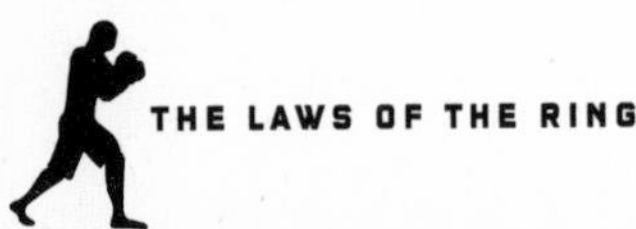

the one, how can I break it off? I was conflicted, and confused, and Michelle was angry. When I finally got up the nerve to tell her my decision, it was very emotional. I knew she wasn't going to be able to break up with me herself, and I felt she was trying to force my hand, one way or another.

I was losing my best friend and someone I considered a family member. The person I was going to start a family with was gone.

I cried. She cried.

"If you do this, I don't want to talk to you," she said. "I don't want to see you. I want you out of my life."

Those words were like knives. I had no response, other than to say I couldn't keep doing this to her. She was working as a marketing manager at a medical firm and she thought she was going to have to relocate. As the Pulver fight got closer, she felt as if the whole town was talking about me. This was my biggest fight, and it was scheduled to take place in my hometown. I was on the local news practically every night. I was in the newspaper. It was a big deal, and she was suddenly no longer a part of it.

As I ran along the riverbank feeling the sun on my back and the rich valley soil under my feet, all of these questions bounced around my brain. The run was much more than training; it was therapy. And so when I watched Push-up Man with his buddies drinking, smoking, joking, and laughing, I realized something: These people had seemingly the worst thing happen to them, they'd lost everything, yet still they found a way to enjoy life and be positive, even if it was only for a few moments on a sunny day. But I saw dignity in their despair, and it made me realize that we're hardwired to be optimistic, and optimism is damned hard to defeat.

I thought to myself:

If lose this fight, so what?

If I lose my house, so what?

If I lose my business, so what?

I'll just come down here and enjoy a beautiful day by the river.

As you work to incorporate passion into your life, it's worth asking yourself a few questions.

What would happen if you lost everything? What if you took a big risk and lost? Where would you be? What's the worst-case scenario?

The answers to these questions are as different as our personalities. Everyone has his own worst-case scenario. For me—single, childless, and freshly wounded by the end of a long relationship—the encampment on the river didn't seem that bad. I could make it work down there.

I made the river run a regular route during the final six weeks of training before the Pulver fight. One day I passed within fifty feet of the encampment and heard hooting from three women sitting near a tent. I then came upon four men sitting near a fenced-in electrical relay station, having a conversation and passing around a bottle of booze. I thought about all the great times I'd had sitting by the river with my buddies, having a few beers and sharing a few laughs. The men were looking at me in a curious, nonthreatening way. I stopped to talk to them.

One of them smiled and asked, "Why you always out here running?"

"I'm training," I said. "I've got a fight coming up and I'm getting ready."

"Okay, *that* explains it. You're a fighter—we've been wondering about you."

The conversation might not have amounted to much, but as I jogged away from those men I was feeling a mixture of gratitude for my outlook and optimism about whatever lay ahead. I had a house, food, and comfort, but I knew that if I lost the fight . . . or my business . . . or *any* material possessions, everything would still be fine.

From my vantage point, the people by the river had gone through horrible times, maybe as a result of their own poor decisions, but while their habits may have been poor—boozing the day away isn't exactly the best way to improve an impoverished living situation—their attitudes weren't. I carry this thought and those visions with me in times of fear and doubt. I know I need to have healthier habits than the folks on the river, but their strength—their ability to survive—rests on a positive foundation and the human instinct to find a way to survive.

Life is a series of choices, and your lifestyle is sculpted by the choices you make. Much like a river changing course over time, the lifestyle alterations you make might not yield immediate, readily apparent results. Small choices

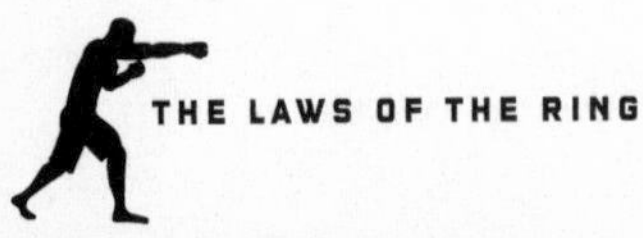

add up, and each positive choice you make increases confidence and dispels fear.

For a professional fighter, a job that not many choose, fear is a constant threat. You can have short-term fears: Can I beat this guy? Will I get injured? But I can't end this chapter without discussing the thing that's on everyone's mind. The *long-term* fears of brain damage. Will I be able to walk and talk when I'm fifty?

The question is uncomfortable but unavoidable. I remember watching a documentary about Muhammad Ali and thinking, *Man, every one of these guys is punch-drunk.* That scared me a little, but then I go into analysis mode and come up with reasons why I shouldn't freak out about my future. We all play these justification games with ourselves, and I'm no different. For one, I'd like to think my sport is different. My background is in wrestling, so I didn't spar or do any stand-up training until I was twenty-four. There are so many different disciplines in MMA and not all of them require taking repeated blows to the head as part of the training.

At the same time I'm not in denial about the dangers. As time goes by, I understand that what I'm doing is taking a physical toll on my body. That means I have to listen to my body. I have to train smarter.

I attended a UFC tutorial on the long- and short-term impact of concussions, a constant worry in any combat sport. As the teachers discussed the symptoms, I started thinking: *Did I get one here? Did I get one in this fight? Is that why I felt that way?* They made me aware of factors I never would have considered—for instance, you don't spar when you have a headache. Protective gear during training is no longer something I use when I feel like it; it's a mandatory part of the process. The potential for head injury has caused me to choose my training partners carefully and to rest on days when I might not want to.

You have to take all of this into account, but in the end I have to remind myself that life is about taking calculated risks. The risk is always going to be there, but the trick is to eliminate the type of risk you can control.

Fear is weakness. Fear is controllable, even though it's not always rational. You can destroy fear through preparation. My landscaper friend who walked into the cage shaking and quivering before getting his ass kicked was really afraid of his own lack of preparation. His refusal to train or put together a coherent plan created the fear. He was in it for the wrong reasons, which meant his sense of purpose was not well defined, and this showed in his performance.

But what was he afraid of? It wasn't his opponent, because he didn't know his opponent from a stranger on the street. He was afraid of himself, and the terrible position he put himself in by attempting to have the life of a professional fighter without putting in the work.

In most cases, fighters and nonfighters alike feel fear when they feel vulnerable. This vulnerability does not stem from a fear of bodily harm, but from a fear of failure. This failure can take many forms: failure to provide for your family, failure to live up to external expectations, failure to progress through the socioeconomic strata at the so-called right pace.

Stop and consider this: Failure, and your sense of it, is in the mind, which makes fear of failure controllable. Until you stop living, you will not fail. Life is nothing but second chances and new opportunities. If you put together a good plan and follow it—whether it's a plan for a fight or for a job interview—your fear will dissolve *substantially.* And if you learn from your failures but eliminate feelings of regret and remorse, you can overcome fear of failure. You just need the creativity and fearlessness to find those second chances and new opportunities.

There are only two things that you have to do in life: You have to die, and you have to live until you die. The rest is up to you.

THE 32ND LAW OF POWER

THE DIGNITY OF THE GOOD LOSS

When I was taking classes in human development at UC Davis, I read a study about kindergarten boys. First the researchers spoke to each boy, individually and privately, and they asked one simple question: Who's the toughest boy in your class?

Their answers were nearly unanimous: "I am."

For the second part of the study, the boys were all lined up in the same room. They were asked the same question.

Forced to look around at the other boys and assess their place in the toughness hierarchy, the boys had vastly different answers. Nearly every one of them pointed to one of their classmates—it didn't matter which one—and said, "He is."

To me, this shows we have an innate ability for self-assessment. These boys talked big and talked to impress when none of their peers were in hearing distance. After all, how was some researcher going to know if he was tough or not? In that scenario, there was really no perceived consequence for boasting of toughness.

The dynamic changes when we're faced with consequences. When all your buddies are standing there, they're going to call you on your boast. If one of the weakest boys in the class stood in front of all the other boys and said, "I'm the toughest," there would be a response. He'd be laughed at, maybe, or someone would tell about the time he saw Little Billy crying in the bathroom when he lost a kickball game.

Worse yet, the other boys might decide to make Little Billy prove his assertion. In that case, it's a far safer and more realistic strategy to point to a kid down the line.

There's always going to be someone bigger than you, smarter than you, or savvier than you. This is part of why developing a who's-who network is so important. Collaboration brings out the best in the individual as well as in the group.

But it also brings up a larger point that is often lost in our win-at-all-costs culture: You have to learn how to lose. Losing is inevitable, and losing with dignity is a lost art. Knowing you gave it your best and leaving without excuses is one of the best traits a person can display.

We all lose. You might be in sales and lose out on a big account. You might be a contractor who gets underbid on an important project. You might be a newspaper reporter who gets scooped on a story.

The hardest thing is to lose with class. We need to teach this to more young people. I have seen kids who are unable to process defeat. Parents don't ever want their kids to be disappointed, and losing can come as a shock. It breaks them down. Parents aren't doing their kids any favors by pretending disappointment is an avoidable part of life.

As the kindergartners in the study showed, it's ingrained in us to understand the harsh realities of our own strengths and weaknesses—our own wins and losses. Teaching self-esteem is valuable, but understand something: Deep down, *the kids know where they stand.* They know who's tough and who's smart and who's attractive to the opposite sex. This won't change, no matter how much society attempts to ignore it or will it out of existence.

The trick—and this is where parents come in—is learning how to deal with the harsh reality of defeat.

My job is the easy part. For me, the worst part of losing has nothing to do with my win-loss record or my status in the sport or how it might affect my future. The worst part of losing is thinking about all the people who follow me and help me and lose right along with me. My ego might take a tem-

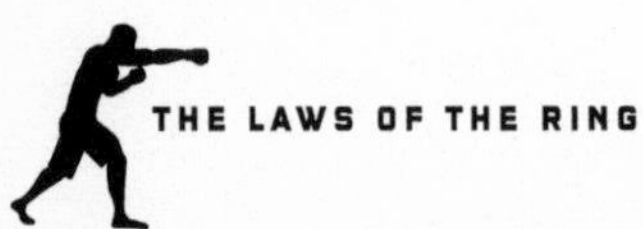

porary hit, especially if I feel I've lost to an inferior opponent, but I can deal with that. The ones who concern me are the people who are attached to my journey and sometimes living vicariously through me. They don't get the release and the rush of competition that I get in the cage. They often feel far worse after a loss than I do. (*Especially* Virgil.)

My philosophy is pretty basic: I know there are times when you plan it right, train it right, and fight it right—and still lose. There are times when the other guy is just plain better. There's absolutely no shame in owning up to that.

I lost twice to a very good fighter named Mike Brown. The two losses couldn't have been more different, but together they provided me with a lesson on how to handle defeat.

Our first fight took place on November 5, 2008, at the Seminole Hard Rock Casino in Hollywood, Florida. In the first round, I was doing really well. I came out strong and felt I was controlling the fight from the beginning.

That all changed when I did a jumping-back elbow that coincided with one of Brown's overhand rights. I managed to clothesline myself, jumping into the air and directly into his fist. From there, it was a quick and inglorious fall to the canvas, flat on my back. Not even close to the way I'd planned it.

It looked really bad. It didn't seem that bad to me at the time, but looking at it from the television camera's point of view after the fight, I have to say it was bad. I went right to the ground, Brown jumped on me and I was on the ground trying to fend off his punches when the referee stopped the fight.

At 2:23 of the first round, it was over. I'd been in far worse situations than that—I wasn't unconscious, for one thing—so immediately after the fight I felt agitated and a little cheated. Remember, a fighter isn't always rational, or even close to it, when it comes to his personal well-being. While I was on the ground, figuring out the angles that would allow me to throw Brown and return to my feet, I wasn't dwelling on the punch that put me on my back. It was history, old news, and all that mattered was the task of righting myself and getting back to winning the fight. You have to forget fast in this business, and part of my surprise at the stoppage of the fight stemmed from my ability to put bad breaks—in this case, a punch to the face following a fluky confluence of events—behind me and move on. It happened, it was over, and I was moving on. But *my* opinion didn't count.

There's an empty feeling that comes with any loss, but the total unexpectedness of this one hit me hard. Making matter worse was not only the fact that this fight—like all fights—involved months of training but also the fact that when I lose, I like to feel I've expended every micro-ounce of energy from my body. The only way to lose is full force, full effort. I like to be stomped out, and to have the ref call the fight with me unconscious, in a heap. In this fight, that didn't happen.

It sounds drastic, even masochistic, but it's the truth. This is the game I chose, and that's how it works. And that's why referees exist—to keep guys like me, who will keep fighting as long as we remain conscious, from putting ourselves in serious physical danger. Someone has to watch out for us because we're too consumed by the moment to do it ourselves.

That's why I couldn't blame the ref. I could sense right away—from the reaction of the crowd, especially—that it looked like I was in serious danger. And of course, after the fight, I had to answer questions about what happened. That's just part of the job.

The only words I could muster as I stood there in the cage, in front of a jam-packed arena, were, "I apologize to all my fans out there. Congratulations to Mike Brown—what a great win for him. I'll be back."

That was all I said, and all I felt I needed to say. I had to acknowledge to myself that the referee did his job; I didn't do mine. I found myself in a bad position, and I couldn't get out of it.

Despite the emptiness that was welling up inside me, I apologized to my fans and congratulated my opponent. When I got home to Sacramento, my pop came up to me and told me he was proud. He might actually have been happier in that moment than he'd have been if I'd *won* the fight.

"'Congrats to Mike Brown, what a great win for him,'" he said with his big smile and a chuckle, repeating my words to me. "That was really cool."

I didn't have any ulterior motives in saying what I said—I honestly felt apologetic about my performance—but apparently, I gained fans that night. Even though I lost.

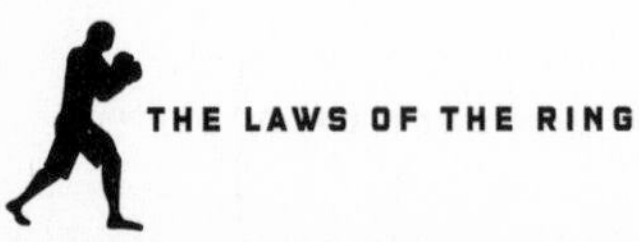

The response after the fight made me think more clearly about my definitions of winning and losing. Don't get me wrong . . . right after the fight I felt the blow to my ego and thought about how this loss might affect my career. But in the end, my simple words, and my acknowledgment of the people who helped get me in the cage that night, strengthened my reputation, and as a result, my personal credit in the fight community grew. Now, I ask you, how can something like *that* be considered a loss?

As a society, we've lost the dignity of the good loss. Everything is win or lose, black and white. The public discourse is shockingly elementary: If you win, you're great; if you lose, you suck.

Just imagine this hypothetical scene: Peyton Manning loses the AFC Championship and says he feels great after the loss. He's happy and wants everyone to know that he and his teammates did all they could do and still lost.

What would be the reaction to that? How would the public perceive Manning? What would sportswriters write about him? He would probably be vilified as someone who didn't care enough, when in truth his words are saying the opposite. If you have a plan for success and execute it to the best of your ability—leaving nothing behind in your quest to achieve victory—you can and should be happy with yourself even in defeat.

The Monday following my loss to Mike Brown, I had to board a flight for Mexico City for a tour promoting the fight I had just lost. There was a one-week delay in airing the fight in Mexico, where it would be shown on free television. I remembered what Dana White had told me the night we had dinner with Lorenzo Fertitta at the Hard Rock after the UFC had purchased the WEC: *Do the PR we have set up for you.* In all fairness, the trip had been planned before the fight, and as the face of the WEC, I understood that I had to be a team player. But it wasn't easy, pumping up the broadcast without letting anyone know what happened: *Hey, everybody in Mexico, tune in to watch me lose a fight and look really bad in the process. Come watch me end my thirteen-fight winning streak and lose the WEC featherweight title, which I've held for almost three years.*

I did interview after interview in Mexico telling the people, "Watch this fight. You're going to love it," but every time the lights went on and the questions started, I fought a lump in my stomach and worked hard not to let my pride get the best of me. It wasn't easy.

I was going through this torture knowing there was a carrot at the end of the stick. Shortly before the first Brown fight, I bought a quarter of an oceanfront penthouse in Puerto Vallarta from my mom and stepdad Tom. The housing market was beginning its collapse, and they needed to get out from under this purchase, so I cashed them out (for a good deal, of course, on the price) to keep the spot for our family.

When the promotional work for the fight ended, I asked the WEC people if they could send me directly to Puerto Vallarta instead of sending me home. They agreed, and I looked forward to spending a few days soaking in the sun and feeling sorry for myself. That was about the extent of my plan.

Predictably, my first order of business when I arrived in Puerto Vallarta was to get some beers and sit on the beach. I was planning on sitting there for two or three days, staring out at the ocean and thinking about the loss.

Within an hour—and maybe two beers—all I could think about was how beautiful my surroundings were. The weather was great, the view was spectacular, and I just couldn't bring myself to feel bad. I tried hard to, I really did. But then I started thinking of all the positives in my life. I was healthy, I was happy, I had gone through my worst night as a professional and come away injury-free and with some new goals. I was—at that very moment—sitting on the same sand that anyone in Mexico could sit on if they had two legs and a butt to plop down on, and it was awesome. Mapping out my next step was easy: get back on the horse as soon as I was back in the States, and hold my head high.

I put the beer down. I got dressed and went out. I met a hot chick and took her out to dinner. I found myself smiling and laughing and forgetting all about Mike Brown. All my plans to hold a three-day pity party went out the window. I just couldn't feel sorry for myself.

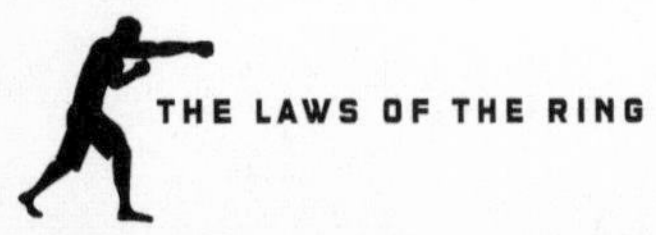

THE 33RD LAW OF POWER

FIGHT TO THE BITTER END: THE POWER OF GIVING YOUR ALL

Seven months later, on June 7, 2009, I got my rematch with Mike Brown. This was my chance for redemption, and I'd thought of little else from the time the first fight was stopped. I was fighting before my hometown fans in Sacramento's ARCO Arena. I entered the cage determined not to put myself in the kind of compromising position that had cost me the first fight.

Midway through the first round, a heavy punch whizzed by my head as I ducked out of the way and answered with an unorthodox up-kick that landed on Brown's head. Frustrated by my speed and elusiveness, he displayed a growing sense of aggravation that led me to believe I could take him right out of the fight. He almost ran toward me, and I responded with a two-punch combination and immediately backpedaled out of reach.

A small cut opened over his right eye, the first physical manifestation of my attack. He rushed in and scored a short-lived takedown. I quickly got back on my feet and forced separation. As he came forward, I unloaded a vicious right hand. He ducked and let loose with a punch of his own. My right hand connected with his forehead, and immediately I could feel the crackle of bones in my two small knuckles.

Four minutes into the first of five rounds, in a fight I was dominating, I had broken my right hand in two places. The pain was searing; my fist vanished and my hand dropped limp to my side. I threw a desperate dropkick that missed and sent me to the canvas, with Brown following. I lay there, my hand throbbing, my mind reeling.

This was the second-worst pain I've ever experienced in a fight. I fought José Aldo for a title at 145 pounds, and José just annihilated my right leg all night long. It was like being hit with a baseball bat for twenty minutes straight. He caught me with a couple of good ones in the second round, and almost immediately two softball-size lumps grew on my thigh. I lost my mobility from there, which allowed one of the best kickers on the planet to unload on me round after round. By the end of the night, my right leg was swollen to about three times the left, and it changed colors three times over the course of the next two weeks. My leg looked like it belonged on a dead body. But I digress . . .

Here I am against Brown, my big fight for redemption having just begun, realizing that I was going to have to beat him with one hand.

There was an understanding, and a calculation, but I doubt you would have seen a change in my heart rate from the moments before I broke my hand to the moments after. It's difficult to describe where my mind goes during a fight. It's a far-off place, where the only thoughts are centered on one thing: keep fighting. It's not like I'm playing a game and I hope it turns out in my favor. It's deeper than that, like a fight for survival. My trainer, Master Thong, knew I could keep going. He doesn't speak much English, but after the first round I let him and Dustin—and *only* him and Dustin—know that I'd broken my hand.

Master Thong gave me a furious look and said, "Shut up—champion!" and punched me right in the heart. I was down with that.

Adversity is always an internal struggle. Surrendering never entered my mind. Creativity and persistence, right? I had to think of a way to make this work. The old battle plan—the one that counted on two healthy hands—was gone, replaced by a plan that depended on my ability to defeat a world champion fighter with one hand.

I made it through the second round in good shape. I relied on elbows and knees, unable to use one of my best weapons. I was hiding my handicap pretty well, until the announcers figured it out late in the second round. First they noticed I wasn't throwing any punches with my right hand. I was all elbows and knees—that's all I had. I couldn't even defend takedowns because of the hand, but I could get back up to my feet.

Then, in between the second and third rounds, one of my corner guys asked, "Why aren't you throwing your right hand?" This was a stupid thing to say. I'd figured Dustin and Thong had let him in on the secret, but I guess not. Just to shut him up, and purely out of frustration, I said, "I can't. It's broken." Everyone else in the corner knew, and here he was, telling me to throw my right hand. Unbelievable.

Early in the third round, things got worse. I dislocated my left thumb. Now *both* hands were useless. The announcers noticed that I was now slapping with both hands. One of them said, "Oh my gosh, I think he might have broken both hands." I was doing my best to hide the fact from Mike Brown that my hands were essentially useless. As it turned out, the emphasis on my hands, and the commentators' disbelief that I could continue, was a good thing for me. I compete in the ultimate masculine sport, and I gained a ton of new fans who were won over by my willingness to keep fighting and my relative success in doing so.

The thumb injury was incredibly frustrating. It wasn't totally useless; it was *intermittently* useless. If I hit with it, it would lose its strength, but then gradually improve until I used it again. The same cycle repeated itself.

Nobody in my corner ever suggested I throw in the towel, probably because they knew the reaction they'd get from me. (If you're curious, go back and read about Dustin and Dave's intervention after my first fight.) I knew I looked silly throwing punches that looked more like schoolgirl slaps, but I'm proud that I made it a fight. I probably even won a couple of rounds with a broken hand, and I almost had him in the fifth round with a standing choke, which I lost when he flopped to the ground and my broken hand was the one dangling.

Afterward I discovered that people thought I was crazy. They wanted to know why in the world I continued fighting for twenty-one grueling minutes with two snapped metacarpals in my right hand and a dislocated thumb on my left. The answer is that from the moment I started training to be a professional, I made sure I was proficient at all the disciplines to allow myself the best opportunity to cope with the worst-case scenarios—maybe not specifically a broken hand and a dislocated thumb, but worst-case positions or situations.

When you approach your passion as a fight for survival, your world changes. I wasn't going to stop just because I injured my hands. What was I going to do, lie on the canvas and bemoan my fate? No, I'm going to try to figure out a way to win with the cards I've been dealt. The worst-case scenario arrived. How am I going to react? How good am I? That's the mentality. Of course, you know by now that my thinking is the same as the thinking of other guys who are truly meant for this profession—I'll fight until I'm unconscious—but I was prepared to adapt on the fly and, in training, created a scenario where I could compete despite the restrictions and the pain.

Don't let anyone convince you that a loss is a loss is a loss. All losses *are not* created equal, and most of the time it's how you handle them—the way you hold yourself accountable afterward, and the way you apply the lessons you've learned—that determines their worth. Approach your own goals, dreams, and aspirations with an undying persistence and don't stop until the final bell. Having passions in life is what keeps us going, even when adversity tries to knock us out.

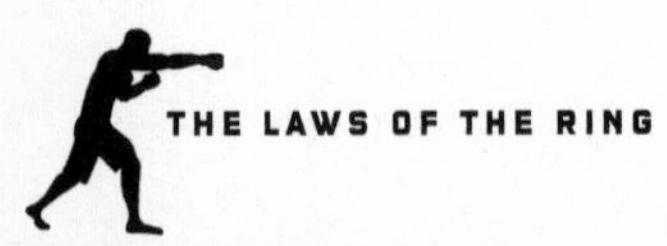

THE 34TH LAW OF POWER

FIND THE GOOD IN BAD SITUATIONS (THE HIDDEN BENEFIT OF TWO USELESS HANDS)

I've never felt a level of helplessness in the cage that compares with my feeling during the second Mike Brown fight. As if breaking two bones in my right hand wasn't enough, I had to go and dislocate my left thumb in the third round. That's a whole lot of rotten luck for one fight, but I made a point of not using those injuries as an excuse for losing the fight. This wasn't just a public front either. There were several times during the fight, after I'd suffered the injuries, when I sincerely believed I could have won the fight. I just didn't.

As I've said, writing this book has forced me to revisit a lot of memorable moments in my life. Some positive, some not so much. Since I am always searching for ways to put a positive spin on a negative topic—making excuses, for instance—I did a little soul-searching to find a way to put a positive spin on this one. I knew there was something I took away from the experience, but I kept coming up empty.

Then my buddy Dave Shapiro reminded me of the Monday after the fight. We went out to lunch in Sacramento, and he now tells me he was all prepared to give me his best keep-your-chin-up speech. He figured I was going to be down in the dumps after losing the fight, so he was ready to spend the afternoon trying to cheer me up.

Instead, he got blown away.

"I couldn't believe all the positive stuff you were saying," Dave later told me. "I'll never forget it: You were even saying that having two busted hands was a blessing in disguise."

It *was* a blessing in disguise. Remember, wins and losses are not the ultimate proof of your effort or ability. The scoreboard is not God, and nobody should worship it. By fighting hard and well against Brown with my hands essentially useless, I learned a lot about myself. I tested myself under the most trying circumstances, and I came away stronger for it.

But it wasn't just about winning a couple rounds with severely compromised hands (which proved to me that my stubbornness wasn't in vain). After the fight, the injuries to my hands forced me to take a break from training and seriously reassess my life and career. For the longest time, I had promised myself I was going to sit back and spend some time addressing some of my business issues. Training for one fight after another, I never gave myself the opportunity to address them. Now, with my hands needing to rest and heal, I could sit down without guilt and put my businesses in order.

The downtime allowed me to organize the gym and hire the kinds of trainers and teachers I felt could provide the most benefit to our members and fighters. I was able to spend some time with Mike Roberts and Jeff Meyer discussing ways to grow MMA Incorporated (our management company) and what my part was in the process. I devoted more time to getting this book under way, and mapped out some great strategies to strengthen Team Alpha Male, which was growing fast. I would schedule meetings with my neighbor Jim and think of cool activities and exercises we could do to strengthen the team's mental game.

Furthermore, before the second Mike Brown fight, I had told myself that I would make some time after the fight to work on my legs. I wanted to devote a serious amount of time to strengthening my legs and improving my kicks. With my hands out of commission, it was the perfect time for that.

According to Dave, our lunch talk was filled with me rolling out all these positive outcomes of my injuries. As it turned out, he didn't have to spend any time trying to cheer me up. I guess I was unknowingly practicing what I've been preaching since page one of this book. The need for an optimistic outlook.

Again, the battle against adversity is a completely personal one. It's fought in your mind and your heart. Unless you face adversity, how do you truly find out who you are? Taking on your passion, especially if it's something out of the mainstream, is bound to create adversity. Excuses won't overcome it, but you know what will? Inner resolve and the personal satisfaction that comes with prevailing in the face of overwhelming odds. Then getting creative so that the odds turn in your favor.

THE 35TH LAW OF POWER

KNOW YOUR ENEMY

The roots of my rivalry with Dominick Cruz go back to the days before our first fight. He and I were doing some promotional work that included signing the official fight poster. This is a standard part of the lead-up to the fight—you sign a ton of posters, most of them are given to charity, and others are passed out to promote the fight. We get to keep a few for ourselves to pass out to friends and family.

Right away, Dominick was upset because his picture wasn't on the poster, only his name. I had nothing to do with this decision, but apparently the WEC felt that the four belt holders were the main attraction and they decided not to include Dominick's face. Dominick protested this in a way that I felt was childish and, for lack of a better term, pretty lame: He signed his name right across my face on each of the posters.

The MMA hype machine makes the most of my rivalry with Dominick, but in truth, watching him deface the poster bothered me on a number of levels. I felt it was unfair to the promoters, the other fighters, and the charities that were going to receive the poster. And I confess that a factor outside Dominick's control increased my displeasure. I had just gotten my gym up and running around that time, and a few days before this incident, it had been hit by taggers. When I saw what he was doing to the posters, I equated it with the tagging. In a way, it felt like vandalism to me, and I was sensitive to this at the time.

Fast forward to the lead-up to our second fight, the headline fight for *UFC 132* in July 2011. Dominick and I, once again, had to do a promotional tour together. One of the stops was at the U.S. Marine base at Camp Pendleton, along the coast north of San Diego.

There were four fighters there—me, Dominick, Phil Davis, and Rich Franklin. When we arrived at the base, we thought it was going to be a shake-some-hands-and-support-the-Marines kind of thing. Man, were we ever wrong.

We were introduced to three drill sergeants, just shy of having one for each of us. I was doing my usual thing, trying to be happy and outgoing and ingratiate myself in as easygoing a manner as possible.

"Hey, I'm Urijah, nice to meet you," I said, sticking out my hand to a guy who looked like he could be an NFL running back.

He shook my hand but didn't smile. Glad I didn't try to high-five him.

Then Phil, always the wise guy, said, "Hey, you were just about to smile."

The sergeant stopped and looked at him without a hint of amusement. "No. I wasn't."

These guys didn't seem interested in happy horseshit, though we still didn't think their rudeness was deliberate given that we were being filmed for an advertising campaign featuring UFC fighters and the Marines. After we were dressed down by the drill sergeants like fresh recruits, they hustled us over to the obstacle course, where they lined us up again.

"You will shut your mouth and listen," one screamed out like he was R. Lee Ermey from *Full Metal Jacket.*

Phil Davis laughed a little, still not sure that these guys were for real—still thinking they were going to start laughing at any minute.

"Phil, is there something funny about the U.S. military?" another of the officers asked.

The third drill sergeant, Sergeant Fuentes, noticed that Phil was having a hard time repressing his smile. He barked in a hoarse shout, "Phil, when he says, 'Stop smiling,' he means hide your teeth!"

At that, I started laughing hard. We were like fourth graders—one guy giggles, pretty soon the whole class is giggling.

The first drill sergeant turned his attention to me and asked, "Urijah, is there something funny about Americans dying in war?"

Okay, so this really *was* serious. I thought there was going to be a little indoctrination scene and then we'd move on, but after we finished the obstacle course, they tossed sixty-pound packs on us and marched us three miles. Later, we had to do a night obstacle course, during which we had to crawl under barbed wire and roll around.

There was no time for petty squabbles between Dominick and me. In this situation, we were forced to spend a good deal of time together and even work together to get through a lot of the exercises.

It was an unusual setup for two fighters leading up to the biggest fight in either of their careers, but I took it as an opportunity to figure out what Dominick was all about. I didn't ignore him or pretend to hate him—"pretend" because I don't hate him. I just wanted to understand him a little bit.

He and I spent a lot of time talking. We were both reluctant at first, and mostly made sarcastic jabs and comments to each other, but eventually we came around. It didn't take me long to realize that Dominick has a huge chip on his shoulder. He felt he'd been mismanaged, and that this had cost him money. He felt he wasn't appreciated enough by the public and the fight community given the amount of success he had.

I could see that Dominick was a little taken aback by how nice I was to him. Given our history, he didn't expect me to engage him the way I did. I might dislike the way some people behave, but I honestly don't hate anybody. Instead of using our awkward proximity as a chance to add fuel to the feud, I wanted to use it to gain a better understanding of who he was and why.

There are bound to be difficult people in your life. You're guaranteed to run across people who have personalities that don't mesh with yours. And these people might be the ones standing in the way of you and your passion. You're going to have to deal with them. But you gain power from knowledge, and confidence from understanding a person's background and motives.

I had felt that the basic difference in our personalities boiled down to the different factors that motivated us. Of course, I openly thrive on positivity

and constructive feedback, and I had believed Dominick was motivated by negativity. But what I came away with from our time at Pendleton was this: Even though it seemed as if he drew strength from things that were seemingly negative—perceived criticisms and slights—he always managed to latch onto something positive.

Here's what I mean: In the cover story about him in *FIGHT!* magazine, Cruz made a point of bringing attention to an after-fight speech in which Matt Mitrione praised Cruz's fighting style and said he would like to pattern his own style after him.

"How many people in the world have other fighters coming out publicly and saying they wish they could fight like him?" Cruz was quoted as saying in the magazine. "Well, Matt Mitrione is a good example of that. He's a guy who recognizes what I've accomplished in this sport."

That's when it hit me. Cruz's negativity is a facade, a motivational *ploy.* Like the rest of us, Dominick wants to be told he's doing something well. That's the power of positivity. We all want to be told we're doing something well. We all want positive feedback, even when we've convinced ourselves that the negative kind is the only kind we'll ever get.

So the whole time we were together, I took the approach that anyone should use with someone who wants to pummel his face in. I made a concerted effort to see the best in him. How did I do that? By showing *him* the best in *me.* It wasn't an act—I try to stay open-minded about everyone, even if—maybe even *especially* if—it's someone I'm fighting. If Dominick, as I perceived it, was motivated by negativity, I was going to show him nothing but positivity. I was going to be relentlessly upbeat. I wasn't going to provide him with any material that might create more animosity between us.

No matter how much you might feed off negativity, a positive message is always stronger. I'm habitually positive. I try not to use anger as motivation. Sure, there are always times when I think about pummeling my opponents in the cage, but it's not because I'm angry, it's because I want to win. What fuels my drive is my belief in myself. My competitive nature will not allow another person to strip that belief from me. *That's* how I get motivated for a fight. There's no anger, but there is a sharp competitive edge. Every fight is an opportunity for me to test that belief in myself.

I am happy with myself even in defeat, which is a difficult concept to grasp unless you see it as I do: When I have given all I can and still lose, I can't be anything but happy. I am willing to concede that another man can be better than me on a given day, and I harbor no resentment in the aftermath of defeat. I try my hardest to avoid jealousy and envy.

On the flip side, I do not see my success as indicative of another person's weakness. I do not use victory as a means of elevating myself above other people, or as license to belittle them.

In the quest to allow your passion to dictate your life, a positive approach is imperative. Train yourself to be positive. Make conscious decisions to be productive and uplifting. I said, regarding Cruz in the *Countdown* show leading up to our fight, "I think the main difference between us is simple: It seems like he's motivated by all these negative things, and I'm motivated by all these positive things." Now, looking back, I know this isn't true. During our time together, I think we were able to bring some positivity to our competitive relationship, and we ended with an epic fight. I'd like to think there was a connection between those two events, and I look forward to fighting Dominick again.

My fiercest rival in college was Matt Sanchez, who wrestled for Cal State Bakersfield and was a two-time All-American. Matt is a year younger than me and we split four matches at 133 pounds while I was a senior at UC Davis. Our competitive, one-track personalities were such that we both assumed the other was a complete jerk *off* the mat because we were bitter enemies *on* the mat. The nature of competition wouldn't let either of us believe the other might actually be a good guy. It made no sense—we didn't even know each other. We competed, but we didn't have conversations or make any attempt to understand each other. That was the way it needed to be in order for each of us to maintain a competitive edge. I didn't want to know if he made regular visits to an orphanage or volunteered at an old-folks home. I wanted to keep our relationship on an adversarial level; it was the only way I could maintain my dispassionate and animalistic mentality.

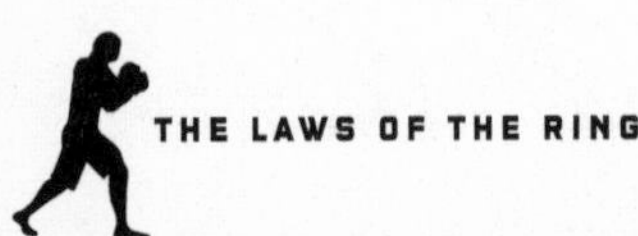

The last of our four matches came at the Pac-10 championships in Boise during my senior year. The stage was set for an epic battle after a back-and-forth year that had me up by one. Matt won our first match in a close decision. I won the second in a close decision and I destroyed him in the third. I was pumped for my final match against him because I was ranked number nine in the country and a win over him would improve that and earn me a spot for a third year in the NCAA Division I wrestling championships. The year before I had missed All-American status by one point, putting me in the top twelve in the nation instead of in the prestigious top eight. I had been training the entire year for the NCAA tourney, and thought it would for sure be the last competition of my athletic career.

Midway through the first round, I had a 2–1 lead. It felt like I was in control of the match, but that didn't last long. We were standing and I lunged in for a sloppy inside trip that got me put on my back; two-point takedown, then a three-point near fall. I fought hard off my back but landed in another three-point near-fall position. In a matter of seconds he was leading 9–2 at the end of the first round. It was a crushing turnaround for me, and I responded by going on a wild spree in an attempt to win by pin, my only legitimate chance at victory. It didn't happen, and Matt won by a technical fall.

I was devastated. I walked away and slumped onto one of the back warm-up mats, crushed. The more I thought about it, the more upset I became. Before long, I was lying on the mat, crying. My athletic career was finished, and it had ended in horrible disappointment.

I couldn't stay on that mat and wallow in self-pity, though. I had to compose myself and return to the main mat for the postmatch handshake. This was tough. I pulled myself off the mat, swallowed hard, wiped my eyes, and tried to remove any last vestiges of my tear-fest. When I lined up with my teammates, the first thing I did was look across the mat to find Sanchez. And there he was, smug as could be, chewing gum and smacking it around in his mouth like a cow chewing its cud. For some reason, this bugged the crap out of me. By this point, everything about Sanchez bugged me—his body, his wrestling style, his smug attitude, his damned gum, and the way he went about chewing with his stupid mouth open and smacking it from side to side. I guess you could say I didn't like Sanchez at that moment.

After the season ended, and I graduated, I was hired as an assistant coach at UC Davis and, that summer, participated at a kids' summer wrestling camp at Lake Tahoe. There I ran into Matt Sanchez. We were in a small group of camp teachers, and when it was my turn to speak, I said, "Can you believe this dopey, scrawny little guy beat me?" The kids all laughed, of course. "Well, it was hard for me to accept that, too, but this man right here is the best technician I ever faced. You can learn a lot from him."

Matt just smiled, and I walked away hoping I'd made my point: I still wasn't happy that I'd lost to him, but he had my respect. From there, it was natural that we'd start talking and getting to know each other in a manner that was different from on-mat rivals. Not surprisingly, we got along great. I even came to forgive him for being the only guy who made me cry in competition.

My professional fighting career took off during my second year of coaching at UC Davis. Once I got the sponsorship from the Dunmores and was being paid to train, it was harder to justify the hours I needed to spend coaching. I enjoyed the work, but the payoff didn't justify the output. However, I didn't want to leave my old coach in a bind by quitting, so I began to think about how I could find a solution that would work for everyone.

I called Sanchez. He had graduated from Bakersfield and had coached there. He needed a job and would be a great addition to the UC Davis program. I had recently bought my first house and Dustin had just moved out, so I added an incentive: six months of free rent for Matt to get settled in the area.

Matt and I could have easily ignored each other at that wrestling camp and held on to our rivalry long after it had officially ended. I could have been envious of his success—I was never an NCAA All-American, and he was twice. I could have held a grudge against him for causing me humiliation in my final college wrestling match.

Instead, he joined us under the umbrella. We became friends and he was the first person who popped into my head when an opportunity arose. He took the job and ended up living rent-free at my house for the six months I promised. He coached at UC Davis for a year, and during that time I started my gym and he got to see the team we were forming both in the gym and on our block of houses. We were doing what we wanted to do without chasing down money, and we were having fun doing it.

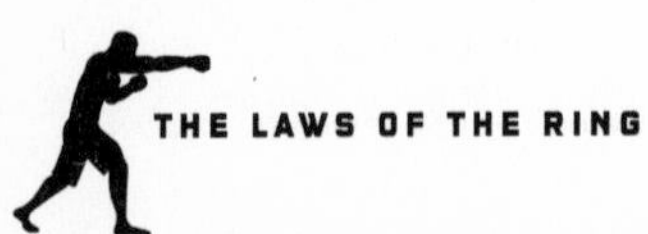

"I like your lifestyle," he said. "I'd like to live the way you guys do."

"Well, then come manage the gym," I said.

And so Matt Sanchez, my bitter rival, ended up managing the gym for two years. He even trained and ended up with two pro MMA fights. He also won one FILA World Championship and several other international competitions in submission wrestling. During the time he was managing the gym, sometime toward the end of 2008, the house next door came up for sale. Matt and I bought it together—I fronted the down payment and he pays the mortgage.

Through a couple of wrestling relationships, Matt came upon a business opportunity in the summer of 2009. With home foreclosures rampant throughout the country and particularly prevalent in the Sacramento region, he started a business that does yard work—mowing, trimming, etc.—for the banks who are attempting to off-load foreclosed homes. Real estate agents and neighbors are happy to see the yards of abandoned homes kept up, and Matt's business exploded. He went from three employees—other friends who lived on the block—to more than sixty. What started in the garage expanded to four different office spaces. It quickly became the biggest company of its type in the country, and in a short amount of time Matt went from being an assistant wrestling coach to the owner of a multimillion-dollar business. He's always in need of workers, so new fighters who come to the gym in need of some extra money can always piece together enough work to keep training by mowing lawns for Matt.

Even though he's not a fighter, Matt is a part of our community of fighters. He still lives next door, now with his girlfriend and son, Jaxon. And there's still a hole in the fence we use to go back and forth. His son is getting the same energy that I got growing up with an upbeat community as part of an extended family. We are still competitive with each other in a bunch of different ways, including land acquisition and business success. We laugh when we reminisce about being crammed in my first house on the block, and the way we would carpool around Sacramento to save a buck or two on gas. It's hard to remember that *this* was my enemy, a guy I wanted to punch for chewing his gum too loud.

At the end of our stay at Pendleton, Phil, Rich, Dominick, and I went to a Japanese restaurant in downtown San Diego with the drill sergeants and the production crew. At first, Dominick hadn't planned to go, but by the end of the trip he was ready to be with his enemy. I was sitting with Phil and the Marines. Dominick was sitting on the other end of the table near Rich and the producers and the television people. Phil and I, especially, were having a blast. We were telling stories and listening to the drill sergeants tell their stories. (They'd relaxed quite a bit by now.)

Dominick was missing out. I could sense him watching us from the other side, and I was happy when he picked up his chair and walked all the way over to the other side to sit with us. It was telling, because it evoked one of the lessons I always try to teach our fighters: If you feel like you want to do something, there's no reason why you shouldn't.

Dominick wanted to be part of the conversation and part of the fun at the end of a hard day. We put our differences aside and sat there and had a great time. At that moment I felt we had become strictly competitors on an athletic level and no longer enemies in life. It took some work to create a tiny crack in the shell, but we both made the effort. I understood him better, and he understood me, and we discovered we had far more similarities than we'd ever have known had we not been forced to spend a little time together. We even held some preliminary discussions about getting him the right management team so he could take his career where he wanted it to go.

I'm not perfect, but I look for the positive and try to make things work. It can be difficult to seek out the positive, especially in difficult people who seem unwilling to meet you halfway. Dominick, as it turned out, wanted to meet me halfway and squash the beef. We both broke through each other's insecurities and gained power from the effort.

So, when you know someone has a tendency to be negative—even someone you might see as a rival in life—call his bluff. Give him a compliment and watch his attitude change immediately. It's powerful stuff.

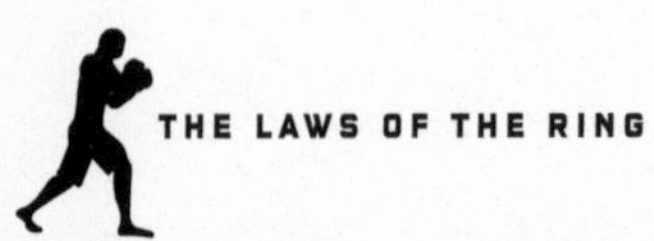

THE 36TH LAW OF POWER

THERE'S NO EXCUSE FOR A LAME EXCUSE

If you've been reading this book from page one, this law might seem redundant, but I really need to drive the point home, because if you want to work toward a more fulfilling, passion-centered life, taking stock is only half the battle. The competency model I wrote about earlier is a great place to start: You need to understand your strengths and weaknesses. But once you do that—once you conduct an honest assessment of who you are and what you can do—you have to begin to eliminate one of life's major toxins—excuses.

That's right—eliminate them altogether. Excuses are an infection. They start in one place and then expand until they become a permanent part of your personality. They hinder productivity because they keep you from honestly evaluating who you are. If you believe there's always some external force at work keeping you from success, whether it's a boss who doesn't like you or a spouse who doesn't understand you, you will never be able to deal with who you really are. And if you can't do that, you can't employ the Laws of Power to improve your life. These unseen forces will forever remain in your way.

Excuses, in many ways, are a form of envy. They're a way to dodge responsibility as a means of explaining why someone else has something you don't. They're a way of avoiding accountability by shifting blame. Nothing good can come from that approach.

Take my second fight against Dominick Cruz. He fought a good tactical fight and won by decision. From my standpoint, I thought I won the fight, because by my estimation, I was the more aggressive competitor. But judges don't always reward the aggressor. My biggest fault, from a *tactical* standpoint, was to fight for the knockout. That was my mentality going into the fight, and I didn't adjust to fight a more tactical, points-oriented fight, which, when it comes to a decision, is what it's all about.

This was my biggest moment: my first UFC showcase fight and my chance to seize my first UFC title. I was proud of my performance and felt Dominick and I gave everyone watching a good show, but two things were key to how I responded. One, I wasn't reveling in it, but I accepted the fact that I lost fairly; two, I wouldn't allow a loss, by external standards, to dictate my self-worth. Dominick and I competed respectfully and fiercely, we walked away without injury, we had a whole lot of fun. I hope we do it again soon.

At the beginning of this book, we discussed passion and how too few people can identify their own. As an exercise, I suggested you make yourself your passion, and assess what you find fulfilling as an individual in order to help you become a contributing and valued member of your community. Focus on your own small daily triumphs and spend some time being conscious of every decision you make. Understand what makes you feel good and what doesn't. In time, you will reach conclusions about yourself and develop a sense of purpose.

Excuses are among the most damaging passion-stoppers. You can find an excuse to avoid doing just about anything, but the truth is, your passion can't wait. It's too important.

When I started my fighting career, I could have relied on any number of excuses to give up on my passion. *The promoter didn't call me back . . . I might get hurt . . . My friends don't think it's a good idea . . . There's no money in it . . . I've never had any formal training . . . It might never escape the shadows of In-*

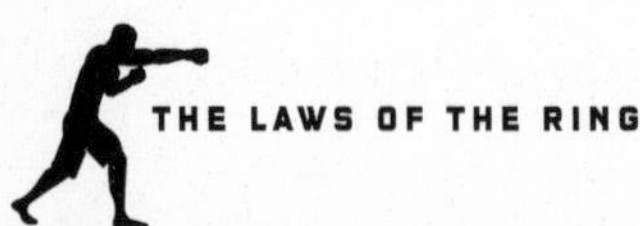

dian casino parking lots and ballrooms . . . It would be a waste of my college education . . . There's no security. Each one of those would have been enough for some people to decide it wasn't worth the time or the effort.

There are undoubtedly a thousand excuses standing in the way of your making the decision to pursue your passion, but there is always *one reason* why you should move forward: It's your life, and you will get more out of it. Is there anything else that even compares to that? You could pile up all the excuses running through your head and I guarantee you that one reason stands taller than all of them combined.

Go slow if you must.

Go easy if you must.

Just go.

A FINAL WORD: LIVE THE DREAM

I'll leave you with this: the ultimate lifestyle. This is the culmination of putting your passion to work. If you're living the dream, you're coming as close as you can come to incorporating your passion into every aspect of your life.

There are many avenues to this destination and it's subjective. My friend Jaimal Yogis lives the dream. From the moment he ran away from home and bought a plane ticket to Hawaii as a high school student, he followed his passion. (I'm not *endorsing* that approach . . . but it's one way to do it.) He studied Buddhism and surfed and wrote a book called *Saltwater Buddha* that allowed him to explain his philosophy to a wider audience. He lives his life on his terms, without regret.

My friend Matt Sanchez lives the dream. He came up with a brilliant business idea—yard maintenance for foreclosed homes—and built it up to the point where it essentially runs itself. He hired like-minded people who are full of potential, and they work in a collaborative, productive environment, with plenty of free time to fill as they please.

To live the dream, you have to have the right focus, the right mentality, and the right lifestyle. You know what you like to do, and you've figured out how to make your life revolve around your passion. You have a job you enjoy doing. You love your work and find fulfillment in doing it.

You have the right mentality. That mentality is believing, *Hey, I can do anything I want if I work hard and I'm smart about it.*

If you're living the dream, you have a job, a career, and a life that revolves around the things you love. You know what you want to do, you know how to do it (that is, you have the talent), and you've taken the ultimate step: You're doing it.

This is where you want to be. From this day forward, you should strive to make some progress toward reaching this goal. It's not always easy, but it is worthwhile.

It's a wonderful feeling. To be positive about something every single day is a gift. It awakens you to the world and all the great things in it. You want to pursue the goal of seeing the world through a wide-angle lens. Living your passion allows you to expand your worldview and live a life that contains far less worry about how you are being perceived. There is less judgment and fewer judges.

Every day when I wake up, I feel I'm living the dream. This doesn't mean things are always perfect or easy. It means I enjoy life and I'm prepared for the turbulence that is inevitable throughout it. It's not just a cliché; it's a way of life. I pursued my passion when that particular passion wasn't popular. I thought positively and acted with persistence. I resisted fear and avoided bad habits and never made excuses. I looked at opportunities and made a point to sieze them. I've won and lost with dignity, and I took notes along the way. I've found joy in sharing my successes with a community of like-minded people. I keep an open mind and I'm always eager to learn. But don't misunderstand me; my journey's not done yet, far from it. Living your dream isn't about perfection. It's about knowing who you are and believing anything is possible. I continue to believe that anything is possible, and I believe you should, too.

This book is written about my laws, things that I've learned and experienced from my life so far. I hope you enjoyed my opinions and viewpoints, however, I encourage you to let yours carry the most weight. Think about what you want from life and determine what laws you want to live by, on your journey. Enjoy the road you travel, look forward to all the destinations ahead, and let passion lead the way.

ACKNOWLEDGMENTS

I learned a lot throughout this process, and I was fortunate to have had some excellent teachers.

First, I'd like to thank my managers: Mark Schulman, Jeff Meyer, Mike Roberts, and Mike Castrillo. My literary agent, Richard Abate, believed in my unconventional idea and stuck with it until it became real. Along those same lines, my editor at HarperCollins, Adam Korn, pushed me to make the book as unique as it could be. Trish Daly at HarperCollins made sure the gears worked smoothly.

And of course, I'd like to thank each of the characters in the book for allowing me to share their stories.